We Are All Treaty People

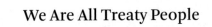

# We Are All Treaty People

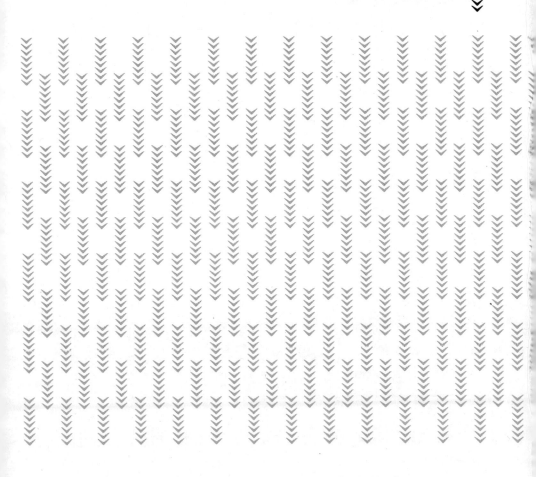

*Prairie Essays*

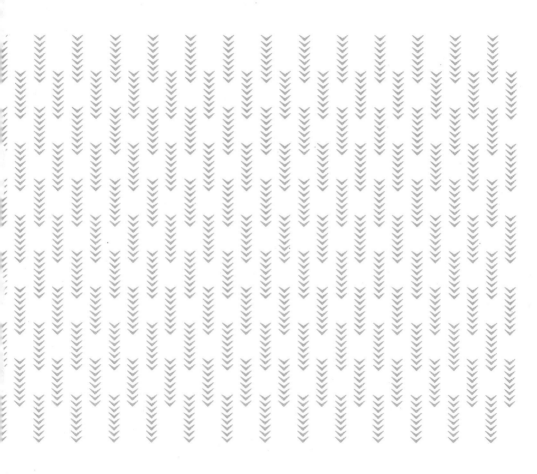

Roger Epp

The University of Alberta Press

The University of Alberta Press

Published by
The University of Alberta Press
Ring House 2
Edmonton, Alberta, Canada  T6G 2E1

**Library and Archives Canada Cataloguing in Publication**

Epp, Roger, 1958-
　　We are all treaty people : Prairie essays / Roger Epp.


Includes index.
ISBN 978-0-88864-506-7


1. Prairie Provinces.  2. Prairie Provinces–Rural conditions.
3. Prairie Provinces–Economic conditions.  I. Title.

FC3237.E66 2008　　　971.2　　C2008-903765-0

The University of Alberta Press is committed to protecting our natural
environment. As part of our efforts, this book is printed on Enviro Paper: it
contains 100% post-consumer recycled fibres and is acid- and chlorine-free.

The University of Alberta Press gratefully acknowledges the support
received for its publishing program from The Canada Council for the Arts.
The University of Alberta Press also gratefully acknowledges the financial
support of the Government of Canada through the Book Publishing
Industry Development Program (BPIDP) and from the Alberta Foundation
for the Arts for its publishing activities.

 Canada Council　Conseil des Arts
for the Arts　　du Canada　　　Canadä　　 Alberta Foundation for the Arts

*For Rhonda, who gave me the creative courage to paint with essays, and for Stephan and Elise, who gave me reason to do so.*

# Contents

# Acknowledgements

This book, perhaps more than most, owes its existence to friendships formed around shared interests in the rural prairie West. The essays it contains, of course, are mine. But I would not have taken the risks involved in writing them, sometimes in unconventional, unacademic, often personal ways, from the isolation of an ivory tower. Rather, these essays have been shaped profoundly by almost miraculous encounters with the right people; by countless opportunities in the countryside to listen; by invitations to speak, write and provide media commentary for diverse regional and national audiences; and, above all, by timely affirmations that there was something worthwhile in my efforts to think about what it still means to dwell on these prairies—the descendent of European settlers, the inheritor of multiple, complex stories. When I write, I unavoidably have real faces and voices in mind. The unexpected reward of the decade of work from which this book has emerged has been an expanding circle of academic colleagues across North America and friends in communities across the Canadian prairies.

Near the geographic centre of that circle is my home campus in Camrose, Alberta. It has been my good fortune, even in dark times, to work in a small academic community filled disproportionately with supportive and venturesome colleagues. Among them, John Johansen, Jack Waschenfelder and Keith Harder accompanied me on foot or by canoe in exploring slices of the Battle River watershed. John has also referred much good reading my way. Sandra Rein, as rural as any of us, made insightful suggestions to improve one essay and otherwise encouraged this work. David Goa at the Chester

Ronning Centre for the Study of Religion and Public Life provided an opportunity to read from the manuscript in its late stages. Tom Bateman is someone whose conversation I continue to miss.

Within the University of Alberta, President Indira Samarasekera has made public citizenship and community engagement a priority for its scholars. I concur heartily. While the position I now hold puts writing and speaking time at a premium, I am fortunate in other ways to have worked with a tremendously supportive and talented group of senior academic leaders in Provost Carl Amrhein and my fellow deans, many of whom are also small town prairie people. They include the late Ian Morrison, with whom I shared a conference platform in Manitoba three months before his accidental death.

A decade ago, Walter Klaassen, Roxanne Dunbar-Ortiz and Mark Neufeld kindly read and affirmed a version of the essay, "Oklahoma"—my first attempt at creative non-fiction. My sister Kathleen read it and several other chapters. Bill Moore-Kilgannon understood the importance of my earliest work on the politics of rural Alberta. Dave Whitson signed on to a partnership that has resulted in a co-edited book, *Writing Off the Rural West*, and a CBC Radio *Ideas* documentary, "The Canadian Clearances," which we produced together with Dave Redel. Those projects and others have enabled me to work with many thoughtful people whose determination to live well, in place, while others would reduce the rural to a resource plantation, has been the most powerful motivation for me to get it right—to make my words count. They include Ken and Sharon Eshpeter at Daysland and all of those friends who meet on winter concert nights at the Palace Theatre; Brian Rozmahel and his irrepressible rural co-conspirators Alvin Sorenson, Vern Hafso and Don Ruzicka, who together will put the community of Viking on the map for reasons other than hockey; and the members of the Kingman Renaissance Research Institute, from whose weekly coffee-shop symposia I have been noticeably truant in recent years.

My circle includes students from rural points across the prairie West through whom I have experienced a farm auction, rodeos, weddings and a wake. In particular, I am indebted to several of them for extended conversations about the ideas found in one or more essays: Robert Lee-Nichols, Cody McCarroll, Tyler Lawrason, Matthew

Hebert, Patricia Macklin, Karsten Mündel, Sandra Read, John Crier and Vern Saddleback. Muriel Lee, an Ojibwa-Cree, first used the evocative words that constitute the title of this book: on these prairies, we are all treaty people.

My circle also includes people like Andrew Nikiforuk, Lisa Bechthold, Elaine and Ted Regier, Darrin Qualman, Nettie Wiebe and Jim Robbins, Ken Larsen, Dick Haydu, Bill Dobson, Cam Harder, Colin Millang, Bob Stirling, Murray Knuttila, Allan Patkau, Francis Gardner, Jillian and John Lawson, Doug Griffiths, Judy Unterschultz, Mark Lisac, Laura Rance, Eldon Funk, and Art and Janet Klaassen. In recent years I have been honoured to have been asked back to Saskatchewan to speak at the centenaries of the Territorial Grain Growers' Association and of Rosthern Junior College, my high-school *alma mater*; from the pulpit at Eigenheim, from which my great-grandfather once preached; and at the 75th anniversary weekend of the country church outside of Hanley to which I refer in chapter four. Kathy Peters, who was there, was among the first to suggest that what I had to say ought to be a book. Her cousin Doug used to call when he heard me on the radio. How I wish that instead of returning to Hanley for his funeral in the spring of 2008 I had been able to put a copy of the book in his hands.

At every stage of this project, I have been exceptionally well-treated once again by the University of Alberta Press. Director Linda Cameron and her staff at Ring House 2 combine the best of both worlds: on one hand, sophisticated, highly-skilled book sense, editorial care and design creativity; on the other, an office as casual as a small town, where it is still possible to arrive without appointment, be welcomed into the conversation around the front-room table, and have Cathie, Yoko, Michael, Alan and Peter come around to say hello if they are not already there. This book has benefited greatly from Michael Luski's ongoing guidance, Zanne Cameron's fresh eyes as copy editor, Marvin Harder's design work and, in particular, Linda Goyette's insightful comments as primary—and, at the time, anonymous—reader for the Press. She grasped what I meant to say and why I needed to say it.

The final words of acknowledgement are owed to members of my family, my mother Louise and late father Clarence, my parents-in-law

Jacob and Hella Harder, and, above all, Rhonda, Stefan and Elise. While I have dedicated this book to them elsewhere, it is important for me also to express gratitude to them for support of many kinds. Not only have they been willing to join me in exploring prairie back-roads, places and powwows, or to read first drafts, find articles and transcribe interviews. Rhonda in particular has lived with my ill-timed bouts of inspiration, my speaking commitments and my sheer determination to write. Without her, I cannot imagine that this project, or many others, would have been completed.

# Introduction
## *A Prairie Accent*

I

In the circle of conversation at a conference reception at the London School of Economics, of all places, something I say—the way I say it—prompts a flash of recognition in a graduate student.

"Is that a prairie accent?" she asks.

"Yes," I say, "it is."

II

On a crystal-clear day in early December, I have a window seat for a flight from Regina to Edmonton. The plane takes off to the southeast and loops back around over the Qu'Appelle Valley and Last Mountain Lake, unmistakably long and slender, sunk deep into the prairie tableland. So far the landscape is identifiable only in broad outline; I find my bearings from what I know of maps. But as the plane crosses over the trickle of Arm River, and then Highway 11, the details are suddenly, strikingly familiar, like the lens of a microscope focussing on its subject, only from a height of 31,000 feet. Below is the small town of Hanley, where I grew up, and to the west, along the road we called the "town line," I am able to gauge by quarter-sections and the creek to spot the smallest specks of remembered farmyards, a church, more farms, then the sand hills, and the South Saskatchewan River. Near the northern horizon, past Saskatoon, I can roughly locate the farming district of Eigenheim west of Rosthern where my first Canadian settler ancestors arrived at lonely homesteads in 1894, and where my parents lived as children.

Minutes west, the plane is above Bill's farm on the edge of the Bear Hills. Then Wilkie. The Eagle Hills. Paradise Valley, and the Haydu farm, which tells me I am now above Alberta, though the land is of a single piece. The Battle River in its spectacularly wide chasm. The traces of the old Grand Trunk Pacific rail-bed north of Kingman, whose tracks once ran into the small city of Camrose, directly behind my house, and on towards a mammoth trestle bridge across the same Battle River valley. The forests and lakes of the Miquelon escarpment.

There is great clarity in this exhilarating, olympian hour. This is where I belong. This is where I am fortunate to be. This is the world, viewed as a whole, in which I dwell and teach and am still learning to think. It is a world set apart by its own aesthetic of light, colour, and landforms; by its own human imprints, reverences and defences— a world populated by people I have come to know. From the vantage point of the ground, this world is something like a large tent with a high, high, blue-sky canopy and a floor stretched across a large piece of the prairie West. It is staked down at many points, many of them clustered close together; one is driven into the ground as far away as Oklahoma. Those stakes are my stakes in this place.

III

There is great sudden clarity in words too. In a real sense the project that is represented by these essays was summoned by these words from David G. Smith: "Most social theory, in the West, especially since the turn of the century, has been generated in urban, highly industrialized environments, places where the only trees and plants available to human observation are products of hyper-cultivation, and the only visible animals are profoundly domesticated, dependent on pleasing human overlords." As a result, he writes, theory and policy generated in such places are characterized above all by "prediction, control, and rationalization." Over against this, he recommends that thinking begin not with abstractions but with an attentiveness to "the necessary geography of all human thought and action," and to "the complexity of human experience in its lived conditions of place, story, and family."[1]

These essays are exercises not in theory, at least not directly, but rather in attentiveness–to a necessary geography, to place, story and family, to the contemporary challenges of living well in that part of the rural West that was once called the prairie grainbelt. They blur the lines between genres. Taken together, they stretch the limits of the academic conventions in which I have been schooled. They wear lightly the influence of political philosophers such as Hannah Arendt, Hans-Georg Gadamer and Charles Taylor; they are as much indebted to novelists, essayists and poets.[2] They aim neither at detachment from their subject nor at cleverly ironic acts of subversion. They could not have been written from anywhere else. Their understanding is placed; it is partial and partisan; it might even be called provincial—in the sense, as Wallace Stegner once wrote, that "encompasses the most profound things a writer has to say."[3] Precisely for that reason, these essays ought to be held to the highest hermeneutic standard of rigour I can imagine: namely, that they ring true for those people whose life-worlds they describe, not by parroting popular opinion to them, but rather by earning their trust and inviting them to interpret their experience differently or more deeply. Some of these essays first emerged in the immediacy of public speech, at occasions as diverse as a centenary symposium, a homecoming, a parliamentary committee hearing and a funeral. All of them have been written with real faces in mind. They are intimately personal at points, for there is no other way to write about place, story and family than to translate one's own life and inheritance into words.

The first three essays in this collection are grounded in those particularities. They probe the ambivalences of home in three rural prairie settings. One is a slice of the Battle River watershed in east-central Alberta, out beyond the province's most identifiable sites of natural grandeur and economic prosperity. The second is that rural district of red-dirt Oklahoma, beside another river, the Washita, where the stories of the Cheyenne and my maternal ancestors run parallel for a generation before our uprooting to Canada as a result of World War I. The third is the town of Hanley, Saskatchewan, where I lived as a boy. Those essays represent some of a life's work of thinking-through what it means to be a settler in the North American West—to inherit a story of locations and dislocations, of longings and obligations. I am aware of Stegner's objection that the word settler is a misnomer, for the simple reason that so few families actually have settled in any one place for more than a generation on a continental frontier occupied by Europeans on the premise of mobility. My family's history bears out his point. But I have deliberately claimed the designation of settler for other good reasons. First, it conveys a sense of historical brevity; it is not so long ago that my ancestors arrived here. Second, it evokes an agrarian connection to land. And, not least, its use points to the settler's historical "other"—the aboriginal—and to the need to remember the relational terms of our settlement that most would prefer to forget.

Thinking-through requires acts of retrieval and retelling in order to answer the most basic questions: Who am I? Why am I here? Who is we? What are the moral sources, the horizons of meaning, more or less shared, more or less fragmented, out of which I act in the world?[4] The first three essays are most evidently personal and familial retrievals. They are written out of a wonder at having once been young, in what seems a very different time, and at having been entrusted from early on with pieces of the stories that constitute a family. They also reflect an orientation to the rural, to the past, and an insistence on telling stories of family and place in such a way that they cannot be disentangled from those of the Cheyenne and Cree.

The subsequent set of essays offers historical retrievals of the settler legacy that are more political in character. The first is the most straight-forward. It remembers a time—now buried at least two generations deep—when rural Alberta was home to the most robust radical-democratic politics in the country and prairie farm movements were associated with fresh, innovative ideas about the meaning of citizenship. More than ever, the rural needs to be reclaimed as a site of politics. My intention, however, is not to leave readers, especially farmers, with a sense of regret that they did not live in another time. There was no golden age. While there is, I think, much to admire in the political history of the frontier, my construction of that period is not meant to be an uncritical or an uncomplicated one. The remaining essays turn the same period over and over to see it from different sides.

In one case, I locate prairie radicalism within a bigger, older inheritance of agrarian practices and ideas shaped around distinctive understandings of land, work and freedom. As the editors of a recent book argue, "we can be neither good citizens nor creative scholars unless we fully engage the rural political tradition."[5] The tradition I have in mind emerges out of European peasant resistance to serfdom and the loss of the commons to new modes of property. It is expressed on the homestead frontier of North America in the identity of the producer-citizen and in the powerful, creative farmers' movements, producer co-operatives and local institutions of self-government that were built from scratch by settlers. It still echoes in the fragments of speech with which farm people struggle to say who they are and why it matters. The strength of that tradition, however, especially its focus on the producer, is also its weakness. At what point, for example, does the moral authority derived from producing food give way to the corporate agribusiness seed-and-chemical pitch to "feed a hungry world" by the promise of high yields?

The second essay considers the exclusions and self-exclusions of agrarian populism, partly through the close-up lens of family history. The third takes up the reality that agrarian thought, though it was forged against the princes and landlords of Europe, found its North American antithesis in the aboriginal; farmer-settlers were footsoldiers in the civilizing mission of cultivation. At least that has been the story we've told ourselves. My claim in this essay is that on these prairies, we are all treaty people—settler and aboriginal. I am not interested in easy self-flagellation. Rather, it is important to recall a more complex historic relationship than mere conquest and to recast the difficulties of accommodation, memory and reconciliation as the "settler problem," rather than, as the policymakers once put it, the "Indian problem." More than that, I venture the claim that it is necessary for old antagonisms to give way to rural coexistence not just as a matter of demographic necessity, but in recognition of profound parallels: policy histories, identities built on land and kinship, and now relegation to the status of ornamental anachronisms within the wider society. Where productive use of land was once a self-sufficient settler rationale, their descendents on the land now struggle, in turn, against the prospect of being displaced for some other, more profitable use by that same rationale.

IV

The final set of essays engages some of the contemporary challenges facing rural communities and farm livelihoods. Since about 1997, I have been drawn into the work of thinking *with*, and not just *for*, rural people across the prairies—in farm kitchens, community halls and churches, coffee shops, Orwellian multi-screen hotel conference rooms and university classrooms. I know that anger, weariness and bewilderment are the currency of a good deal of rural speech, and that tears are often close to the surface. Rural people feel increasingly on their own. They struggle with political indifference, a loss of cultural respect and a global economy that systematically extracts wealth from their communities. Many of them have been led to believe that this is somehow natural, that the logic of consolidation and the displacement of people with skills to produce food on a human scale is just the way the economy works. Indeed, displacement serves some interests well. Across North America, rural landscapes are being refashioned from the outside as resource plantations, industrial zones, transportation corridors, dumping grounds for big-city waste, or, if they are pretty enough, as resort destinations or recreational properties that drive land prices out of reach for agricultural use. The link between rural and agriculture has become increasingly tenuous. Land- and water-use conflicts have intensified. Not surprisingly, between 1998 and 2001—that is, before the worst summers of drought and bovine spongiform encephalopathy (BSE)— Statistics Canada recorded a precipitous decline of almost 40 percent in the number of people in Alberta and Saskatchewan who declared farming to be their primary occupation.[6] Nothing has happened since to reverse that trend. Those statistics simply aggregate the personal stories that rural people know all too well.

Bleak depictions of loss capture an undeniable reality. There is the black-and-white photograph of rural Saskatchewan on the controversial cover of the national newsmagazine *Maclean's* in 2002. Or there is the geopolitical travel writer Robert Kaplan's *Empire Wilderness*, which anticipates a future West, on both sides of the border, consisting of "suburban blotches separated by empty space."[7] But those are outsiders' depictions. There is something incomplete about them, something lifeless, too easily fitted into the modernist presumptions in which, after all, urban is destined to displace rural as surely as the future displaces the past, as surely as economic life is to be organized on industrial lines and concentrated in the hands of corporate owners. We have been trained to call this progress. The think-tank economists and business columnists are ready with advice: why not just move to where the jobs are? Almost always, any other response is dismissed as nostalgic. As the political philosopher Alasdair MacIntyre has written, with a reference to agriculture that is exceptionally rare among his profession, the range of acceptable political alternatives has been successfully narrowed so that "fundamental issues" are routinely excluded from public consideration:

> An example of just such an issue is that presented by the threat of the imminent disappearance of the family or household farm and with it of a way of life the history of which has been integral to the history of the virtues from ancient times onwards. Good farming has required for its sustenance, and has in turn sustained, virtues that are central to all human life, and not just to farming.... The destruction of the way of life of the household farm has therefore great significance for all of us and powerful statements of that signficance... have not been lacking. Yet these statements have had no effective political impact, and this is not because they have been heard within the political arena and then rejected. They have gone politically unheard.... [T]here has been nowhere in the entire political process where the members of modern political societies have been invited to confront systematically the question: 'What do we take the significance of this transformation to be and should we or should we not acquiesce in this loss of a way of life?'"[8]

There is precious little nostalgia, and plenty of fatalism, in the rural communities I know. I do not want my work to contribute to either.[9] That work—some of it represented in this collection—has resisted the notion that there is anything necessary about the displacement of people with the skill to produce food on a human scale. It has focussed instead on the human choices and the

7

structural economic forces involved. It has traced a history of political deskilling that has left rural people with a hollowed-out populism that swings ineffectively between rage and resignation, easily roused on gun control and same-sex marriage but complicit in the exclusion of serious economic issues from public policy discussion.[10] Most recently, my work has followed the emergence of renewed forms of rural political activism and community enterprise across the prairie West.[11] My examples include campaigns to challenge massive corporate hog-barn developments, oil-field flooding and school closures. They also include grain-car loading facilities, theatres, museums and direct-marketing food co-operatives. The people involved in those ventures—thoughtful, articulate, community-minded—defy all of the caricatures through which the rural is now most likely to be encountered. They know that what is at stake in the countryside touches on the most basic questions of our time, questions about the future of technology, work, food, the environment and democracy. That and the survival of what they are coming to call a distinct, minority culture—a way of life that is as rooted in the spaces in-between as it is difficult to put into a language that can be widely understood anymore.

The essay, "Two Albertas," marks in a related way the divergent trajectories of urban and rural. The essay's point of reference is the year 1996. It was commissioned for a provincial centennial history that assigned particular years to numerous authors. In my case, the year 1996 was a vantage point from which to observe that Alberta had become a very urban province, that its real countryside was increasingly an industrial one, but that, curiously, its mythology still drew on the pioneer farmers, ranchers and wide-open spaces that were quickly disappearing

v

The concluding essay in this collection reflects on what it means to be part of a university at home in the rural. Living and teaching in the prairie West, on Treaty 6 land, near the Battle River, has taught me the truth of Wendell Berry's insistence that a university and its professors need a beloved country. By that he means a point of reference outside the university, to which a sense of obligation, accountability and critical affection can be lived out within the context of a scholarly vocation. Without a beloved country, he writes, professors are prone to the narrowed horizons of careerism, insulated peer-review processes and incantations of excellence.[12]

The rural prairie West is, for me, such a landscape, a history, an economy, a set of complex communities encountered at close range and sometimes through enduring friendships. Its accent is one that I share.

One

# The Measure of a River

*Once in his life a man ought to concentrate his mind upon the*
*remembered earth.... He ought to give himself up to a particular*
*landscape in his experience, to look upon it from as many*
*angles as he can, to wonder upon it, to dwell upon it. He ought*
*to imagine that he touches it with his hands at every season and*
*listens to the sounds that are made upon it. He ought to imagine*
*the creatures there and all the faintest motions of the wind.*
*He ought to recollect the glare of noon and all the colors of the*
*dawn and dusk.*

    N. Scott Momaday[1]


I

Western Canada is carved by rivers whose headwaters begin in mountain glaciers, whose reputations have been made by the furs borne on
them, the cities built beside them or the distant ports reachable by
them. The Battle River can claim none of this. It flows from a small
lake in the west-central Alberta parkland and eventually into an over-
sized valley, hollowed in a geological instant, whose broad floor it
can only occupy respectfully by means of looping oxbows. The river
relies on whatever rain trickles down a thousand creeks to sustain
itself after spring run-off. It figures in no great exploration narratives.
While the explorer Anthony Henday in 1754 is thought to have been
the first European to set eyes on the river and to travel west along
its valley, he did so by foot. Having professed in his journals that
"I cannot describe...the pleasant country I am now in," he gave such
little account of its features that his turn-of-the-century editor judged
his route to have been far to the south.[2]

The Battle likewise has no significant commercial history. A Blackfoot map sketched for fur traders appears to give it the discouraging name "snake." The first wave of ranch and homestead settlement east of the railroad station at Wetaskiwin did follow the river on which, unfathomably, in the most literal sense, lumber and dry goods were floated downstream and passengers could travel on a 30-foot steamboat. But those first settlement villages—Duhamel, Heather Brae, Ferry Point—were soon bypassed in the railroad boom. They are now historic-site cairns. Indeed, the Battle runs through few towns before it joins the North Saskatchewan some 400 twisting miles from its source, surely the slowest feeder river in the great basin that drains into Hudson's Bay. Any canoeist knows as much, having struggled even once with its serpentine form, its beaver dams, and its shallows, against what turn out to be wildly optimistic projections of arrival time. In the prolonged drought of a recent summer, no flow was recorded along stretches of it. In other words, the Battle is insignificant by measures that judge a river by where it is going and by its power and sweep in getting there. Its appeal is not linear at all. Like the Jordan, it is a river defined by what it separates and what it joins, by what life it draws to itself and what life it releases.

II

To look upon the Battle River from the angle of the water itself, from a canoe, is to imagine that you are the first to come this way, having found a secret passage through a familiar place.

It is to stop paddling while a deer swims across the river in front of your bow and emerges, thin and muscular, to climb the opposite bank.

It is to learn the lie in hardened dichotomies like wild and domesticated: watching coyotes weave through a herd of cattle grazing in the flats; or tracing the eastward spread of maples from the abandoned farm around which evidently they were first planted. It is to hear intimations of an antiquarian quiet.

It is to understand why the Cree word for river, *sipiy*, is an animate noun.

It is to collect a Chauceresque pilgrimage of ducks, shorebirds, even a hawk. It is to be entertained—distracted?—by orange-tufted grebes skittering left-right-left across your path as if on the two-dimensional track of a carnival shooting gallery.

It is to accept the leadership of a heron, perhaps several, waiting stick-like around every bend, unfolding angular, prehistoric wings to keep a comfortable distance and lift mockingly over the narrows of an oxbow that will take twenty minutes to paddle. It is to glimpse a heron rookery in the tops of the tallest aspens.

It is to wonder at nature's diversity: pockets of spruce, cactus-studded badlands, and, on the sun-facing side, grass thin as threadbare cloth through which pale brown knees shine.

It is to skim the bacterial progeny of cattle manure.

To look upon the Battle River from the angle of the water itself, from a canoe, is unforgettably to join forces with my son the summer I turned 40, when he was 13, for a trip that began with an owl's smooth christening on the downward descent into the valley, then surprisingly easy talk about important things—careers, religion, the school year just ahead—all of it silenced by the slow realization that this would take more time and concentrated paddling than we had planned. It is to steer around deadfall, to find the gap in a beaver dam, to duck fence-line, to judge the depth of a stony patch, to form a habit of watchful steering so disciplined it continues into sleep that night.

### III

Walking away from the river, we catch a doe in the open with a fawn that cannot be more than a week old. The fawn struggles to stand on new legs, then collapses, as if injured. We are within 200 feet. I have a firm grip on the dog who, for once, doesn't notice a thing. But the doe has seen us. She implores the fawn to follow to the safety of hillside brush. She makes a two-step start, turns back, starts, turns back, each time with greater urgency, until the fawn is coaxed forward for a short advance. The doe resumes her pleading. It takes several tense minutes for doe and fawn to complete their arc around us and disappear.

Somewhere in this encounter is a lesson about grace and danger, and how little stands between them. Or there is grace itself, a gift, which looks like danger from the other side.

IV

*Kahkewak*—Dried Meat Hill—is one of those subtle surprises that
confound conventional notions of prairie. Approached from the
north, a dirt road overhung with trees rises unassumingly before
opening to a panorama of sky, fields, and a long lake bending to the
west and south, where the river is pinched and widens across the
valley. This view alone holds your attention for a long time, like a
complex painting in which, even looking away, you see something
new and are drawn back. But the hilltop beckoning beyond a fence
surpasses it with a clean curve of horizon in every direction.

This hill is where I have come to understand physically where is
here, to face the sun, to revel in the wildness of a coyote den, and to
impress mountain-bound British Columbians with the elongated
shadows of sunset.

This hill is where I have come with university classes; for it is
easier and more powerful to talk about treaty-making with an eyeful
of land. For the same reason, local people commemorated the Treaty
6 centennial in 1976 with a re-enactment on this hill, to which they
invited representatives of the Cree communities around Hobbema,
not far upstream on the Battle and joined by the same treaty-making story, but, in the way the river also separates, worlds apart in
everyday life.

This hill was a crucial site in the buffalo economy. It was used for
drying meat to be mixed with local berries for pemmican. It was a
strategic look-out, too, part of a chain of high points along which sig-
nals could be relayed when Cree migration into Blackfoot territory
and conflict over buffalo and access to Fort Edmonton made a border
region out of a long stretch of the Battle—east to the Neutral Hills—
and gave the river its name. Not far from here, the black-robed Father
Lacombe made his famous foray into a cloud of bullets to plead for
peace during a Cree attack on Blackfoot lodges.

In the sea change of settlement, Cree names for hill and river
passed awkwardly into English. The first settlers who picnicked at
the hill recall bleached buffalo bones knee-deep around the base—
cleaned up, no doubt, by scavengers selling to American fertilizer factories. By 1903, the hill was the site of a dance hall which was dismantled a dozen years later for lumber to build a barn. It has served since

as pasture and gravel pit. A fresh sign posted last spring on a fence-line stretched tight spelled out its present status: THIS GRAVEL PIT IS THE PROPERTY OF THE ALBERTA GOVERNMENT. TRESPASSERS WILL BE PROSECUTED.

This hill is where I came with my father at the end of a drive through the country, when Parkinson's and arthritis had slowed his step and curved his spine. I guided him through the fence the way he must once have showed me—step down on one strand, pull up on the one above, slide a hand on his unsteady back to protect him from barbs. We climbed past the buffalo beans and the dragonflies thick and blue as cornflowers on the hillside. Why? Not just to show him an eyeful of land, but to let him see for himself who I'd become, who I was, how I was at home.

To invest oneself anywhere in the world is to live with the possibility it will be lost.


V

For two weeks in October the harvested fields between the southern rim of Camrose and the river are a staging area for migrating Canada geese. The evening skies are noisy with geese swirling in formation, "Vs" unfurling like large ribbons, maybe 20 swirls or more visible at a time; landing, foraging, taking off, building strength. And then one evening, unpredictably, just as their presence has become a familiar part of the landscape, they are gone; the novelty of silence does not register at first.

The geese are gone, and we are left to face the winter.


VI

In the long interval between harvest and spring thaw, which is to say at least six months of the year, the field that is just one block west and across the ring-road from our house is walkable. This pleases our dog, though she is less fussy about the coarse, high cut of canola scratching at her underside than she is about wheat stubble. Packed snow is best of all. She came from a farm near the river: part golden retriever, part terrier, lesser parts unknown. In the field she is unfailingly alert, running ragged, nose down, following a track, expecting something.

The field rewards human attentiveness, too, to light, colour, and the grade of the land, though it is a place of jarring juxtaposition. To the north horizon stand the first big-box commercial markers of everycity. To the south is the distinct, blue-haze line of hills. To look towards the river is to accept that discovery comes slowly. About colour, for example. About how fleeting are the greens. About how quickly in fall they are purified into blues and yellows. About how those primary colours dominate even in mid-summer in the play of canola flowers on a pale sky. Left to themselves in September they brighten each other, so that a slough is never so blue and the aspen leaves around it are almost afire. In winter angled sunlight makes waves of blue shadow on a snow-covered field and turns protruding yellow stubble soft as mohair. In winter too, pink smudges the southern horizon in mid-afternoon, and a mirage turns the hills south beyond the river and north, along the Miquelon Lakes escarpment, into speckled arborite counter-tops rounded up against a kitchen wall.

"It is only in the place that one belongs to, intimate and familiar, long watched over," writes Wendell Berry, "that the details rise up out of the whole and become visible."[3]

VII
*Indifferent to, or contemptuous of, or afraid to commit ourselves to, our physical and social surroundings, always hopeful of something better, hooked on change, a lot of us have never stayed in one place long enough to learn it, or have learned it only to leave it.*

Wallace Stegner[4]

One of the enduring attractions of our suburban bungalow is the line of tall old aspens behind our lot, curiously preserved from development. The trees have grown in around a Grand Trunk Pacific rail-bed cutting diagonally across the township grid to what was, in 1910, a wooden trestle bridge across the Battle River valley—the largest in the British Empire, perhaps the world.

You can see that tree line from the air. Or you can walk it. Not that the walking is easy. This abandoned rail-bed, unlike others in

Western Canada, has not been converted to a gravelled recreational trail. There is no path at all. The trees are the only guide, which means threading between them, ducking electric fences where landowners have annexed this strip of pasture, or, where the trees flare out, doubling back after following the wrong side through an overnight deer-bed into a slough. At the rim of the valley, where the treeline disappears, bushwhacking through gullies is the only option.

A friend and I took more than four hours to arrive at the valley bottom near the spot in the river where bridge pilings are still visible: 10 feet across, 80 feet wide, at the base. The bridge was built in a spendthrift era using four million board-feet of foot-square B.C. timbers, hauled from the train in Camrose by exhausted farm horses, and set on pilings driven deep into the ground. The bridge was almost 4000 feet long, with a wide bend at the north end that unnerved passengers when the once-a-day train between Edmonton and Mirror leaned into it. The bridge was a famed engineering marvel, though vulnerable to fire (a local man walked it after each train to check for sparks) and, above all, to the GTP's precarious financial position. It was a costly redundancy when the company was folded into Canadian National; it was dismantled in 1924 and the timbers sold off.

The small slice of valley where the bridge crossed represents a rich confluence of cultures and a reminder of the provisional nature of all of them, indeed, of all human work. Within half a century, it was witness to the construction and dismantling of a bridge and, before it, a clapboard town; to cattle-ranching's brief heyday; and to what local histories describe as the last Cree sun dance in which "torture was used"—this in about 1892, on the north rim, where officers of the North West Mounted Police arrived from Fort Saskatchewan to break it up. Before that, this slice of valley was witness to a flourishing Metis settlement, surveyed in river lots. Part of the Red River diaspora of the 1870s, Metis families bridged old and new prairie economies. They were the area's first cultivators and merchants. But they were also buffalo hunters and ox-cart freighters. Hunters returned to this settlement with meat from the last big hunt on the central Alberta plains, and freighters returned each fall from Fort Garry in noisy caravans, wheels screaming and staggered in order to minimize ruts, loaded with supplies exchanged for furs. In the aftermath of the 1885 rebellion at Batoche and the displacement of freighters by the railroad, however, the population dwindled. Metis surnames like Laboucane, Salois, and Dumont have no current local presence except in the cemetery of the church built in the early 1880s. Cart tracks can still be found in the valley. And the land is still divided into the long, narrow lots on either side of the river.[5]

One October afternoon I came to the flats with two busloads of Grade three students to find the bridge pilings. The idea was to study local history in a place where it could be visualized. Our group was joined by the grandmother of one of the students, who had married into an old ranch family in that part of the valley. She told how children a generation before her had climbed and walked atop the trestle bridge. Then she took us to the bench halfway up the north slope on which a Belgian engineer-entrepreneur had built a ranch house complete with imported marble for the fireplace. She passed around a picture of the house in which she had lived until it burned down in the early 1950s.

The children fidgeted through the storytelling, hers and mine, and seemed unimpressed by the bridge pilings. They were impatient to play in the hills.

One wide-eyed girl later declared this was her first trip out of Camrose to the country.

VIII

*The world is full of places. Why is it that I am here?*
Wendell Berry[6]

A decade and a half ago our family returned to the Saskatchewan River watershed in which I have lived most of my life, though this time to a small city, a small university, and a tributary I did not know. I carried a Ph.D. from a top-notch Ontario university, and with it the unspoken disappointment of professors who expected I would land something better, even in a tough job market. One of them mused that everyone should spend a couple of years in the hinterlands before returning to the centre. After five years, my forays into the countryside had become more deliberate. They could easily be interpreted as an admission of defeat, a coming-to-terms with the narrowing of prospects, a small-town boy's defiance of the metropolitan snobbishness of his academic guild, or perhaps a mid-life release of restless ambition for the safer waters of belonging. There is enough truth in each of these explanations to call them to mind. Since childhood I have known the unsatisfied pulls of ambition and belonging; and if I seem to tilt now towards the latter, I do so recognizing them not as rivals—a choice of standing out or fitting in—but as different expressions of the same human aspiration to be remembered, to be saved from obscurity at death.

While such psychological accounts can be rehearsed to the point of self-absorption, they are not enough to answer Berry's profoundly human question. They construe a relationship of one-way desire. They discount the possibility that a place can exert its own influence. Tellingly, what now requires justification is the full-bodied work of knowing a place, seeing it from many angles, finding its beauty, stories and human imprints. The times are against it. In the global village, linked by computers and mobile capital, place is inconsequential. Locality is condemned with faint praise to a pedestal from which it cannot disrupt the consumption of name-brand culture. Why indeed?

From the intellectual hinterland of western Montana, Albert Borgmann writes that against the technology-driven, "glamorously unreal," "virtual," and hyperactive frenzy of a society in which we are made sullen, disposable, less mindful and less connected to our place in the world, we must recover a "world of eloquent things"— whether wilderness or human artistry or communal celebration— that "may *speak to us in their own right*."[7]

Eloquent things, real, humbling things. A heron rookery. A fawn in an open field. The commanding presence of a hill. The departure of geese. The remains of a trestle bridge. A pink smudge above the horizon. The ancient singing and drumming of a pow-wow. The feel of the bones in Cree hand-games. The familiar banter around a softball diamond at Edberg, with its spectacularly distracting view from the first-base coaching box. Harvest season. The hospitality of people on both sides of the river from Gwynne to Paradise Valley. This world of eloquent things is not easily or instantly won. Borgmann writes that it requires us to "[settle] down in the land that has come to be ours, to give up the restless search for a hyper-real elsewhere, and to come to terms with nature and tradition in a patient and vigorous way."[8]

Why is it that I am here? Where is here? What does it mean to *dwell* here, as the philosopher Heidegger once put it, in the sense of preserving and staying-with it?[9] What attentiveness does dwelling entail? What inherited obligations? What does it mean, in particular, to be a fourth-generation settler on Treaty 6 land, one who feels obliged to mediate respectfully between the settler and Cree worlds that in this place are separated—and joined—by a river? What needs preserving and staying-with?

How is it that a river can collect and carry along the disjointed fragments of lived experience, solitary and communal, that have come to constitute this place for me?

What is it to know a river?

IX

On what turned out to be the last warm day of September, sign or no sign, I returned with a class to the commanding presence of Dried Meat Hill. My expectations, as always, were high. We sat cross-legged in a circle at the top above a patchwork world of primary colours: blues, yellows, the red leaves of berry bushes. Harvest was in full swing in every direction. Again, I told the story of the signing of Treaty 6 at Fort Pitt on the North Saskatchewan, though it was easy to imagine the lodges erected at the base of this hill that day. At one point I looked up to see, in the clump of trees just beyond our circle, a large bird against a dead branch, its shape at first indistinct, then clearly that of a giant pilleated woodpecker, almost two feet tall; until I could confirm it later, I was unsure that a woodpecker could be that size.

But that was not all that happened on the hill that morning. A middle-aged aboriginal student, a woman who had sat apart from the circle, facing east, came back down with tears in her eyes and gratitude in her voice. Somehow, she said, the anger she had carried a long time was gone. Days later, she ventured that "the grandfathers were there on the hill," whispering words of consolation.

The possibility of a world of eloquent things capable of speaking does not seem at all far-fetched along the Battle River. Meandering as it does at the geographic margins of human utility and consumption, in a prosperous, increasingly urban Alberta, it sustains real counter-possibilities for those who approach with patience and vigor, senses alert, expecting to be surprised.

Author's note: An earlier version of this essay appeared in the magazine *Alberta Views*, March/April 2000.

Two

# Oklahoma
## *Meditations on Home and Homelessness*

*From my family I have learned the secrets of never having a home.*
   Linda Hogan, *Red Clay: Poems and Stories*[1]


I

Long before I had ever been to Oklahoma, I was no stranger to it, to its
ruddy soil, to the pleated banks of the Washita River; I was no stranger to the longing for home. Oklahoma I learned in my grandmother's
house. More than any words spoken, Oklahoma was the melancholy in
her eyes and voice. In the early morning, though this may be the com-
pression of childhood memory, she combed through her waist-length
hair, uncut since she was a girl, while I feigned sleep on a make-shift
sofa-bed. And she sang wistfully, if not precisely, about Oklahoma.
*O beautiful for spacious skies/and amber waves of grain.* She had lived
there less than the span of childhood, not even one-half the years
between land rush and dust bowl. Home and not home it was. And is.
Oklahoma.


II

*The land is always stalking the people.* The words are those of an elderly
Apache woman, repeated in my hearing and scribbled in my note-pad.
The stalking is real, intense, personal. I am being stalked. The land has
taken the form of a story that reveals itself, on its time, in tantalizing
fragments, as if testing my willingness to follow; and now it insists on
being told. Apparently the story must begin with a grandmother, too,
although at one level it is about two men—one, a Cheyenne chief; the

23

other, my maternal great-grandfather—who are themselves linked only by geography and 19th-century Indian policy. Why a grandmother? Why start with one who did not, could not as a woman in her culture, choose either to go or to stay, one who followed and made accommodation? The story is opaque; I am ready to abandon it. But then I am drawn back to N. Scott Momaday's *The Way to Rainy Mountain*, whose beautiful retelling of Kiowa myth and history also begins with a grandmother remembered in the intimacy of long unbraided hair. She had been present as a girl, Momaday writes, at the Kiowas' last Sun Dance on the banks of the Washita in 1887. She was present at the same site three years later when no buffalo could be found to sacrifice, when soldiers rode from Fort Sill to disperse the people. She was his living historical link to the Plains culture of the Kiowa.

Momaday's description on this occasion also recalls a rudimentary map, photocopied from a community history that is part of a profusion of papers and books before me. In small print, befitting historical minutiae, the map marks a sun-dance site. Could it be the same one? It is just across the river, perhaps three miles, from where in March 1894 my great-grandfather Jacob Klaassen claimed a homestead. So the land stalks; a story must be told, or rather retold. But why this land I had not seen, why this story? And how to explain its attraction?

Antonio Gramsci writes in his *Prison Notebooks* that the "starting point of critical elaboration [is] 'knowing thyself' as a product of the historical process to date, which has deposited in you an infinity of traces…Therefore it is imperative at the outset to compile an inventory."[2] That is a partial answer. The story, of course, will have its own purposes. But in the silt of the Washita is a confluence of traces: manifest destiny, of course, but also the Lockean hierarchy of cultivation over wilderness, the biblical exodus and Mennonite pacifism wedded to premillenialist German piety, for a start. The traces may sometimes stand in contradiction, but each in its own way is imbued with expectations of home: a continent emptied for immigrants, with reservations to fence in the wild; productive property wrested by labour from wasteland; a promised land; and, finally, heaven. Nothing but heaven. These tributaries of the Washita collect the lives of the Cheyenne people pushed southward by settlement and of my maternal ancestors arrived in vagabondage from points as distant as Samarkand in Central Asia. They empty imperceptibly in me and in my children.

III

*The prairie is the palm of an outstretched hand,*
*not flat but hilled with calluses;*
*world rubbed against*
*world, hardship against*
*hardship, then grown over.*
*Layers of story resist peeling back,*
*come all at once or not at all.*[3]

IV

By the time Black Kettle fell from his horse to the chill of the Washita, his body splintered by the guns of Custer's Seventh Cavalry, he was ready to settle for a home. Even if it was his reservation in Indian Territory. Even if the promised provisions for eating and hunting did not come. The year was 1868. Black Kettle was tired. The power of his speech he could feel slipping away, and he had nothing else. He was a peace chief in the way of the Cheyenne. He had made his reputation as a warrior...carried the sacred arrows into battle...took treaty with the first chiefs...listened hard to Lean Bear, back from Washington and the Great White Father (what kind of name is Lincoln?) without pockets for hiding his words...fingered his medal...believed the promises...saw Lean Bear ride out to meet the bluecoats, shot dead; a medal is no shield at twenty paces...rumbled like a fool into Denver on a wagon without a horse beneath him...sat in a photographer's aim: *I have not come here with a little wolf's bark, but have come to talk plain with you*...believed the promises...calmed his people at Sand Creek as the soldiers closed in...dressed his lodge with the Stars and Stripes...watched White Antelope step out to stop the bullets, never forgot his death song: *Nothing lives long, except the earth and the mountains*...escaped up the creek, returned at nightfall for his wife's body, carried her still living to camp...kept on putting himself in between...used up his words stopping the young men's anger...

spoke less to the commissioners, pushing west, always wanting the same thing: *Your young soldiers, I don't think they listen to you. You bring presents, and when I come to get them, I am afraid they will strike me before I get away*...made his point at the head of 500 Cheyenne mounted in five columns, they in crimson and eagle feathers—so said *The New York Tribune*—he in dingy blanket, directing their movement by turn of the hand...took land in Indian Territory on the lie that his people could still hunt buffalo...waited for treaty provisions... couldn't stop the whiskeysellers...couldn't keep his young men at home...lost face...appealed again for peace...wanted to believe the promises...returned to the lodges along the Washita, called a council, urged a move down-river to safety in waste-deep November snow... never had a chance...couldn't even shield his wife riding with him from the bullets.

*Moka-ta-va-ta.* Black Kettle. A name given in adulthood, a story, flattened in English translation into the two dimensions of an immutable ledger entry. A name that in translation suggests something at once faintly comical and dangerous—sooty, burnt, overheated, domesticated. A name flattened, not unlike his speeches, translated and recorded by government scribes, preserved not by telling and retelling, but in the files of the War Department and the Bureau of Indian Affairs. They are recorded without gesture, inflection, or tone, as if only the words themselves matter. But they are not easily discounted, or romanticized for that matter. Here is Black Kettle, addressing the treaty commissioners one year after the massacre at Sand Creek:

> *When I come in to receive presents I take them up*
> *crying. Although wrongs have been done me*
> *I live in hope. I have not got*
> *two hearts.*

The commissioners, at his request, have counted the wounds on his wife's body. There are nine in all:

*Now we are together again to make peace.*
*My shame is as big as the earth,*

*although I will do what my friends advise me to do.*
*I once thought that I was the only man*
   *that persevered to be the friend of the*
      *white man, but since they have come*
   *and cleaned out our lodges, horses, and everything else,*
      *it is hard for me to believe white men anymore.*
   *These lands that you propose to give us*
      *I know nothing about.*
   *There are a great many white men. Possibly*
      *you may be looking for someone with a strong heart. Possibly*
         *you may be intending to do something for me better than I know of.*

Here is Black Kettle the next autumn, summoned to defend the
Cheyenne against charges of murder and horse theft:

*Notwithstanding the promises made to me had not been fulfilled,*
   *when we heard that Commissioners were here*
      *and had sent for us, Chiefs and soldiers*
   *got on their horses and came to hear what you had to say.*
*It is very hard for us to move so often,*
   *and we are without proper clothing. What is right is all we want.*
*The reason why we moved from this place as soon as we did*
   *was to get away from trouble.*
*Your talk is good and we are going to listen to you.*
   *Will it be true, or*
      *as heretofore not come out as you represent it?*
*We will leave once again.*
*There may be some jumping around yet but we will trust you.*[4]

After the "battle" of Washita River, the U.S. Army moved 3,500
Cheyenne to the block of land reserved for them in Indian Territory,
next to the Kiowa. Home and not home.

    v

By the time Jacob Klaassen paid the auctioneer, said goodbye to his
neighbours and his land above the Washita River, weeping as he
had only twice before, and departed by train from Oklahoma, he was

leaving home. Defying it. The year was 1918. The oldest boys were gone away, and a father should follow. He had been granted his boyhood dream, nourished in the watermelon field of a German enclave in Russia: to own a big farm. Now it was finished. He would not look back. In his life he had buried his father dead of typhus in Turkestan...pulled axles from quicksand in the wagontrain to the Second Coming...seen Ellis Island and Niagara Falls...chafed as a farmhand...looked for cheap land in Nebraska and Colorado...heard of Cheyenne land opening up: $10 for title...took his brother to pick a homestead, 70 miles from the train...ignored the worrisome back in Nebraska (he knew wild: tigers and Asiatic bandits, unrestrained by God-ordained authority)...loaded everything on a rail car, livestock too, got off at Minco, assembled the wagons...built a sod hut, shared with animals...hauled water from neighbours...survived a January storm that caught him in the open...stopped Sundays for services at the Mennonite mission seven miles by horse where, to his disgust, women suckled infants in plain view...brought his bride from Kansas, fearful all four days from the train what she'd make of the farm... sliced the land with his plough-blade...sowed corn and wheat... became a father...built a house, at last, of wood...accepted, reluctantly, election as a minister in the Herold Mennonite Church, where on Christmas Eve in 1903 almost 120 sacks filled with apples, oranges, candy, and nuts were given out to the children present...promised not to preach in vain lofty words...wrote out his sermons...buried his mother: O death where is thy sting?...buried a first daughter, lived twelve days: *O death where is thy*...begged Katie to rest...called for the doctor...could not sleep...cradled her until death *tore through my spirit*...sting: *Now I was alone with my six boys. How was everything going to go on?*...lost words to preach...shovelled wheat onto a wagon...watched Herman his youngest run alongside, fall under the wheel, crushed...carried limp to the house...remembered no more: *You are a God who hides Himself*...battled doubt, feared judgment... rented land for the boys in the valley from the Indians: made it produce...built a barn, paid cash...picked ripe fruit...heard war news... felt hate in the town...decided it was time for his sons to go to Canada when his nephew was shipped home from Fort Leavenworth in a box, in a uniform he had refused to wear.

A Mennonite pulpit was not a Cheyenne council fire. On a Sunday, it gave only one man the authority to speak free of interruption or concern for time. Jacob Klaassen by his own account was almost overwhelmed by the awesome responsibility attached to the office. Preaching was a dignified business. Somewhere, no doubt, copies exist of his sermons that would attest to his preoccupations—whether in the Old Testament he favoured the texts of exodus and deliverance over exile and dispersal, whether he preached a God of sternness or blessing. I suspect that he leaned towards exile, towards sternness, exemplified it in his eyes, his stance, in the confidence of a voice unwavering until it was silenced in a chain of sorrows. That was his preacher's role. And the father's role, with no mother to soften it: *always so afraid that we would go to pieces socially and morally, since we were, after all, as far as other people were concerned, left quite to ourselves.* The trademark sternness that some of his sons inherited, including the grandfather I faintly remember was, for Jacob Klaassen, a protective mask, formed, layered, and worn in three continents. It was a mask; the honest emotion expressed in his memoirs suggests as much. But once he left Oklahoma, he was inclined—this, at least, is the impression I have— to keep that mask on, to reveal himself only in what he put to paper for his children and grandchildren.

On his last Sunday afternoon in Oklahoma, Jacob Klaassen was persuaded back to his farm where, unknown to him, the Herold congregation had gathered for a last farewell:

*I could not help weeping. Had I not lived the most beautiful part of my life*
     *on this little piece of ground?*
*There were several short speeches; I thanked them all again*
     *for the love and friendly participation,*
        *And said my farewells once more.*
*And how heavy this farewell became! And yet*
     *when a brother asked me if I did not still feel*
     *quite at home, and if I was not sorry about my decision, I had to say no;*
     *it had required such incredibly hard struggles which I had to fight*
        *all by myself to separate myself*
     *from all this, and after I had finished the struggle*
        *I was actually rid of everything*

*and a stranger,*
*and would remain a stranger everywhere from then on.*
*And this has been corroborated until this day.*
*In spite of all the good that I have received, I have never felt*
*at home in Canada.*[5]

Jacob Klaassen lived out his remaining thirty years on a farm in the district of Eigenheim, Saskatchewan, on land ceded to the Canadian government by the Willow Cree, a field away from where his son, my grandfather, raised a family with my grandmother. They were betrothed secretly in his last days in Oklahoma and agreed to marry, she once told me, when he was settled on a farm. *Eigenheim*: home of one's own. Could promises flattened into English be true, or as heretofore not come out as represented?

VI
*Police make it hard wherever I may go/*
*And I ain't got no home in this world anymore.*
*This dusty old dust is a-gettin' my home/*
*and I got to be drifting along.*

Is it any coincidence that Woody Guthrie also came from Oklahoma? How many of us are there displaced on this continent? How many with ancestors buried there?

VII
If this story must have a point, beyond its yearnings for home, its coincidences of geography, its parallels of male defeat, could it lie in the fact that its two principal figures nowhere converge, that their lives must be forced into juxtaposition so that the latter can never be understood apart from the former? In Jacob Klaassen's pioneering horizon, the Cheyenne and Arapaho of west-central Oklahoma were incidental: a mission-field, rocking-chair landlords. If he swapped stories with any of them around the fire at the creek-side campsites on the trail to El Reno; if he forded the river down the hill at Big Jake Crossing—named for a Cheyenne chief of Black Kettle's council— to walk the sun-dance site; if he read Custer hagiography; he left no

account. He did not look for the Canaanites on taking possession of the promised land. He was a farmer. And this, by force of will, was to be home.

The story of my great-grandfather has been with me, at least in broad outline, since childhood. Homesteading in Indian Territory surely was part of its romance. The story of Black Kettle I first heard from Lawrence Hart, a Cheyenne peace chief. He told it—why? expecting what?—in the heart of Alberta's God-fearing, wealth-blessed, white-skinned Bible belt; and I have never forgotten it. Hart was present on the banks of the Washita in November 1968, the anniversary of the "battle," when the Grandsons of the Seventh Cavalry arrived unexpectedly from California in authentic costume and full weapons, intensifying what was already an uneasy re-enactment. His children were in the lodges. Hart writes of the instant and deep hatred he felt on that occasion.[6] But he was also a peace chief, chosen for his temperament, expected to put himself in between. He was the one who, on behalf of the other chiefs, put the commemorative blanket over the shoulders of the Grandsons' Commanding Officer, although it had not been his choice. The ceremonial gesture loosed a hundred years of tears and embracing. My family, however, was nowhere near. Custer hadn't died for our sins. We had no blood bad enough to need reconciliation; we had come too late, left too soon.

Home, in the restlessness of North America, is what you leave to make your life as an autonomous individual; thereafter you live wherever you choose. Homesickness was Nietzsche's diagnosis of nineteenth-century Europe's fatal attraction to nationalism, and the word recurs as part of the urban, postmodern sneer at any "nostalgia" of place, offered from the superior vantage-point of ironic detachment, that is, from nowhere. Even common sense advises not to expect home so you won't be betrayed in a century, like the one before, of mass migration.

I did not grow up in Eigenheim, although its country church, where I first discovered Jacob Klaassen's intense, bearded face in a large, framed photograph, and its cemetery, where all of my grandparents and most of my great-grandparents are buried, still hold a powerful attraction for me. Where I grew up, eighty miles south, no one had known my parents as children; and I, in turn, had resolved to leave perhaps by the time I was six. It was not home, although the immensity of its near-treeless sweep of land and sky left a mark such that I cannot imagine living anywhere other than the North American prairies. Leaving is the way it has been with us for a long time. Leave-takings are what we expect. To find maternal ancestors who knew one place over a lifetime—and most of them were farming people—I would need to go back at least six generations and nearly two centuries to the Vistula delta of West Prussia. Prospects for the future are no better. My children have already moved from their places of birth, and now from home, and are growing up in a society and an economy that assumes their mobility.

When I had not yet been to Oklahoma, I knew that someday I would go make my peace with it—at the farm, at the river below. Home and not home.

VIII

The land, it turns out, has more to tell.

In the summer of 2000, our family drove north to south across the Great Plains, temperatures crowding 100 degrees, two teenagers in the back, to the part of southwestern Oklahoma that was at once so familiar as an imagined place, so crucial to my sense of belonging, and yet, on first impression, so spectacularly sparse and so bereft of any markers of that historical imagination. Not only that, as talk radio on the highway made clear, politically this was now hardcore Republican country—alien and intimidating. The point of entry, however, proved no more threatening than a telephone call to a distant relative, Robert, who had just moved off the farm, my great-grandfather's farm, after fifty years. All it took was mention of family from Canada. By the next morning, Robert, his sister and brother were waiting at the Herold church to welcome us to the Sunday service. Even the usher knew to expect us. This is extended family: stretched tight across a continent for generations, but not broken.

In the sanctuary where Jacob Klaassen once preached and where, outside, overgrown cedars shaded the graves of his wife, son and infant daughter, the preacher speaks on the Old Testament text from the Book of Joshua in which God assures the Hebrew people that they will take possession of the land that was promised to their forefathers. This of all texts. The sermon, however, is scarcely triumphal. It is inflected with the same sense of fragility found in rural churches across North America: "If you farm, the future can be scary....We're hanging on out here in the country." Before the service ends, the preacher informs the congregation that one of its elderly members, a distant relative, a rancher with a reputation for colourful stories and plain language, is in hospital. The invitation for volunteers to help finish the summer fieldwork draws affectionate interest. Evidently, the pull of community and the reciprocal code of neighbourliness temper the impulse to judgment.

Robert is part cowboy too. After lunch, he removes his necktie (his "rope"), changes to blue jeans and swings his bad hip into the driver's seat of his 1983 Lincoln. His worn-white Stetson sits on the dash. Robert is taking us—not quickly, not directly and certainly not in air-conditioned comfort—to the farm, which we are anxious to see and he, though obliging, is not. We stop first at brother Eddie's in Clinton. We drive past the place where Robert has coffee with "working people, not your doctors, lawyers and teachers"—the words are out before he remembers that his sister had proudly introduced me in church as a college professor. We stop at a kitsch Indian trading post off the interstate highway. We stop at Big Jake Crossing to see the cottonwood, deformed by lightning, where 19th-century cattle rustlers, horse thieves and rapists met justice at the end of a rope. Robert points out the sundance site across the river. Back in the Lincoln, running rough, its radiator hose about to blow, we drive past the hill—*Steinerberg*—on which my grandparents played as children.

And then we are at the farm. Robert has not been back since he sold it two months ago to a young couple from the community. He is only here now because we asked. He bought that farm from his wife's parents, who bought it from Jacob Klaassen. He had held onto it through the loneliness that followed the death of his first wife and through divorce settlements that followed two short-lived marriages to women who, he says, "took him to the cleaners." He had only sold it because at his age, near 80, no bank would give him the loan he needed to make improvements to the farm and his custom haying operation. The first thing he notices is that the line of trees he once planted as a windbreak for his daughter when she waited for the school bus at the end of the lane has been removed. We lavish our attention instead on the hip-roofed barn that was built by my great-grandfather and his sons, complete with an inventive pulley elevator, in the prosperous years before World War One. Remarkably, it shows no sign of sagging. There are also fruit trees on the farm that my great-grandfather would have planted and nurtured; they are loaded with the apricots he learned to appreciate as a boy in Central Asia. Robert, however, cannot help but scrutinize the farm for signs of recent change and, by implication, disrespect. Already, it is home and not home.

IX

The land has one more surprise, one more juxtaposition to reveal. Robert's sister Helen has taken us to the county museum in Cordell, just north of the domed courthouse where an antagonistic judge once sent the boys of the Herold church to military prison rather than accept their claims as conscientious objectors. On a display table is a 1913 map of Washita County. After two days of backroads exploration, I have bearings enough to locate the quarter-section squares belonging to my great-grandfather, his brother and, several miles south, my grandmother's parents. There is another familiar name or two. But I am not prepared for what else I see. Within two miles or so of the river, the map is a checkerboard that alternates between Mennonite and Cheyenne owners. Among the latter, there is also a familiar name: that of White Buffalo Woman. She was a girl in 1868 when the Seventh Cavalry attacked the Cheyenne. Her description of the event is an important piece of its oral history.[7] In 1913—though I cannot say for sure it is the same person—she is listed as the owner of two 80-acre blocks of land. One straddles the river. The other borders Jacob Klaassen's farm.

Author's note: An earlier version of this essay appeared in *Conrad Grebel Review* 16 (1998): 61–69. It is reprinted with permission. I have been indebted subsequently to the encouragement of Roxanne Dunbar-Ortiz, another transplanted Oklahoman and to the inspiration of her fine memoir, *Red Dirt: Growing Up Okie* (London: Verso, 1997). This essay also reflects the work of Wallace Stegner, the foremost literary interpreter of the themes of home and homelessness in the history of the North American west. His family had not yet abandoned its Canadian homestead when my draft-dodging grandfather would have passed by it in 1918 on the road from Hydro, Montana, to Maple Creek, Saskatchewan.

Three

# Hanley, Saskatchewan

I

*To the person who lives in a modern city with all the*
*conveniences that go with city living, our pride in our town*
*might seem rather strange and unexplainable. Our town is not*
*new. Most of its buildings are not modern; in fact, many are*
*old and perhaps a bit shabby. And many small prairie towns*
*can boast of a more beautiful location. These are the*
*observations which are probably made by the newcomer to our*
*town, or by the highway or railway traveller as he passes*
*through our town. But these are actually the facts which form*
*the basis of our pride in our town. Hanley possesses the dignity*
*of an older prairie town; its buildings reflect both the prosperity*
*and hardship which it has experienced in more than fifty years*
*of existence.*

Hanley: The Story of the Town and District, 1955 [1]

Small prairie towns and perhaps, by now, the entire province of
Saskatchewan are steeped in defences that are no less skilful for
being familiar. For every audience, every situation, those defences
must strike the right balance between conflicting core elements: a
self-deprecating honesty; a near-fatalism about the forces that determine prosperity and hardship; a scepticism that outsiders—city
people—are fit to judge, much less understand, what they can see
only in passing; a desire, nonetheless, for respect from those same
outsiders; and, as a last resort, a pride in one's own, in simple endurance, as if the alternative of self-loathing is not an option. I know

those defences from the inside. Hanley is where I grew up, mostly in the 1960s, when its prospects already seemed far removed from the boomtown "picture of prosperity verging at times on opulence" recalled in the 1955 Diamond Jubilee history—when, indeed, even that book represented a grander, more ambitious, and more literary town than the one I knew. I have deployed those same defences with limited success on my own children when, on the way to somewhere else, we have detoured through town. In size alone, it impresses them mostly by its insignificance. Not knowing the stories that give life to human landmarks, there is not much to see.

Three blocks by six, more or less, set diagonally against the survey grid, parallel with the Canadian Northern tracks—its lifeline. By 1906, two or three homestead trains a day deposited settlers and their effects into tent villages and ox-carts headed for land as much as 100 treeless miles away. In the legendary prairie winter that followed, desperate people shovelled drifts of snow off the tracks—in April—so that food, coal, medicine and mail could finally come through. In 1959, Queen Elizabeth II stepped from a rail-car on her cross-country tour to receive flowers from a local girl. Now, along those same tracks, there is no more grain delivery. When the last Wheat Pool elevator went up in the late 1960s, it had filled out a respectable skyline by any prairie standards.

Main Street shrunk long ago to a single, gap-toothed block, having never recovered from a series of fires, the most spectacular in 1947, and then from the arrival of a four-lane highway to Saskatoon. Certainly there is nothing left to match the extravagance of the druggist's glass display case that was devoted to a collection of bird's eggs, the largest an ostrich. The whole store was carted off as a museum piece to Heritage Park in Calgary in the late 1960s. One of Hanley's architectural wonders, a red-brick Opera House built in 1914 by the town and rural municipality as a bold $26,000 promissory note to the future, was once the site of vaudeville and Chautauqua shows, and later, in my memory, of Royal Purple teas, election polling stations, and blood-donor clinics. It was boarded up in my teens. It has been gone for two decades.

There is, to be sure, a hockey rink on a corner of Main Street built to replace the one I remember: a corrugated tin structure that on the coldest winter days managed to sustain a lower temperature inside than outside. The houses along the residential streets are less shabby now, less improvised than I recall, having grown up in one whose kitchen, according to rumour, had been the town's first jail. Suburban-style bungalows are commonplace. But the overall visual effect, I know, is such that my children can scarcely imagine a life lived in that place, which means they can scarcely imagine their father at their age, or, for that matter, know him now.

Hanley is the sort of small prairie town that the *Globe and Mail* columnist, William Thorsell, could easily have had in mind when—who knows what provoked him?—he wrote that parents commit an immoral, "profoundly aggressive act" against their own children by raising them in rural or remote places, where their horizons will not be sufficiently broadened and their career prospects will be limited by poor schooling.[2] He would have found plenty of damning evidence in my time. Hanley offered little exposure to the arts, even measured against its own pioneer standards of vibrant amateur theatre and a community band. There were no enrichment programs. There was no art gallery. There was no "cinema," no longer even a run-down movie theatre at which to watch Roy Rogers on Saturday afternoons. There was no bookstore—the druggist's comic-book rack held the only literature for sale on Main Street—and only a hole-in-the-wall library that opened with the provincial government's financial sponsorship in about 1971. Advanced music lessons required weekly trips to larger centres. The school's half-hearted attempts through a succession of teachers to teach French proved futile. As for cultural diversity, Main Street lacked even the standard Chinese restaurant. Hanley's population had slipped below 500 people. No more than a handful of them had a university degree. None of them, safe to say, read the *Globe and Mail*. Some of them lived off welfare, or off the winter-works jobs that governments once paid for, or both, depending on the season.

So much for self-deprecating honesty. What about the defence that is implied in making such rhetorical concessions? Having left thirty years ago, and being hard-pressed to recall my own childhood in more than fragments, it may be that I am entitled to nothing more than Wallace Stegner's conclusion about Eastend, Saskatchewan, in his classic work of return, *Wolf Willow*: namely, that it was "a seedbed, as good a place to be a boy and as unsatisfying a place to be a man as one could well imagine."[3] But Stegner's paradox is not mine. Hanley was not always such a good place to be a boy; I was happy to leave when I did. Yet, in mid-life, I have committed myself in various public ways to the defence of rural communities. I am prepared to claim that good people lived and still ought to be able to live in, and near, small prairie towns such as Hanley, and that there are important human truths at stake in the survival of such places, difficult as they are to articulate in what is now a very urban Canada and a culture of individual mobility. So I am drawn back to see that town, to show it, to piece together an understanding of it and my life there, to think about the truth of it, about the marks it has left and what binds me to it still.

II

*In the fall of 1909, at a large and well-attended meeting, it was unanimously decided to build a brick schoolhouse of four rooms, designed in such a way that it could be enlarged to six or eight rooms. It was thought that $16,000, the estimated cost of the new school, was not too large an amount for the people of Hanley to spend on educational purposes, and the result is that today we have one of the finest schools in the West, and one that does credit to the architects who designed it, and the men who carried out the work....*

*A small stair leads from the hall to a large, well-lighted library in the Tower. This room commands a splendid view of the surrounding countryside.*

*The Hanley Herald*, June 24, 1910

In those days my father occupied what might have been the highest office in town. At the age of six and seven, at the end of most weekdays, I crossed the street from my classroom that was one of a row of country schoolhouses just moved into town. I walked up the stairs of the big school. Inside, there were more stairs. I would spiral up the bannistered staircase, advancing timidly against the flow of older students, onto a landing above the front entrance—the base of the belltower—and finally into his office. He would be in his suit coat, tie not loosened even at the end of the day. His dress, the building, and his office all said this was a place of important work, purposeful, mysterious, honourable work. It was not so glamorous as working in the Nabisco factory in Niagara Falls, making Shredded Wheat, as he had done one legendary summer in the 1950s, before he married, as part of the post-war wave of prairie migration to Ontario industrial jobs; but it was much more important.

I would enter with a sense of awe and privilege. Not just anyone got to come here. More than that, as the oldest child with two younger brothers at home, I relished the chance to be the only one with him, to wait while he filled out his lesson-plan book for the next day, while he conferred with other teachers, while the janitor's broom swirled up the green cleansing compound sprinkled on the well-worn maple floor. Then it was time to walk home, across town, stopping sometimes at Simonsen's Shop-Rite for a quart of milk or fresh-sliced bologna; and I would listen with pleasure, learning how to be an adult in the world, while he talked easily with the woman who ran the store. When her son was younger, and his legs too weak to carry him, my father carried him up the stairs into school; in winter, he pulled him in a sled. That was how he had made his way as a newcomer and a teacher in that town. That was how he earned respect.

It was my father who taught me the value of words. He showed me the work they could do, the pleasure they could bring in a well-timed witticism, the importance of finding the precise one. He was well-spoken; his clipped, careful speech hinted, I thought, at a BBC English accent. He was sometimes asked to read in public. He was a demanding grammarian. He wrote letters and typed minutes from meetings on a compact green Smith-Corona typewriter. He spent his share of evenings at meetings: the library board, the church, the teachers' federation local. He kept careful records. He lived out the old-fashioned idea that a teacher with his education ought to be a resource person for the community, even before teachers' salaries were high enough to allow much generosity with money or time.

He taught for 30 years in Hanley. That was why we lived there. Once, in his last year, while he struggled in hospital for health and peace of mind, I expressed admiration for his example and asked him questions I had never asked before about what it was like to teach in that town. He talked about the differences that were exposed in anticipation of a teachers' strike, about the improvement in the academic and social climate of the school when farm kids were bused in to the new composite school, about principals he had appreciated and those he hadn't. In particular detail, he described one principal, concerned to build a reputation for tough standards that could take him somewhere else, who made it clear to him one June that he was required to fail students, even if it meant scaling back one girl's grades to achieve it. The principal soon left the community. My father had to live there with the knowledge of what had been done. He taught the girl again next year, followed her progress in higher grades, and could not avoid her parents. He carried his regret a long time. He had never told it to anyone.

III

*The Yankees in the land abound/For Uncle Sam gets all around*
*And with his push and grit and go/Is sure to make the*
*country grow*

Grain Growers' Guide, September 20, 1911

In those days it was not thought odd or unpatriotic that all but one of the north-south streets in town were named for American presidents: Washington, Lincoln, Grant, and, most obscure, James Garfield, shot and killed soon after taking office in 1881. It was not thought about at all. The last great American land rush, after all, had occurred on the Canadian prairies—more than a million emigrants in the early part of the twentieth century, many of them a generation removed from northern and central Europe. The Hanley district was settled mainly from the south: from the Dakotas, Minnesota, Nebraska, Iowa, and elsewhere on the western plains, where the agricultural potential of inexpensive land with no trees to clear was pitched at state fairs and in newspaper advertisements. In nine months, the Saskatchewan Valley Land Company had sold most of its million-acre grant—some of it to small speculators who waited for demand to build. In the new prairie economy of hard spring wheat, more money was made in speculation than in grain production. By 1914, the boomtown era was over. The farm failure rate was high. Many of those first settlers, like Stegner's family, began drifting back into the U.S. before the First World War. More left during the Great Depression. In the 1928–29 crop year, 643 grain cars were loaded at Hanley, in 1937–38, that number had dropped to three.[4]

In those days, when we lived on Grant Street, we counted on the summer arrival of the neighbours' relatives from California pulling a silver Airstream trailer that announced they had made it somewhere else, but also that they had not forgotten whence they came.

IV

*The "Unemployed All-Stars" baseball team...travelled the length and breadth of the province during the height of the depression, taking in tournaments, and winning many of them. Rumour has it that when the winnings were a bit slim, the boys were obliged to do a bit of "living off the land."*

Hanley: The Story of the Town and District[5]

In those days Hanley was a hardball town, a good one, its teams built around intimidating pitchers who attracted the notice of big-league scouts. As a result, the ball diamond was one place where respect-ability could be earned by a reserved teacher's kid who had learned to field grounders by endless afternoons of throw and catch against the back of an unused old garage. Saturdays in spring were reserved for sports-day tournaments in the communities within an hour's drive throughout Gardiner Dam country: Davidson, Loreburn, Elbow, Outlook, Hawarden, as far as Central Butte, where, in our faded, baggy grey flannels we once eliminated a cocky city team from Moose Jaw in one inning by the so-called mercy rule. We showed absolutely none. We won money consistently, enough to buy bats, balls, and equipment, and, one year, to buy modern, green-and-gold stretch polyester uniforms.

Often we drove to games in our coach's Meteor. Once its engine burst into flames and we watched, frozen, in the backseat while he leapt into the ditch with uncharacteristic speed for a pail full of dirt to extinguish it. More than once, that Meteor, packed with 12-year-old ballplayers at the end of a long day on dusty diamonds, got parked in front of the Hawarden Hotel, twenty minutes from home on gravel, so that our coach could replenish lost liquids in adult company. The poet Glen Sorestad once wrote an elegy to that hotel, about drinks and lies spilled gracelessly between hunters and local farmers in the fall.[6] I never saw the inside of it. But I can attest to gracelessness, squeezed in the back seat beside the beery old man who was invited to ride home with us, listening to him lurch from line to line of what I know now was a well-travelled parody of a revivalist hymn, sung by harvest hands in Kansas and military trainees during the Spanish-American War, partisans of the International Workers of the World, the Wobblies, in the 1920s, and hoboes in the Great Depression:

> *Hallelujah, I'm a bum,*
> *Hallelujah, bum again,*
> *Hallelujah, give us a handout*
> *Revive us again.*

In those days the hard work of childhood was shielding parents from the truth of my existence. It was not simply the drive home after a couple of beers, though that much, if revealed, would have complicated any future in sport with parental anxiety long before ability and desire had reached their peak. It was also the sacrilege of being unable to erase the old man's lyrics from memory.

v

*Und führe uns nicht in Versuchung, sondern erlöse uns von dem Übel...*

  (And lead us not into temptation, but deliver us from evil...)

In those days we lived as exiles cast out of Eden—cast with an unspoken shame into hardscrabble dryland, away from extended family and the green relief of poplar bluffs that dotted the landscapes of my grandparents' farms, to make a living in an inhospitable place. Hanley was a tough town. It was a tough town in which to be a teacher's son. We learned to dread Hallowe'en. It was a tough town, too, in which to be identified as Mennonite, pacifist, German-speaking. Its civic identity was steeped in the patriotic memory of great numbers of recruits and casualties in two world wars; it was as worldly as Passchendaele and Vimy Ridge. Its residual resentment of "yellow-bellied krautlovers," chickenshits, those who were unwilling to fight Hitler, was still expressed roughly on the playground a generation later through its children. My only defence—a secret defence, for I never dared speak it—was my father's young uncle Peter, who had enlisted with some of his brothers in the Canadian forces during World War II, against the strong disapproval of his family and community. He was killed in Europe in the last stages of the war and, as a result, there is a small lake named for him in northern Saskatchewan. I found it in an atlas. While I could not have claimed Uncle Peter as my ticket to local respectability without betraying the greater weight of family history and principle, I had learned the link between war, belonging and separation.

In Hanley, we lived always at a slight distance, wary, more private, more pious, as if unsure when the world would turn against us. My father neither curled nor socialized at the beer parlour. My parents did not attend the parties at the Legion from which the last vehicles pulled away early on Sunday mornings. Instead, wearing shoes that had been polished black the night before in ritual preparation for worship, we drove through streets empty as the rapture, imagining—silently, disapprovingly—what kept the "English" in their beds, or, once we were free of town, what kept them in the fields when they should be going to church like the Mennonite men.

Our destination was a white-clapboard church ten miles west of town; the psychological distance was much greater than that. On the far side of the divide, we were also outsiders. We were not farm people. Here we had no graves to tend and no close cousins. We were not *Russlaender*, that is, those Mennonites who had only left Russia in the 1920s. We did not dance at weddings. We were a generation further immersed in the English language, among people who still spoke and sang their deepest reverences in German. We carried with us no recollection of how my great-grandfather had come here often by train to visit, how he had reclaimed friendship with families from the same cluster of Old World villages after half a century apart, or how, in the early 1930s, he had gathered potatoes and sought out pasture in his home district for these people. Every week, we crossed from one world to another, then back, in time for Sunday dinner.

We could see that church as a bright, sun-lit beacon from an upstairs window. Which is to say that on that long slope towards the South Saskatchewan River there were no trees, save for the willows along a creek and the lines of caraganas planted as windbreaks by the Prairie Farm Rehabilitation Administration. It could still happen in the spring that the west wind would raise an enormous, moving wall of dirt, a black-brown blizzard that engulfed that house of worship and, within minutes, the house next door. The worst of those dust storms left body and mind besieged. They deposited a gritty film indoors despite all hurried efforts to seal doors and windows. They filled ditches with topsoil, leaving patches of bone-white land, too thin, too hard, for roots. Or so it seemed to me then.

What theological adaptations had been demanded of those who had learned to worship in that clapboard church, framed so elementally by wind and sky, so defenceless against them? As the Cree people had found, moving from the forests, the natural theology of the prairies was monotheistic. The seamless transition from the English-language benediction ("The Lord make his face to shine upon you") to the singular warmth of the sun waiting outside said as much. Tellingly, half the men in the congregation would quickly huddle in the shade of the building, away from the sun's stern glare, to smoke a cigarette—a *Russlaender* habit of which our family also disapproved.

Rain, in turn, was a blessing not to be squandered. It was not unusual on a Sunday morning to pray for it. And so the congregation's economy of salvation was shaped accordingly. It eschewed revivalist hymns filled with scarcely resonant metaphors about being "washed whiter than snow"—who could imagine that much water?—in much the same way that it eschewed dramatic immersion baptisms. There was water enough for its candidates for baptism to be sprinkled, as I was at 17, like seeds, planted trustfully and without anxiety for the harvest. It was an attitude that very much described the reputation of our leading minister, Henry Peters, as a farmer.

He was a gentle man. I remember how, as an adolescent at the *faspa* table, I mustered the courage to ask as rebellious a question as I dared ask a minister in the presence of my parents: so why can't we wear jeans to church? The question could easily have evoked fears of youth rebellion at a time when denim was a counter-cultural flag. His response was not defensive. Instead, it was about the older association of denim with the overalls worn over good clothes in the time of horse-drawn travel to church, and also with farm work, the barn, corrals that needed to be cleaned out—work from which the Sabbath was a day of rest. His response was an invitation into local memory and culture.

Paradoxically or not, it was in that clapboard country church that I saw a slide-projector image of a water fountain in Gulfport, Mississippi, beneath a sign that said "Whites Only," and I knew for the first time that the world needed fixing.

### VI

In those days it happened once, after a school dance, that we crowded four in the cab of a half-ton truck. The girl driving was the only one with a licence. It was her farm truck. There was no drinking, just adolescent fearlessness, hormones and the exhilaration of speed on darkness on a country road south of town. Stupidly, in the three seconds of that night I still remember clearly, I pressed my foot to the foot already on the gas pedal to go faster, then backed off. It is a wonder we did not hit a patch of loose gravel and roll the truck. We could easily have been dead. Some years later, in different circumstances, teenagers were killed in a truck accident on a country road near Hanley— the kind that becomes a cautionary tale for a generation.

The next morning my father and I were standing beside the pumps at a local garage while the gas tank was being filled.

"Your mother," he said, thrifty with words as always, "was worried about you last night."

### VII

*Only local and regional history satisfied the need to remember the most intimate matters, the things of childhood.*
Joseph Amato, *Rethinking Home*[7]


Those who imagine small rural communities as places of child abuse or mere deprivation are allies of a kind with those who romanticize them, and, for that matter, with those journalists who patronizingly insist on describing them—typically in reports of shocking crimes—as "tight-knit," as if social relations in them are uncomplicated. Such sweeping images are revealing mostly about those who resort to them. Small rural communities are not alike; they are marked by distinct, slowly-sedimented, highly localized cultures. More than that, small rural communities are arguably the most complex of places, though this claim flies in the face of much metropolitan pretence. The very word "community" is a case in point. It is now typically used to describe self-chosen clusters of people who, in a world of strangers, share some essential characteristic, for example, profession, ethnicity, sexual preference, or, behind gates, wealth. In rural contexts, however, it continues to mean something quite opposite: living unavoidably with, and having to rely upon, *people who are not like you, and doing so possibly over a lifetime.*

That reality is a demanding one. It requires small-town people to live in face-to-face proximity with the identities they may have inherited, as someone's son or daughter, with unspoken hierarchies of respect, shame, and social class, with the reputations they make for themselves, and with the histories they make with others. It requires them to manage social relations over long periods of time, perhaps into a second or third generation. It presses them to measure their words, to avoid public conflict, to hope that time will heal things (as it sometimes does), to keep up appearances, to suppress differences, to the point that the writer Kathleen Norris, in a perceptive essay, asks: "Can you tell the truth in a small town?" Indeed, she says, a community's most important, most formative stories—the ones that shape it over time and make its responses understandable—are precisely the ones that never get told, whether out of respect, self-defence, or neglect.[8] They are softened or omitted entirely in local history books that instead celebrate the hard work of founding families and their descendants who have stayed around. They do not necessarily make headlines in the weekly newspaper—a matter of smug criticism on the part of those who rely on mass media to confirm that an event has happened and to determine its significance. This web of silence is part of what makes small towns inaccessible to newcomers, who have no initial access to the formative stories and are prone to stumble into them indelicately. There is, of course, a century full of fiction devoted to the dark underside of small-town life. It is much rarer to find a respectful, nuanced literary treatment.[9] The truth is that not everyone is capable of living well in such places, of learning the artfulness that is required to do so. As current trends intensify, fewer people will need to do so—or even have the opportunity.

Small rural communities are hardly places of refuge from broader economic, cultural, and political forces. They never were. They exist on the Canadian prairies as a legacy of the National Policy, which made the territorial occupation of the region a primary purpose to be achieved through widespread agricultural settlement. Their prospects, like those of Hanley, have always been tied to the complexities of commodity markets and the placement of railroad lines and roads. They are now increasingly subject to decisions made in far-off political capitals and corporate boardrooms. Prairie towns are being reconfigured by investment flows in a ruthlessly extractive economy, by the pressure placed on prices for primary products by processors who can scour the world for the cheapest raw materials, by the consolidation of public services and by the related retreat of governments from traditional roles that balanced opportunity across a whole society. Vast stretches of the grainbelt are being emptied out of people. While the prettiest parts of the rural countryside are bought up for tourist resorts, golf courses, acreage developments, or preserved as parks, the most disadvantaged regions become vulnerable to the most divisive, dubious schemes: urban landfills, massive hog barns, open-pit coal mines, or low-wage manufacturing. Municipal politicians often see no other choice than to accept or compete for such investments, as the local tax base shrinks—thanks in part to grain elevator closures—and as populations decline. The message is that the future, if there is one, will depend less on the traditional agricultural base. Already, the subtler social implications of this shift can be observed in places like Hanley, as the relative rank of farm and town is reversed. Where it was once simply understood that the town existed to serve the farm economy—an understanding reinforced by that imposing line of elevators—farm survival may now depend on the availability of part-time work in town even at jobs that once would have been considered demeaning. There is less time for community, perhaps less expectation of it.

None of this sense of dislocation is a matter for regret for those who defer to the "natural laws" of the economy or who, like Mr. Thorsell, declare it a good thing that "towns wax and wane," because it encourages people to move to someplace better. The favourite word of reproach for these impatient critics of rural communities is sentimental, the foil for their hard-headed realism. But there is more at stake here than misplaced, shallow affection. I am tempted to say—as I have heard rural people say, more or less—that Canada as a whole has lived for a long time off both the economic *and* cultural capital that was generated in places its governments have abandoned and its opinion leaders now disdain, and that it will be impoverished by their decline and disappearance. The contents of that cultural capital are difficult to capture in a compact definition or to convey in an overwhelmingly urban society. They require an on-going familiarity with worlds that are genuinely foreign to many people; and, conversely, their description, like any claim of difference, is prone to exaggeration—as if urban and rural were isolated realities. This is not, however, a time to be tentative. It is a time to count the costs.

One is the *possibility of a robust sense of human action*—of sustained involvement in the life of a community, and of everyday collaboration across differences. This is not mere nostalgia. My friends in Daysland, Alberta, for example, have lived it out. They formed a society to take over the town's boarded-up theatre, learned to operate its antique arc-light projector, volunteered their time to select and show movies, and, more recently, built a live concert stage to broaden the facility's scope for community use. The local concert series now draws packed audiences from neighbouring towns. As Raymond Williams, the late social theorist and son of a Welsh village, who never forgot his origins, once wrote: "It is not so much the old village or the old backstreet that is significant. It is the perception and affirmation of a world in which one is not necessarily a stranger and an agent, but can be a *member*, a discoverer, in a shared source of life."[10] For Williams, such experience of membership and mutuality, of a stake in a place, is the basis for a critical understanding and a critical politics. In a somewhat different way, Kieran Bonner has identified the small town as most approximating the ancient Greek *polis*—not in its municipal government, but in the public opportunities through which people can reveal their character, be remembered for words and deeds, and also be held accountable for them.[11] To amend Socrates, it is not the unexamined life so much as the unanswerable life that is not worth living. This face-to-face accountability, of course, is the flip-side of the more familiar, negative image of the informal surveillance of the small town, from whose watchful gaze and gossip its youth are lured to the anonymity of the city in order to "be themselves" or to "make a life for themselves." A life lived as an active member of a community generates its own informal credit and security provisions. I am told that when Henry Peters, the farmer-minister, had retired into town and would sometimes grow disoriented when he walked to the post office, others would make sure he got home. They knew who he was and where he lived.

A second cost is *routine contact across generations* among people who know each other as a grandparent or grandchild, or as someone else's grandparent, parent, or grandchild. Sometimes this contact happens in the context of meaningful work for sake of the household economy. By contrast, cities are disproportionately youthful and segregated by age, which only reinforces the illusion of self-creation. People formed out of a community-minded, inter-generational ethos are not just being old-fashioned, prudish, or nosy when they express disappointment at young couples who choose to marry in private (or not at all), or, for that matter, at individuals who instruct their survivors not to have a public funeral. They understand weddings and funerals as singularly important events in the binding of communities and families.

A third cost is *proximity to the working countryside, and particularly to the sources of food.* The summer I turned 16, I worked on a friend's farm, stooking and loading bales, feeding cattle, shovelling a load of grain into the truck and riding along to the elevator at Dundurn. I hope I earned my keep at the Olsons. What I received in return was a sense of the pleasure in hard, physical work and a glimpse into the rhythms (and stresses) of farm life that I have not forgotten. That kind of coming-of-age experience is no longer typical, and not just because farm machinery has further reduced the need of manual labour or because it is too expensive to risk in the hands of untrained teenagers. Most people simply do not have contact with the farm. That disconnection is evident in the way that the celebration of Thanksgiving in October is no longer linked inextricably with harvest. At that austere white-clapboard country church west of Hanley, Thanksgiving Sunday was a visual cornucopia of gold and orange, of bundled wheat, pumpkins, garden vegetables and flowers sprawled across a table at the front of the sanctuary. I suspect it still is. This conjoining of necessity and beauty was offered in deep gratitude by producer families who did not take their daily bread for granted, and who impressed that same gratitude on all who worshipped there.

A fourth cost is the *possibility of return*—to live, or more likely, to claim an historic connection to particular places and people. There were thousands of communities built on the Canadian prairies during the settlement era: villages built around grain delivery points, post offices, and stores; postage-stamp school districts in rural areas (by which people still identify themselves in community histories). In retrospect, it can be said that those communities served, and continue to serve, as points of dispersal. Many no longer exist, though even in those cases there is usually a cairn, a cemetery, a weathered, unused church, concrete footings from a barn that no longer stands, some physical landmark that bears witness to those who once lived there, who belonged there, and who, as a result, may confer a relation to that place even on those who have never lived there. Walter Klaassen captures this sensibility in the opening lines of his history of the prairie settlement community of my ancestors: "Eigenheim is a place of which we know the centre but not the circumference."[12] So does Alistair MacLeod in the novel *No Great Mischief*, which traces a family story through generations in Cape Breton back to the Scottish highlands, where an old woman assures a young Canadian just arrived: "But you are really from here. You have just been away for awhile."[13] There are still some among us who respond knowingly to such an encounter because we have had similar experiences; we know who we are partly because of the way that identity is formed out of stories handed down about people in particular places. To those who are entirely at home in the brave new memory-less world of individual opportunity, this kind of rootedness will seem anachronistic. But it is hardly a spent force. In recent years, indeed, the Saskatchewan government has begun reinstating place-names on its highway maps, rather than deleting them, even for towns that have no remaining inhabitants—this to accommodate those who go back.[14] All the same, it is a bleak, sobering thing to visit a cemetery or a cairn in an open field, away from the continuity of a living community. Reminders of the fleetingness of human settlement are common enough on the prairies. Like Dickensian spirits, they haunt those who live in rural places whenever an elevator is torn down or a school is slated for replacement with "portable" classrooms. The truth of a century's experience is that many have left, and will continue to leave. Far better that homecomings are made possible because some have been able to do the important work of dwelling in a place, staying with it, and learning to live well there.

VIII

In those days, on one long spring evening, I rode my bicycle with a group of boys to the Old Park—a field on the edge of town enclosed by trees. We lay on our backs, as instructed, shirtless, arms at our sides, eyes tight shut. We were waiting for the nighthawks. If we could stay perfectly still, we were assured, they might land on our chests. It might have been a set-up. What difference would it make that our eyes were shut? I had never seen nighthawks or heard the distinctive, whip-saw sound of their flight, to know if they were near. I desperately did not want one to land on my chest. But I did not want to be proved a coward. And so I lay there,

*wild grass bristling my back, obedient now,*
    *visioning a tightened circle overhead, tensing*
*for the rip of talons, the instant rush of wings.*
*Would I hear or feel them first?*
    *Waiting...until*
*defiant restless stricken still,*
*eyes broke free to empty twilight,*
    *arms pressed downward for the land.*

53

IX

You can now go to Hanley a thousand ways on the information high-way. Setting aside the many fill-in-the-location searches for hotels, restaurants, jobs, golf courses, real estate, and mates for seniors, as well as the genealogical references that confirm how Hanley was just one more point of arrival and dispersal, an internet search suggests that reports of its demise are exaggerated. The town's population finally has risen slightly above 500. Its gasoline prices are famously low. The demolished opera house has been remembered properly with a cairn that is listed as a *bona fide* Large Canadian Road Attraction. The National Hockey League Players' Association has contributed financially towards the installation of glass around the perimeter of the new hockey rink. The regional library branch is active. People with whom I went to school advertise exotic cattle breeds and prize quarter-horses; they sit on the boards of provincial and national organizations. Students at the high school have produced a multi-media history for the 2005 Saskatchewan centennial that generously blends First Nations drumming, Metis fiddling, homesteading photos, letters home from a soldier and a Tommy Douglas speech. Hanley gets a favourable mention in a Calgary-based journalist's account of a visit to town for high school graduation festivities ("as much fun" as his trip to Central America).[15] The caption of a soft-focus television commercial implies that it was at Hanley in 1945 that a small group of farmers pooled their resources to form what became a national co-operative insurance company. I have no idea if the claim is true. While the commercial sells heritage, the orderly groves of maple trees in the background belong to another landscape.

No amount of internet voyeurism, however, is the equivalent of actually going back. It is neither as satisfying nor as difficult. I have not lived in Hanley for even part of a summer since I was 18. The last routine opportunities to develop an adult relationship to the town evaporated when my parents moved away at the point of retirement. Since then, I have seen individuals periodically but have come back only rarely for events in the community hall: one a retirement tea for my father. I have been inside the town's wood-panelled beer parlour exactly once. What keeps me away is neither resentment nor indifference, and certainly not snobbery. It is more a matter of the childhood reserve brought back to life, the fear that if I showed up unannounced on Main Street or at the Agricultural Fair I would be unrecognized and hard-pressed to explain who I was. It has been a long time. Our family did not really live there long enough—only 30 years and one generation—to belong as insiders. This I know. And now my father has been buried among his ancestors at the country cemetery in the district he left as a young man, in another part of the province where, it turns out, I am most likely to experience the rarity of meeting people who will have known my parents *and* my son and daughter.

All this is true enough. But on a warm Saturday afternoon in October, I am back. Uncoerced, my daughter is with me. We might have been the lead characters in the standard small-town drama of the strangers who must be watched to the destination that explains their business, except that the streets are almost deserted. The encounters for which I am ready do not materialize. On Main Street— Lincoln Street—we stop in the hardware store that doubles as a liquor vendor and then in the grocery store whose check-out counter, floors and at least one freezer look strikingly like those I remember from three and four decades ago. In those days, I say, there was a drug store and a closed-down movie theatre on this street. The rink was there, pointing east, and the opera house in front of it. We are back in the car. In those days, there was the Old Park and the junk collector's house and the tiny Matthews yard where we played foot- ball and the bridge over the spring creek where I held my first frog, then stomped on it in fear, and our house on Grant Street, where we lived when tap water and flush toilets came to town, and the spot where the livery barn once stood, and the two-room house where I delivered groceries to an old maid and the site of the former Lawrence mansion, with its stately columns and porch,[16] and the house to which we moved from Grant, where the paint is now faded and a combine sits in the yard. There is the first modern split-level in town, the school, the Case implement dealership whose sign was once an eagle perched on a globe; there is the one remaining elevator where I once saw my first rat.

We do not take the highway out of town. Instead, we cross onto a gravel road that curls north, away from the garbage dump, and follow it to the Olson farm, where only the dog is home on a harvest day, and then down across the causeway over Blackstrap Lake, where I once saw a grain truck lose a wheel and dig its axle into the asphalt, past the Hutterite Colony, which is forever associated in my memory with the first Apollo moon landing because we were here on a family drive, listening on the car radio, when Neil Armstrong took his famous walk.

I wonder at the complex geography of houses, farms, roads, stories and family relationships that I carry in my head like old phone numbers that can be recalled in the moment when needed. Then I wonder whether my daughter, age 18, having grown up in a different time and place, bigger than three blocks by six, has a comparable geography to which she will return one day. I cannot imagine that she has, or that she will miss it. Or what kind of knowing will have taken its place.

Four

# "Their Own Emancipators"
## *The Agrarian Movement in Alberta*

I

In July 1933, two farm boys from the Wetaskiwin area of central Alberta—eager to be part of history—packed food in knapsacks and hopped a series of trains for Regina. When they arrived at the hotel at which the Co-operative Commonwealth Federation convention was to be held, they were disappointed to find a large crowd ahead of them. They wondered whether they would even get into the room. So they went around to the back of the hotel and helped each other climb up a metal fire-escape stair-case, then through a second-storey window. It might have been a linen closet. Instead, the boys tumbled into a front-row seat for the meeting that produced the Regina Manifesto.[1]

In the same room was Chester Ronning, who in a by-election in 1932 had become the first member of the legislature elected in Alberta under the Farmer-Labour ticket that became the CCF. He sat with the United Farmers of Alberta government. In his first speech in the legislature, duly reported in the Edmonton and Camrose papers, he pronounced that "capitalism had outgrown its usefulness" and "was into its death throes"; his constituents, he said, desired something else.[2] Ronning returned from Regina to Avonroy Hall just east of Camrose. This UFA local hall—still standing—was, like many others, the site of meetings, lectures, debates and annual spring picnics, where between three-legged races, ice cream and songs from the college choir which Ronning also conducted, speakers would promote co-operation in place of greed, people ahead of profits. At Avonroy Hall, which still stands, dilapidated and overgrown, Ronning declared the Regina

Manifesto a "document in which any red-blooded Canadian can take pride."[3]

Needless to say, Alberta is now a very different place in its highly urbanized society, its political (or anti-political) culture, its oil-based economy and its prosperous national profile. In many respects it typifies what the political theorist Sheldon Wolin calls a "post-mnemonic society"—one that has "no interest in remembering its past," or in which inconvenient aspects of that past are "publicly unrecalled."[4] Alberta's lively history of rural activism is now buried at least two generations deep in local memory, or is present only in the thin residue of the UFA farm-supply co-ops and, until recently, the Alberta Wheat Pool. Sometimes, indeed, that history seems to have been deliberately whitewashed, as in the case of Ronning's own political career, of which, curiously, there is no mention in the two-page biography that describes him as a member of Alberta's Order of Excellence. It glosses over the period in which he was MLA and later CCF leader as having been "spent in peaceful and productive work," as a college principal, a parent, and as a devotee of the arts.[5]

From a contemporary perspective, it is a challenge—and per-haps a surprise—to remember that Alberta was once central to the agrarian movement on the Canadian prairies, and home to some of its most radical elements. When David Laycock concluded in his fine study of agrarian populism that it had "contributed more to Canadian thought about the nature and practice of democracy than did any other regional or class discourse,"[6] he had Alberta very much in mind. Similarly, a recent history calls the UFA and the United Farm Women of Alberta "one of the greatest mass democratic movements in Canadian history"—one in which farm people "sought popular political control and wanted to protect their families, communities, and way of life from corporate control."[7] In Alberta, in the first third of the twentieth century, the agrarian movement:

- elected a provincial government in 1921, and again in 1926 and 1930;
- elected a slate of UFA members to the House of Commons during the same period, where they pushed success-fully for reinstatement of the Crow Rate and collaborated

increasingly with Independent Labour Members of Parliament like J.S. Woodsworth—the alliance on which the national CCF was founded (in a meeting held in Calgary, no less, by UFA invitation);

- led in the formation of the prairie wheat pools and other producer co-operatives;
- gave intellectual as well as political leadership through such diverse personalities as Henry Wise Wood, William Irvine, Robert Gardiner, and Irene Parlby.

By the mid-1930s, however, the agrarian movement was mostly a spent force in Alberta—long before it crested in Saskatchewan within the CCF. In broad-brush terms, the political wing was brought down by the Depression and by Social Credit, which, in its messianic 1935 election campaign, usurped what remained of the UFA's populist energies and left sharply divided rural communities in its wake. But it would be a mistake to concentrate solely on the period of direct party-political involvement in an account of the agrarian movement in Alberta. Its distinctive character, internal tensions, and historical trajectory might be unfolded across at least three phases. The first saw the building of the movement, the second the election of a farmers' government and the third its political dissolution.

II

The agrarian movement across the prairies was formed from diverse, often conflicting, sources—ideological and organizational—around which regional and class grievances coalesced. Their targets included the near-monopoly power of the railroads, banks, and grain companies, and a seemingly indifferent national government in Ottawa. Initially, the movement was not so much a single entity as a loose amalgam of groups, overlapping memberships, newspapers and self-appointed pamphleteers. It drew on sources that leaned towards either co-operative or state forms of social ownership; towards either an agrarian or a more inclusive, industrial self-understanding of farmers' position in a capitalist economy; and towards either a parliamentary or a radical-democratic politics. All of these tensions were present from the start.

In Alberta, partly due to immigration patterns, the influence of recent American populist ideas and political experience was somewhat stronger than in the other provinces. Most notably, the Society of Equity was organizing at local and provincial levels by 1907 (though it had to add Canadian to its name to overcome suspicion in some communities). The Society was one of the main groups—the Territorial Grain Growers' Association was another—that merged in 1909 to form the United Farmers of Alberta, Our Motto Equity. The UFA adopted and continued to press several important political demands associated with the Society, including provincially-owned packing plants, grain elevators, railroads, and hail insurance.[8] The Non-Partisan League was a second significant American source in Alberta. Having formed a farmers' government in North Dakota in 1916, it supplied a sharper analysis of both the economy— reinforcing demands for state ownership in key sectors—and the party system, corruption, and patronage. Eventually it helped prod the UFA into electoral politics. The NPL elected two MLAs in 1917 in the face of widespread red-baiting. (One of them, Louise McKinney, was a former temperance organizer, who, with Parlby, would later be part of the "Famous Five" associated with the so-called Persons Case.) As Paul Sharp put it, the NPL injected "an aggressive group consciousness" into prairie politics, one that was open to labour allies as well.[9] At first it posed as a rival to the UFA, whose Missouri-born leader, Henry Wise Wood, had resisted direct political action for fear it would distract and divide the agrarian movement.[10] But the League was persuaded to bring its members and its programme into the older organization. Among those members was William Irvine, a labour organizer and Unitarian minister working in Calgary, and later a federal MP for the Wetaskiwin constituency. It was Irvine who reformulated Wood's idea of economic group organization in political terms as group government.

Irvine's widely-circulated tract, *The Farmers in Politics* (1920), proposed that the party system was merely a "tool of the wealthy." It offered little real choice and did not represent farmers' interests, but rather ensured that the voices of working people were seldom heard in parliaments and legislatures. In its place he proposed a "co-operative commonwealth" in which organized occupational groups would elect their own representatives to a distinctly non-parliamentary assembly. Already, farmers' struggles had given them the self-confidence—men and women both—to "become their own emancipators." While this might sound like class politics to the newspaper editorialists, Irvine suggested that the country already had precisely that: "[Farmers] have been ruled for a long time now.... Would it be any worse for Canada if the farmers should rule for a change and if, for a change, the oppressors should be oppressed?" At the very least, rule by farmers would be more democratic. Irvine was confident, however, that group government would be marked not by antagonism but by harmony among sectoral interests, led by farmers—whose members had "discovered the higher law of co-operation."[11]

Irvine's book, like much of the UFA literature and Wood's speeches, reflected a broader search for an alternative political vocabulary and institutional framework. In 1918, for example, the American social reformer Mary Parker Follett published a book, *The New State*, which advocated neighbourhood- and group-based forms of participatory "non-partisan" democracy—this against the "dead-wood" of "ballot-box democracy," "crowd patriotism," and, in effect, party and business domination. She wrote: "The immediate problem of political science is to discover the method of self-government.... The organization of men [*sic*] in small local groups gives opportunity for this continuous political activity which ceaselessly creates the state."[12] Irvine, Wood and others developed parallel ideas in Alberta: the solution was not just group government. It was also the cultivation of a capacity for self-government as an antidote to a political system that kept people suspended in weakness.

The UFA movement was steeped in the idea of democracy as capacity, liberty as co-operation, for which the local was the most immediate site. A 1919 pamphlet with a matter-of-fact title, *How to Organize and Carry on a Local of the United Farmers of Alberta?*, addressed in careful detail the practical questions it posed. Then, as now, it could not be assumed that people knew how to run a meeting or serve as officers. But the pamphlet also encouraged locals to plan programs for "community betterment"—moral and intellectual. Among its suggestions was this: "Making your school house a social centre where the community can regularly meet and discuss all public questions, thereby helping to fulfill and carry out the ideals of democratic government, which should be not from above, but from the ground up, from the deliberations of the people." The pamphlet recommended, *inter alia*, the purchase of small libraries, sharing of newspaper articles, members' presentation of papers at meetings, and formal debates, for which it proposed a long list of topics: "It should always be remembered that the local unit is the training ground for leadership in the organization and the country, and our programmes and plan of work should aim to develop the mentality, public spirit and power of self-expression of every member."[13]

The United Farm Women of Alberta was integral to the success of the movement and shared its political ethos. Founded in 1915—but *not* as a mere auxiliary—the UFWA's locals were actively involved in community life. They also took the lead in pressing the provincial Liberal government of the day on issues such as rural health care and homestead property rights. They campaigned for women's suffrage along with the UFA. And, at the local level, they "not only encouraged women to develop knowledge and skills for participation in public affairs, they also gave their members opportunity to do so."[14]

In the 1921 election, UFA candidates won 38 of 61 seats in the legislature. The result negated any need for group government or, indeed, the possibility of it; for there were few opposition legislators—and none claiming to represent occupational groups—with whom a farmers' government could co-operate. Obviously Alberta was a predominantly agrarian society. But it would be wrong to imagine that the UFA formed a government simply on the strength of numbers, or, for that matter, superior leadership and compelling political-economic analysis. As Brad Rennie has demonstrated, its success lay in the building of what he calls a movement culture in the period prior to 1921.[15] This culture emerged not so much from a shared ideological outlook, though the widely-read *Grain Growers' Guide* contributed on that side, as from common farm-frontier experience and community work in building halls, cemeteries, roads, churches, schools, and, not least, co-operatives. It was solidified by social events like UFA picnics and school concerts. It brought together farm people across significant dividing lines: religion (at least evangelical and social-gospel Protestantism), nationality and, to some extent, race. While nativism resurfaced in the late 1920s, the UFA in its building phase encompassed locals in several Metis communities and one Oklahoma black community. The movement also brought together relatively large and small farmers on the understanding that they were fundamentally in the same vulnerable position. Rennie suggests that the UFA movement gave farmers a sense of self-respect, strength, and participation in a great cause.

### III

The UFA's move into electoral politics at the provincial and federal level may have been unstoppable, despite Wood's reluctance, especially after the formation of a farmers' government in Ontario. But political success also exposed tensions within the movement. While the UFA had been a populist party without a leader in the 1921 provincial election—Wood had not run for office, but retained his influence in the background—its new cabinet settled comfortably and conservatively into the powers of the parliamentary system. It initiated no significant political reforms. Moreover, it implemented no significant legislative agenda on behalf of Alberta farmers—nothing remotely like the ambitious NPL program in North Dakota. By 1926, the first UFA premier, Herbert Greenfield, had resigned in favour of John Brownlee, a lawyer whose farm credentials were limited to the legal work he'd done for the organization and for the United Grain Growers, and whose subsequent reputation, at least prior to the sex scandal that ended his political career, was one of able, prudent administration, with one eye always on the province's credit-rating.

The UFA government did press Ottawa in the early 1920s for reinstatement of the Canadian Wheat Board. When that failed, it underwrote the establishment of the Alberta Wheat Pool by guaranteeing that the treasury would cover the banks against losses incurred on loans advanced for initial payments—a commitment that almost bankrupted the province when wheat prices plummeted in 1929–30. The UFA government also extended public health services in rural areas and encouraged the creation of mutual telephone companies. It should be remembered for having backed the five women in the Persons Case, Parlby being a cabinet minister, to the point of having the province's attorney-general travel to London to assist in presenting the case before the Judicial Committee of the Privy Council—this while some other governments, notably Quebec's, supported the opposing side. There may be no better historical refutation of "redneck" stereotypes applied to rural Albertans.

That said, the UFA government fell short of rank-and-file expectations. In the early 1920s, and then again in the early 1930s, it resisted demands from UFA locals and the provincial convention for such measures as a debt moratorium and an end to land forfeiture for municipal tax arrears. It explained that it did not want to jeopardize rural access to credit, and, if anything, timidly followed the legislative lead of the other prairie provinces on these issues at the onset of the Depression.[16] It also deflected demands for monetary reform and curbs on the banks as federal matters. As one long-time UFA activist recalled: "When these matters were discussed in the school houses and living rooms of farm people in Alberta, there was disappointment."[17] What was the point of a farmers' government if it governed so conventionally? The tensions between movement and cabinet surfaced especially in tough times. They were sometimes expressed by UFA backbenchers angry at the "despotic sway" of the "money kings of our day."[18] They were commonplace among delegates to the powerful provincial convention, to which the cabinet still had to answer. Indeed, at the 1931 convention, once Wood had retired as president, the party manifesto was amended from the floor to include a clause calling for "public ownership of all land and all natural resources, possession being granted for use on lease." While the UFA's new vice-president defended use-lease as enhancing, not abolishing, security of tenure for farmers faced with foreclosure, the government could not simply ignore the convention; it was forced to refer the idea to a commission for study. (The clause was not rescinded until 1934, when the national CCF had already pulled back from so controversial a land policy.)[19]

Within the UFA/UFWA, however, the provincial government was understood as only one arena of political activity. For the most part, the movement's creative, radical and oppositional energies found other outlets. The first was the House of Commons, where UFA Members of Parliament elected with the Progressive bloc, but at odds with the "soft Liberal" Manitoba group, as well as with Brownlee, could advance positions more appropriate to federal jurisdiction— on grain handling, for example, or monetary reform.[20] The second outlet was the Wheat Pool, with its parallel structure based on delegate democracy. The third was the entire range of local institutions— municipal councils and school boards, mutual telephone companies, creamery and other co-operatives—that constituted the fabric of self-directed community affairs in which democratic politics was an experiential reality. Agrarian populism in Alberta had inherited two contradictory impulses from the American experience: on one hand, towards technocratic, honest, business-like government; on the other, towards local autonomy and direct democracy in a Jeffersonian vein. Within the UFA, it was an open question whether the aims of the farmers' movement were to be carried out primarily at a local, as opposed to a provincial or national, level. Certainly there was a level of office-holding and participation in rural Alberta reminiscent of ancient Athens. There was also a fairly sophisticated understanding, regularly promoted in *The UFA* newspaper, that farm people had "learned much in their own schoolhouses of democracy, obtained a deeper insight into the methods and possibilities of democratic political action" and "gained a quite confidence in their own ability to carry on their own affairs in their own way."[21] The contrast with the Board-of-Trade boosterism that passed for politics in the neighbouring towns is particularly striking.[22] Numerous instances of local political and economic initiatives particularly in the 1920s bear out the claim that Alberta farm people, even in the midst of hardship, had developed the collective capacity and self-confidence necessary for democratic self-government.

IV

The Social Credit era has generated no shortage of historical interpretation,[23] which cannot be rehearsed here. While the kind of vigorous, radical-democratic agrarian populism that had grown up in Alberta would languish in that era, it would be a mistake to draw too sharp a line at 1935, the year that William Aberhart's dramatic campaign to "put aside politics" and put purchasing power in people's hands swept the UFA from the legislature—and from the House of Commons. Obviously the Depression had already taken a considerable toll on the agrarian movement. And in that context, the UFA had already prepared the ground for Social Credit during the early 1930s. Influential individuals such as Irvine had expressed public interest not simply in monetary reform, but in Major C.H. Douglas's woolly debt-and-underconsumption theory, as a possible cure for the present crisis; UFA backbenchers had succeeded in bringing Douglas to Alberta to appear before a legislature committee; and UFA locals undertook the study of his ideas. Some of those locals simply turned themselves into Social Credit clubs when the UFA government in Edmonton—protesting, justifiably, that a province had no authority to introduce Douglas-style reforms— was unwilling to take up the mantle. While the UFA in 1935 was itself sharply divided over alignment with the CCF, Aberhart could unequivocally point to the Fifty Big Shots of Eastern Canada as the enemy of ordinary people. Not only that, the ideological character of Social Credit at least in the Aberhart years was fluid enough to allow some rural activists to imagine that it had come to fulfill the promise of the agrarian movement rather than to bury it. A series of interventionist measures implemented in the new government's first term—controlled marketing, a provincial bank—reinforced this impression. Aberhart, however, represented a distinctly different kind of *plebiscitarian* populism, one that pushed the centralist, technocratic, leader-dominated elements to the fore. The role of "the people" was simply to demand "results," which government experts could then implement. Already in the days before the election, Aberhart instructed Social Credit candidates and study groups not to debate their opponents. Social Credit supporters, meanwhile, brought numerous UFA rallies in country schoolhouses and halls to a premature end by honking automobile horns or pounding on the walls.[24] The 1935 campaign left a bitter aftertaste in deeply divided rural communities. While the CCF absorbed some UFA members, many others withdrew from active politics. Aberhart himself did not make a speech in the legislature until 1939. His preferred medium of political communication—not debate—was radio. The leader's role in this truncated democracy was to interpret and invoke the general will of the people as the occasion required. As Laycock puts it:

"The vacuity of public life contemplated for the average citizen in this vision indicates that Social Credit ideology also exceeded other Prairie populisms in projecting frustrations with current politics into an antipathy towards 'politics.'"[25] W.L. Morton's judgment is no less sharp: "Social Credit was the end of politics in Alberta and the beginning of popular administration."[26]

Centralization of power in the hands of the provincial government was entirely consistent with this orientation, though it struck squarely at the remnants of the older, participatory rural populism. Social Credit's first piece of legislation had nothing to do with monetary reform or dividend cheques; it consolidated almost 4,000 local school districts into 50. While the government could claim economic efficiencies in fiscal hard times as a rationale for the amalgamations, the *10,000* local trustees and the ratepayers who crammed into schoolhouses to petition against it—to no avail—detected a political motive as well. A similar consolidation of municipal government soon followed. The result in each case was to push further from reach the experience of local self-direction and the settings in which political skills could be exercised. In an important sense, Social Credit embarked on a project of rural political pacification.

The point is often made that populist parties in Saskatchewan and Alberta each moved in technocratic directions once elected. There are differences nonetheless. In Saskatchewan the CCF after 1944 was still bound to some extent to follow the policy established by delegates to party conventions; it attempted no equivalent consolidation of local government; and it relied politically on the support of a strong co-operative movement in which democratic practices were also sustained. Co-operative membership in Alberta was significantly lower by mid-century. The other factor that would set Alberta apart economically and culturally was oil. Already by the 1950s, half of government revenues were derived from oil. The province's population grew rapidly and the composition of its work-force changed, putting farmers in the minority.[27] Politically, oil created a dependence on American companies with the capital to develop the resource; it provided a focus for uniting "the people" not against corporate power but against real or imagined federal encroachments; and it gave the government the means to spend generously on health, education, highways, and seniors' housing, without having to resort to high levels of taxation.[28]

All this weakened the agrarian movement over time, as much as the consolidation of farm units with mechanization after World War II. But the retreat from electoral politics after 1935 was not the end of rural activism in Alberta. Though the UFA and UFWA could not always be revived at the local level, and though a unified movement proved elusive for rival or successor organizations, farm people still demonstrated flashes of social power—or perhaps frustration—at least in the 1940s. The most spectacular was the non-delivery strike of grain, milk, and eggs organized in 1946 by the Alberta Farmers' Union to press the case for parity pricing. Oldtimers still recall the tensions surrounding the strike in communities in north-central and eastern Alberta. A second instance was the largely rural campaign for electrification under public ownership. The UFA convention had endorsed the idea at its 1948 convention; and the CCF, which had received almost 25 percent of votes in 1944, with support primarily in rural Alberta, pressed the same demand in the legislature. The Social Credit government was pushed into a plebiscite coincident with the 1948 election partly in an attempt to distance its own political fate from the public power question, though it is not clear that it intended to honour the result. In any event, the result preserved the status quo, but only by a 151-vote margin out of almost 280,000 ballots cast. As expected, support generally was strongest in rural areas, and weakest in Calgary, which set the stage for years of grumbling about being deprived of public power by "city people." The demand for public power—and also for public vehicle insurance on the Saskatchewan model—was reiterated in subsequent conventions of a merged UFA and AFU, demonstrating again that rural Albertans have never really lived up to their anti-government image.[29]

V

The classic work on the UFA and early Social Credit periods remains C.B. Macpherson's *Democracy in Alberta* (1959). Though it has been effectively criticized on several important counts, and was too inclined to understand the province's political history through the retrospective prism of Social Credit under Ernest Manning's leadership, it continues to serve as a primary point of reference for research on the subject. Its insightful conceptualization of plebiscitarian democracy and the "quasi-party system" is still useful in making sense of the peculiar patterns of Alberta politics. Moreover, its judgment of the agrarian movement is, at one level, highly compelling: that radicalism gave way to conservatism because of the inherent limits set by the sanctity of individual property in small-producer ideology; and that the insecurity of farmers' position made them alternatively hostile and acquiescent to the established economic order.[30]

There is nonetheless a patronizing, unsatisfying quality to this conclusion. Despite Macpherson's admiration of the UFA experiments in delegate democracy and his rich account of the resulting tensions with cabinet government, his own theoretical commitment to historical materialism seemingly could allow no other conclusion. The achievements of the agrarian movement in Alberta had to be treated as a short-lived anomaly; for *petit bourgeois* small-holders were destined to disappear, and their position could not be the basis for a critical understanding of society: "They conceive society in their own image, not realizing or not admitting that the day of that society is past."[31] The steady decline in the number of farmers is a statistical reality. At the same time, the slim history of sustained, self-conscious, radical-democratic mass movements in North America would be much slimmer without the farmers of Alberta—or Saskatchewan, North Dakota, Minnesota or Oklahoma. That they ultimately failed does not discredit them. If anything, their experience urgently needs to be recalled and rekindled, especially among those of their grandchildren and great-grandchildren who have been politically pacified, deskilled and fragmented since the 1930s, but whose deepest desire is to preserve the possibility of farm livelihoods in rural Alberta.

Author's note:
This essay was first presented at a symposium marking the centenary of the formation of the Territorial Grain Growers' Association, University of Regina, November 2001. An earlier version is published in the volume resulting from that symposium: Murray Knuttila and Bob Stirling, eds., *The Prairie Agrarian Movement Revisited* (Regina: Canadian Plains Research Center, 2007). It is reprinted with permission.

Five

# Statues of Liberty
## The Political Tradition of the Producer*

*The wood elevator that charts its outline against the evening
sky may be considered the farmers' Statue of Liberty. It is true
no outstretched arm bearing a torch reaches aloft from the
tall silent figure. That torch is carried by the more than
100,000 members.... [T]hese structures serve as monuments to
commemorate the drive and foresight and determination on the
part of Saskatchewan farmers to improve their lot by doing
things for themselves.*

Saskatchewan Wheat Pool (1946) [1]

I

My friend Ken is an extraordinary farmer. It's not that he has a bigger
operation than his neighbours or that he lives a stress-free life. He
doesn't. He's a middle-aged man in a tough business. He sometimes
wonders how long he should keep knocking his head against the
wall. But he's also a community leader, an arts society impresario, a
rural activist, an experimenter. He's built a labour-saving auger attachment. He was an early adopter of zero-tillage grain farming and pion-
eered fava beans among other high-nitrogen pulse crops. He's tasted
slow food in Italy. He's given his time to local and farm causes. He's
been a county councillor. He served as a director of the farmer-run
Battle River Research Group in east-central Alberta. More recently,
as elevators disappear from the landscape, Ken has been active in
efforts to build a farmer-owned producer-car loading facility on the

Alliance line and then to convince the Canadian National Railway to keep allocating grain cars when the corporate preference is to abandon the line altogether. Someday he and his associates may have to run a short-line rail company.

Ken is often on the road, attending meetings and rallies in defence of things he believes in. He organizes some of them. He writes his share of letters to the farm papers. He also sings at weddings and funerals. His bass-voiced, finger-snapping, grain-farmer's adaptation of Tennessee Ernie Ford's coal-mining lament about the company store is a favourite even with city audiences, though they have to be primed for its agribusiness references: "You load a thousand tonne and what do you get/Another year older and deeper in debt/Oh Cargill don't you call me cause I can't go/I owe my soul to Agricore." He cannot say the name Monsanto politely. He is intimidated by neither title nor rank. When he reads something that intrigues him, he calls the author. One month it might be Wes Jackson at the Land Institute in Kansas and the question of shifting to perennial grains and intermixed "prairie grasses"—sunflowers, legumes and cereals—for conservation reasons. Another month it might be Eric Schlosser, author of the best-selling *Fast Food Nation*. Or it might be me, just after 8 a.m. on a Saturday morning, or on a harvest night when he's on the combine—"just thinking." The topic doesn't change much. Why does the rural, as he calls it, keep getting beat up? Why do governments keep trying to take away farmers' market power? Why are farmers their own worst enemies?

## II

On a July afternoon, in the shaded veranda of a farm home, still in Alberta, my friend Reg is giving a passionate, pessimistic account of the state of agriculture and its effect on community life for a visiting member of parliament. The high-profile politician from Toronto interrupts to ask him to look ahead twenty years: What will farming be like? Where will the trends lead? Reg does not hesitate. He has thought about this a long time. What's coming, he says, is a "new feudalism," one in which corporate lords control access to everything from seed to markets, and "producers" are reduced to the status of "serfs."

In the meantime, he too is working on behalf of the loading facility, drumming up delivery pledges from farmers in his district to make the case for trains.

III

There is a story I've tried to tell, though I've told it the wrong way, starting with the wrong people. It's been presented as a densely-footnoted paper for academic symposia and as a course for undergraduate students. Those audiences have liked it well enough. But it was meant, all along, for Ken and Reg and all those farmers who ask similar questions in coffee shops, beer parlors, community halls or their own kitchens. The story invests them with a rightful significance. It invites them to recognize themselves inside a much bigger, older tradition of rural-agrarian political action and ideas. That tradition spans centuries and continents. It is set apart by related understandings of land, work, freedom and political subjectivity—*that of producers or producer-citizens*, as opposed to *serfs*—that are woven through historical circumstances. It is still possible, in my experience, to hear the echoes of those older understandings in the words farmers use when they struggle to describe their highest purposes, their anger, their bewilderment and their fears. Who else, for example, still worries about serfdom? Or bio-serfdom? The enduring self-identity of the producer is itself a curious thing in a post-agrarian, post-industrial society; it has no currency outside of farm circles. Historically, in the story I want to tell, it has sometimes been a powerful source of shared grievance, radical politics and creative self-defence. At the same time, its strengths have also been its weaknesses.

Modern agrarianism emerged several centuries ago in Western Europe. Its setting was the struggle against serfdom, the imposition of new taxes, labour demands and higher crop-shares, and the loss of the commons—forest and pasture, fish and game—to the exclusive claims of the nobility.[2] One of its first signal events was the march from the English countryside to London that tested the reign of Richard II in 1381. The peasants' demands were straightforward; they included fixed rents and a charter abolishing serfdom. After some skillful royal manoeuvring, those demands were answered by brute force and summary executions. The rebels retreated to their fields and the hierarchical authority of king, nobles and bishops. But the pattern of imposition, rebellion and suppression would recur in other places. The medieval world was changing in fundamental ways. The nobility, in defiance of custom, had begun to revolutionize property relations as they jockeyed with kings to extract resources from the countryside to support their political ambitions.

In this long time of transition, peasant resistance involved much more than spontaneous and futile eruptions against authority. Grievances and demands had to be put into words so that kings could be petitioned, crowds could be moved to act and, once the printing press was invented, broader movements could coalesce around common ideals. The peasants appealed to custom, of course, and to the desire for a truer, uncorrupted Christian order, but not simply to restore some better feudal past. They would not be satisfied with gentler lords. The terms of rural resistance included some strikingly modern elements: freedom and equality.

In 1525, at the start of the so-called Peasants' War, one of the articles of a widely-circulated south German tract declared plainly: "we no longer wish to be burdened by lordship."[3] The peasants' levelling tendencies were rooted in two theological affirmations: first, that all authority came from God to be exercised for the common good, in which case, as another tract put it, "poor pious Christians" were not obliged to obey "false rulers" who "want to be lords for their own sake"[4]; and second, that the earth and its fruits were created for human sustenance, in which case it was wrong for some to hoard access to them while others went without. Sometimes those affirmations were mixed with what might be called rural millennialism. One pamphlet attributed to Hans Hergot, written in the dispirited aftermath of the uprisings, looked forward to a time when castles and social estates would be levelled, cities would be humbled into "instruments of the countryside," and a new, bottom-up order would be established. Its primary units would be self-sufficient agricultural villages that elected their own "sustainers." In turn, sustainers in a region would elect a supervisor, and so on, all for the sake of the commonweal. Thus "the small villages will be able to defend their land from the big cities and lords. *And what they get from the soil will be theirs.*"[5]

Hergot's vision upheld the dignity, virtue, intelligence and political authority of the common people. They were fit to rule themselves. Moreover, they could be imagined as a body of producers joined in interest against the lords, merchants, and the higher clergy—the "soft-living people," as the pamphlet put it, those who lived off their labour and abused power to protect position and property.

While the German peasant movement dissipated, its arguments resurfaced in England in the 17th century. Civil war had temporarily dethroned the monarchy and put political power in the hands of Parliament. The result was a victory for the "men of property."[6] It did nothing to reverse the pace of commercialization and enclosure in the countryside that displaced the agrarian poor who had also fought with Oliver Cromwell's republican side, but were then shut out of political power. In this turbulent context, the most famous act of resistance on the part of those loosely organized as Diggers and Levellers, though it was not an isolated one, was the establishment of a colony by squatters who planted vegetables on "wasteland" at St. George's Hill in 1649. The authorities promptly destroyed it.

The Levellers' most influential thinker and prolific pamphleteer was Gerrard Winstanley, a self-taught labourer and cattle-herder. Winstanley too distinguished between the common people and, against them, the landed gentry, clergy and professors who were known by their "parrot-like speaking from the universities." All those who fed and clothed themselves by others' labour, he wrote, were "not righteous actors in the earth"; there was no obligation to obey them.[7] Winstanley insisted that the earth was meant to be a common treasury, not a mere commodity that could be bought, sold and consolidated into the hands of a few to the exclusion of others. He drew clear links between labour and entitlement, land and freedom. In a series of open letters, he appealed unsuccessfully to Cromwell and Parliament to grant commoners access at least to Crown and other uncultivated lands, in order to feed themselves and, in the process, increase the national food supply. In other words, land should be made productive, not left idle, and people should have opportunity to be producers; none should be deprived of the benefits of the earth. True freedom, Winstanley proposed, lay in the ability "to plant or build," to enjoy the fruits of one's labour, to pay no rent to a landlord, and to elect one's overseers. The free commonwealth required that "every household shall keep all instruments and tools fit for the tillage of the earth, either for planting, reaping, or threshing," and that none, as equals, "give hire or take hire for his work."[8]

Winstanley's equation of freedom with farming has an odd-sounding ring to it, but his producerist starting-point could lead to a more conventional position in answer to the question: how could some individuals come to own property in land when there had been no consent to such a change? This was not a settled question at the time. One prominent answer went as follows: the earth may have been given in common for human preservation but, as the philosopher John Locke put it, God did not mean that it should remain "common and uncultivated. He gave it to the industrious and the rational."[9] Because such acquisition increased the food-stocks available to all humankind, there was no necessary limit on property. Instead the standard was efficient, productive use. In England this argument could make common-cause with the Leveller claims directed at idle Crown or gentry lands. In the American colonies, however, where land was to be wrested not from the gentry but from wilderness and aboriginal inhabitants, it was taken up much more enthusiastically. It gave cultivators pride of place over hunters and herders (and, later, ranchers).[10] It still resonates, for example, wherever European settlement is justified on the basis that "there was nothing here when we came," that "we made the land productive" and thereby that "we help feed the world."

I do not want to suggest, however, that agrarianism in North America has been primarily or consistently Lockean in inspiration. If so, its sense of community would have been much thinner and its political conception of the producer as citizen would have remained undeveloped. For generations of European immigrants, land ownership represented more than—or something other than—the chance to be lord on a small scale. It meant freedom from subservience. For this reason, the power and novelty of the freehold experience should not be underestimated, despite the physical hardship and loneliness associated with it. One of its most romantic expressions is found in Jean de Crevecoeur's *Letters from an American Farmer* (1782). Crevecoeur, a French officer who had settled in New York, wrote that he was grateful to be "an American farmer"—not a peasant—since he enjoyed "freedom of action, freedom of thoughts" and knew "no other landlord than the lord of all land." That much a Leveller might have appreciated. Crevecoeur described his farm as the basis of his social and political standing: "[N]o wonder that so many Europeans who have never been able to say that such portion of land was theirs cross the Atlantic to realize that happiness.... [O]n it is founded our rank, our freedom, our power as citizens, our importance as inhabitants of such a district."[11]

My interest in Crevecoeur's account lies in its equation of land, freedom and political standing. Otherwise, it is strangely silent both about his own political position—he turned out to be a monarchist who fled to England to publish his book—and about the undercurrent of rural conflict in colonies like New York, which had been founded on large land grants to prominent families, over leases, tolls, debt and access to freehold property. The number of landless poor swelled. The spectre of a return to feudal tenancy was a persistent and real one. During the War of Independence, the key question for many colonists was whose tyranny should be resisted as a first priority: that of the king in England or that of the colonial elites in Boston—the "non-productive" merchants, bankers and lawyers who lived off the "honest labour" of farmers?[12] The drafters of the Constitution tilted in favour of the elites by strengthening central and state governments and making no formal provision for the local authorities and township assemblies that had been the bedrock of rural democratic practice.[13]

This is the context in which it is necessary to situate Thomas Jefferson's political thought and his presidential defence of "cultivators of the earth" as the "most virtuous and independent citizens."[14] Otherwise he is easily sentimentalized. Jefferson's reputation as a "magnet for those who advocate a special moral or political status for farmers and for country life,"[15] is built on a slim, sketchy and not particularly original set of writings. His place is complicated further by his own status as an active, experimental agriculturalist, to be sure, but scarcely a smallholder, and a slaveowner at that. All the same, Jefferson was clear that "dependence begets subservience and venality"—the opposite of democratic virtues—and that the young

American republic's prospects would diminish should farmers no longer constitute a majority of the population. They were, in short, "the most precious part of a state." In 1785 he wrote from France that, having seen immense wealth, wretchedness, and aristocratic lands left idle, "legislators cannot invent too many devices for subdividing property."[16]

The Jeffersonian idea of the political primacy of producer-citizens has a much older but mostly unacknowledged history. It dates back to the first self-consciously democratic politics in ancient Greece. In this respect, the familiar translation of the word *polis*, the root of politics, as a "city-state" is misleading. First, it wrongly highlights a geographic place rather than a particular way of life that brought citizens together. Second, it hides the agrarian origins of the leading Greek democracy, Athens, which emerged after a program of land reform and debt emancipation had created, at least temporarily, a society of smallholders.[17] Philosophers like Xenophon and, more cautiously, Aristotle ventured arguments that would be associated 2000 years later with Jefferson. First, farmers comprised the best, most stable democracy, because their independent position, skills and experiences matched the requirements of citizens. Second, such a democracy required limits on land acquisition in order to preserve its fundamental character.[18] Though Athenian society would again become increasingly class-divided, its democracy more aristocratic and its citizens less likely to get their hands dirty, the fundamental idea that free individuals owned property so that they could participate in the public life of the community did not disappear. As one commentator has put it: "If the property-owner chose to enlarge his property instead of using it up in leading a political life, it was as though he willingly sacrificed his freedom and became voluntarily what the slave was against his own will, a servant of necessity."[19]

For Jefferson, the justification for property in land was conditional not absolute. It did not take away the underlying natural right, on the part of the poor and unemployed, to labour the earth for food. It rested not on the standard of efficient, productive use—in which case there was nothing necessarily wrong with large landholdings—but rather on the full-bodied freedom it created for smallholders as citizens. There was, therefore, a legitimate public interest in maintaining a certain kind of agrarian society. Consequently Jefferson as president favoured progressive taxation against large estates and fretted about industrialization—"let our workshops remain in Europe"[20]—because the factory, unlike the farm, invariably meant economic concentration, hierarchical relations and a narrowing of workers' intelligence around routine assembly. In the same spirit he opened "vacant" western lands for settlement in order to maintain a predominance of small producers. In concluding a land sale in 1802, he urged a Seneca chief to "persuade our red brethren to be sober and to cultivate their lands," that is, to step up on the ladder of civilization. The place of aboriginal peoples in settler-agrarian thought is an important and difficult one that is considered elsewhere in this volume. Suffice to say that for Jefferson there was no contradiction between territorial expansion and the vision of a nation of smallholders. There was only an obligation, he wrote, to those peoples whose "ardent love of liberty and independence" had been overwhelmed by an unstoppable tide of settlers—an obligation, that is, to "teach them agriculture" and "enable them to maintain their place" by cultivating the land.[21]

IV

The homestead era was the occasion for large-scale territorial ambition in both the U.S. and Canada. To that end, governments sequestered aboriginal peoples by a combination of negotiation and force, surveyed land and harnessed the aspirations—realistic or not—of "small colonists" recruited from North America and Europe to serve their geopolitical and economic interests. In Canada there was none of the Jeffersonian gloss sometimes attributed to the *Homestead Act* in the U.S. The National Policy was decidedly not a project in the outward expansion of a robust democracy, which then scarcely existed at the centre of the country. Indeed, as the ranks of those colonists included greater numbers of sturdy peasants in sheepskin coats, some of the sharpest protests came from radical voices. They were concerned not so much that the young country's British character was being diluted but that the new immigrants, unaccustomed to democratic politics, would be easily enlisted at the ballot box against any prospect of change. The survey grid itself, in the way that it dispersed settlers, presented further spatial challenges to the emergence of any political life in what were often multilingual, multiethnic districts.

The greater challenge, however, but also the moment for the emergence of a broad-based agrarian politics of producer-citizens, arose as western settlers were backed into a corner by new economic realities: the age of monopoly capital, steam transportation and fluctuating world markets, along with the closing of the frontier, first in the U.S., then in Canada. This was a time, as one historian has written, when "throughout the Western grainary the increasing centralization of economic life fastened upon prairie farmers new modes of degradation."[22] In the circumstances it is not surprising that farmers, like miners, railroad workers and others, should have drawn on new socialist ideas as well to make critical sense of their world. But they did so in unorthodox, distinctly agrarian ways. Some of them read Karl Marx.[23] His idea of exploitation was not so different, after all, from the long-standing agrarian distinction between producers and those who lived off of the value that their labour produced. Notwithstanding his dismissals of rural life and of peasants as unreliable revolutionaries, his brisk analysis of land reforms in France—in which feudal lords were replaced by bankers—might have rung true in farmers' own experience: "The smallholding of the peasant is now only the pretext that allows the capitalist to draw profits, interest and rent from the soil, while leaving it to the tiller of the soil himself to see how he can extract his wages."[24]

What came to be called agrarian socialism, however, in places like Oklahoma, North Dakota, and later Saskatchewan, was invariably more agrarian than socialist. In the first place, farmers had a stubborn attachment to individual land ownership. Thus in 1912 the Oklahoma newspaper *The New Century* fixed the terms of its socialism in a decidedly Jeffersonian way: "Without land, man cannot exist. It is the first necessity of being. It is the exclusion of wage workers from the soil that places them at the mercy of their employers and binds the chains of slavery upon them. There can be no solution of the economic question that does not restore the land to the people."[25] In other words, those reduced to tenancy needed to be restored to ownership. While socialist arguments continued to inform a fierce debate over the land question in the desperate circumstances of the 1930s, when state ownership and lease-use arrangements were proposed as a way of increasing security of tenure for farmers, they did not prevail. For some critics on the left, this remains the great failure—the inexplicable sacred cow—of radical agrarian parties in office.[26]

In the second place, farmers rejected the gratuitous political advice that sometimes came from big-city socialist organizers to defer to the industrial working class. In the same way, they would have been baffled by the Marxist theory of history that relegated land, agricultural production and producers to an increasingly marginal place in the shaping of human society. By all appearances they had numbers on their side. Increasingly convinced that the party system did not serve their interests, they were drawn into organized efforts to achieve economic self-defence through the ballot box, beginning with the populist campaign of 1896—"the largest democratic mass movement in American history."[27] While that campaign failed, or was co-opted by other interests, the next five decades represented the political high-point of the agrarian movement at state and provincial levels. On both sides of the border, this period saw the energetic building of farmers' parties, producer co-operatives, newspapers and a movement culture of well-read, politically-skilled men and women.

The fact that settler farmers on the North American prairies would describe themselves and their situation in ways strikingly similar to 16th-century south German peasants illustrates what I mean by a tradition. They were the "plain common people," as the farm activist and *Western Producer* columnist Violet McNaughton often put it.[28] Against them stood the "23 money kings" of William Irvine's classic *The Farmers in Politics* (1920).[29] Less politely, Saskatchewan farm leader and newspaper editor E.A. Partridge's *Manifesto of the No-Party League* (1913) targeted "the rich grabbers of...the choicest portions of the public domain" along with their "mercenary-minded hirelings" in parliaments and legislatures.[30] In *A War on Poverty* (1925), Partridge wrote that society was "divided into those who produce and do not possess"—farmers and wage labourers—"and those who possess and do not produce." He too envisioned a better future, a co-operative commonwealth, but proposed that such a change required nothing less than a radically new political context: an independent Western Canada. This new country, predominantly rural, would be governed by a bottom-up, delegate-based polity of local "camps," regional assemblies, and a High Court of Control that had much in common with what Hergot had imagined.[31] In fact, the closest working models of that structure that would emerge would be the prairie wheat pools.

The farmers' movement at its most creative relied on two other rhetorical themes in shaping producer-citizens and assigning them a lead role in society. One was more directly political. As Irvine had announced in *The Farmers in Politics*, farmers alone could represent their interests; they had "resolved to become their own emancipators"; they were "the most important democratic unit in the country"; and they were "driving home the shaft of conviction to the plutocratic heart."[32] In that effort, the party system was a barrier, not just because it was a "tool of the wealthy," but also because, as Henry Wise Wood, Irvine's collaborator in the United Farmers of Alberta, told his audiences, it suspended the people in a state of weakness. It denied them "opportunity for self-development through active organized effort." The farmers' movement, on the other hand, had a contrary interest in cultivating in its members both an "intelligent understanding of their common social interest" and a "capacity to speak intelligently for agriculture." Self-government, in short, could only be achieved if the capacity to think, speak and act was broadly distributed. This was the higher, democratic form of citizenship towards which society would evolve from its "primitive" forms of politics, farmers leading the way.[33] This was not just self-congratulation. Already in 1916, an eminent Queen's University professor had identified farmers' organized responses to the inequities of the grain trade as "the strongest force making for real democracy in present-day Canadian life."[34]

Co-operation was the other related theme. In this period, the idea of co-operation became virtually hegemonic ("the true social law") over against "wasteful" capitalist competition that put profit ahead of human need. The idea might have had European immigrant roots, but it was borne out in the practical life of settler communities. It was preached from country pulpits and outdoor platforms.[35] To its advantage, the idea of co-operation was elastic enough to stretch over a range of positions. It could mean no more than better prices for farmers as producers and consumers through collective market power. For others, though, it meant social transformation, defence against class exploitation, self-help and a form of social ownership of the economy that could be locally and democratically controlled. The purpose of agrarian activity therefore was nothing short of remaking whole societies as *co-operative commonwealths*—a phrase at least as old as Winstanley. Irene Parlby, a cabinet minister in the United Farmers of Alberta government, reflected the optimism of the times and the ambitiousness of the goal: "Co-operation is not fundamentally an economic movement. It has its roots in the things of the spirit.... [I]t can in time transform a world made hideous by the competitive system into a democracy of hope, justice, and happiness for all."[36]

The prairie wheat pools were close to the centre of this distinctive political blend: democracy as capacity, liberty as co-operation. Though they cited impressive business achievements—members, elevators, lakehead terminals, billions of bushels handled, millions of dollars saved in handling charges and more returned to members as patronage dividends—they continued to present themselves in terms that were broader than that. Their country elevators were statues of liberty. Their country meetings held during the winter were meant to provide "adult education for the development of rural citizenship," especially among young people, and a deepening of the co-operative ideal.[37]

V

The farm movement on the North American prairies, it is important to say, never experienced a golden or unified age—but it did respond to the challenges of the frontier in creative and intelligent ways. Farmers never achieved anything like a steady state against the winds of economic, geopolitical and technological change. By the 1950s, the Depression and mechanization had already produced a decline in the number of farmers relative to the rest of the population; the modest-sized, mixed-farming base that sustained farm organizations and co-operative institutions had begun to erode and, with it, any pretence of unity or a lead role in society. In North America, national governments set down the terms of the new dispensation in the late 1960s. A U.S. presidential special commission and a Canadian task force reached essentially the same conclusion: the problem with farm incomes was that there were too many farmers. The future lay in high-volume, specialized, input-dependent and capital-intensive production for export—a "cheap-grain Olympics."[38] The political message was, in the words of the U.S. Secretary of Agriculture, get big or get out.

This policy shift was the culmination of a complex, incremental history of change—and sometimes resistance—involving government, industry and farmers. Obviously it was designed to appeal to select farmers *as producers*, though in a much narrower sense. From the start of the settler period, with its uneconomically small homesteads, government programs had assumed and promoted the idea that "if agricultural output could but be doubled the farmer would be twice as well off as before."[39] Agronomic experts did their best to nudge "progressive" farmers towards industrial models of production.[40] Then, as now, volume was the preferred substitute for a stronger and sustainable market position. The wheat pools' eagerness to report their success by the bushel reflected the same producerist tendency. Though their eagerness was tempered by goals of citizenship and, on rare occasions, by environmental doubts—"Is it possible that we have produced too much?"[41]—the pools never really developed a policy framework that would have sustained a different prairie society.

The new farm policy of the late 1960s amounted to a rival, more selective definition of producers according to what and how much they produced. In both countries it deepened existing divisions among farmers; the remnants of earlier agrarian movements were placed on the political defensive. During the homestead era, farmers had tended to look to industrial workers as their likeliest allies, but organizationally and ideologically found it most necessary to clarify their relationship to the left—especially those who did not understand the singular importance of land and agriculture. As Irvine wrote, farmers were neither bolshevists nor Wobbly syndicalists; they answered to the higher law of co-operation. By the 1960s, however, farmers were invited to take their place as business stake-holders inside agriculture as an industry joined in a shared interest in production and profit. As a consequence, the agrarian response on behalf of small-scale producers has tended to define itself over against right-wing advocates of market choice, possessive individualism and corporate efficiency. Those responses typically have adapted Jefferson in defence of the *family* farm as a *social* unit that generates more than economic values. But their political ambitions have been scaled back considerably from the heyday of producer-citizens.

The best-known and most prolific agrarian writer of the past generation is Wendell Berry. All of his major arguments can be traced back to his classic, *The Unsettling of America*, which was meant as a response to the U.S. special commission's "powerful attack" on agrarian values and the national government's delivery of agriculture, by design or not, "into the hands of corporations." The book's point and its polemical passion recall the pamphlets of Hergot and Winstanley. Recalling the Cold War outrage in the 1950s over the forced removal of rural villages in communist states, Berry proposed that in the U.S. only the method was different: a "totalitarian" economy.[42] Against this kind of planned economy, with its cult of bigness, its doctrines of efficiencies of scale, its faith in expert knowledge, its cheap-food consumer society and its "community-killing agriculture," Berry invoked Jeffersonian notions of liberty and agrarian virtue. A "free-enterprise system" was not at all the same thing as personal liberty. The latter required a genuine, practical independence. It required people who were "producers"—that is, able to furnish some of their household needs, and entertainment, from their own resources and skills—in contrast to those who were "passive" consumers only, able to do little for themselves and at the mercy of the food industry in particular. The price of specialization, he argued, was not just a loss of freedom; it also meant a "scattering out of the various functions of character: workmanship, care, conscience, responsibility."[43] As agriculture became increasingly dependent on chemical inputs and sophisticated technologies, farmers' liberty was diminished; as their units of production grew in size, they were pushed to take on the values of the technician or the banker, rather than the steward, while others were simply pushed off the land; and as food became an industrial rather than a cultural product, their "intelligence of the earth"—inter-generational, communal, experiential—was devalued. Governments had been no friend of farm people in this revolution.

Berry's politics confound the standard ideological categories. He has described himself as an agrarian and a Jeffersonian. His personal liberty is lived out, first, at the level of local communities or neighbourhoods, where responsibility and care can be exercised and, second, within the limits of nature: "To put the bounty and the health of our land, our only commonwealth, into the hands of people who do not live on it and share its fate will always be an error. For whatever determines the fortune of the land determines also the fortune of the people."[44] In *The Unsettling of America* he claimed a kind of conservatism, but strenuously distanced himself from so-called conservatives in agribusiness who wish to conserve "nothing less than the great corporate blocks of wealth and power, in whose every interest is implied the moral degeneracy and economic dependence of the people. They do not esteem the possibility of a prospering, independent class of small owners because they are, in fact, not conservatives at all, but the most doctrinaire and disruptive of revolutionaries."[45] In a more recent essay Berry proposed that an alternative political division was more realistic—that between the parties of the global economy and local community. The latter, he said, is more scattered and "only now coming aware of itself." It is comprised of "people who take a generous and neighborly view of self-preservation"; who know that work "ought to be good," satisfying, useful and dignifying; and who "know that things connect": farming, nature, food, health, even citizenship.[46]

Berry's agrarianism has had limited or at least delayed appeal in Canada, it is fair to say, for at least three reasons. First, its traditionalism around work and technology makes high demands of rural people. As a rural student of mine once wrote, "no one wants that kind of life anymore"; it is "too frugal, too difficult, too labour-intensive."[47] Second, at least in the prairie grain-belt, where agriculture was export-oriented from the start, the idea of a primarily local or regional economy has no real antecedent. Third, small-producer agrarianism in this country has mixed its Jeffersonian influences with a greater measure of social-democratic ones, which since the

1930s have assumed an important role for the state in counter-balancing corporate economic power through regulation and market instruments such as the Canadian Wheat Board. As those protections have been rolled back, however, the case for the family farm has been renewed with a fresh urgency. To be sure, that work has been left largely to farm people. The conventional voices on the urban right and left are, for their own reasons, plainly discomfited by the language and priority of the family farm. Likewise they are, I think, genuinely puzzled by the claim that the outcome matters, not just because family farms produce food but because they are the "last holdout," however besieged, "in a long war over who will own the economy: local families or distant investors."[48]

In the age of globalization, it is perhaps not a surprise that the most energetic defences have been mounted on other continents where property relations are undergoing the most rapid, radical transformation. The Indian scientist Vandana Shiva has become a prominent writer and speaker on subjects like biodiversity, intellectual property rights, development and trade. She represents a distinctly agrarian strand of eco-feminism that posits as a goal the regeneration of the "real economy, rooted in the earth and community"[49]—and it is none other than Berry who has come to her public defence against criticism by a leading American scientist.[50] In China, an exposé bestseller has documented peasant struggles against high taxation, official brutality, poverty and declining real incomes in the countryside.[51] In France José Bové became a familiar figure for his symbolic attack on the local McDonald's. A recent presidential candidate, he has distanced himself from other political parties—especially the left's dismissal of "the world of peasants"—and defined a distinctive three-point struggle: against the exploitation of farmers as primary producers; against intensive farming systems; and against biopiracy.[52] In Brazil, the Sem Terra squatter movement has echoed Winstanley and the Levellers with its rationale: large tracts of unused land are an "insult to society"; land belongs to those who work it as its guardians; seeds are the property of humankind not corporate patent-holders; and, throughout the world, agrarian reform that would "democratize the land" is required as a basis for food sovereignty and political citizenship.[53]

One important international face of small-producer agrarianism is the organization *Via Campesina*. What is striking about the documents issued from its assembly in Bangalore, India in the year 2000, is how much they bear out important elements of the agrarian tradition I have sketched. Again, land is distinct. It is a "good of nature," a "supreme good" that "needs to be used for the welfare of all," including future generations. It is the basis of culture and community autonomy. Its ownership must be broadly distributed, and on the principle that "only those that work the land, depend on it and live there with their families, have the right to land."[54] Land, food and genetic materials cannot be crudely commodified. *Via Campesina's* proposed charter of the rights of farmers and rural communities begins with a claim for the importance of those who "are the repository of the effort and knowledge of the generations that created the biological richness" that exists in the world, and for their related right to make fundamental decisions about genetic resources against the threat of "monopolization and inappropriate use." In words reminiscent of 16th-century peasant demands against the enclosure of the commons, the document declares: "Patenting of plants, animals, and their components means that peasant and indigenous communities lose control of the resources that we have traditionally used and known."[55]

### VI

My fascination with the great agrarian arch I have reconstructed in this essay lies partly in the light it shines, surprising to most, on rural settings for political words and deeds. We have all become accustomed to the idea that political power is located in and flows from metropolitan capitals. On the prairie frontier, however, it was none other than producer-citizens—concerned for their own livelihoods—who produced a vigorous, creative, tough-minded and self-aware democratic politics, *in and for the countryside*. This claim, of course, comes with a puzzle: those same regions on this continent are now characterized, not just by conservative voting tendencies, as Thomas Frank has noted about Kansas,[56] but by a fatalistic absence of any meaningful sense of political skill and critical agency. The democratic frontier that was once so important to the continent as a whole closed several decades ago. Farm people are poorer for it in every respect. The countryside is seldom a place where people meet to consider a course of action and then do a new, memorable thing together. The economy that isolates them as individuals and extracts wealth from their communities also suspends them in weakness. Rural communities, stripped of meaningful authority, suffer government and corporate decisions made from a distance by people who will not live directly with the consequences. The old "statues of liberty" and "schoolhouses of democracy" have been dismantled or left to deteriorate without regret.

With that in mind, my interest in recollecting an agrarian tradition is to consider whether it can still offer critical resources to farmers like Ken and Reg, who live out the old-fashioned ideal of the producer-citizen, and whether it can inform an open, new agrarian politics for all people who care about land, community, good work and food. Historically, that tradition has been both conservative *and* radical. For its own reasons it has been suspicious of the state *and* sometimes demanded that it protect farmers against the vagaries of commodity prices and the near-monopoly position of railroads, banks, grain companies and packing plants. In North America it has settled on the paradoxical position that farm land is best owned by individuals—more of them, not fewer—for the sake of greater political, community and environmental goods.[57]

The same agrarian tradition has imagined producers as citizens.[58] But that blend, like the difficult balances in the preceding paragraph, has proven unstable over time. The self-identity of producer, as this essay has demonstrated, has proved malleable and two-sided. Therefore its use requires some care. The word producer is, at its core, a claim of *entitlement*, against those who profit unduly from the work it represents, and of *respect*, especially when it is associated with so basic a human good as food. This self-identity represents potential common-ground with farm people around the world. But, as recent experience shows, producers can be thrown off course. Their positive culture of hard work and self-help, individual and communal,[59] can shift its focus away from those who extract wealth from their communities, so that society's soft-living parasites are not the clergy, gentry, railroad barons or bankers of the past; instead, they

91

are the poor, the unemployed and the aboriginal[60]—all of them light-ning rods for rural resentment. Producers can be co-opted by agri-business and government strategies that make production an end in itself and deference to agronomic experts a matter of routine. They too can aspire to tame nature with the help of the latest chemical advantages in hopes of achieving marginal improvements in yield. Most of all, though, producers can define themselves narrowly, indi-vidualistically, so that they lose any sense of themselves as citizens.

Flashes of agrarian action, when farmers freely do something new, are now rare. They occur, if at all, well beyond the fence-line of formal politics—like that producer-car loading facility on the Alliance line. They are made possible when farmers combine a clear assessment of their situation with effective leadership, broad partici-pation and sympathetic non-farm allies. Nowadays farmers may have neither the political strength of numbers nor deep pockets. Whatever they do is precarious. But there is also a sense in which, daring to act at all, they reclaim their own history, their own practices, their own power, their own conception of freedom—older, more profound and more communal than the simple "choice" of free-market ideologues, and the opposite of serfdom in any form.

Author's note:
Earlier or partial versions of this essay have been presented at small conferences at the University of Guelph (2002) and the University of Nebraska (2007). I am grateful to my colleague Sandra Rein for comments on a penultimate draft.

Six

# Populists, Patriots and Pariahs

I

The political paradox of my ancestors is this. On one hand, they could trace a spiritual lineage to the "revolution of the common man" in 16th-century Europe.[1] On the other, they had learned to trust kings against commoners long before they settled on the North American plains with its fertile soil for agrarian radicalism; and so they remained aloof from—and sometimes were vilified by—the most energetic, broad-based democratic movements in this continent's political history. They had emerged out of the violent cauldron of the Reformation as a distinct Mennonite people and faith. They had broken not only with the authority of Rome, but also with the idea that certain persons, places, or days, had been set above others as holy. In their first generation, they had tended towards an egalitarian communalism; they stressed local autonomy in decision-making, the sharing of members in the work of scriptural understanding and, in some cases, in a common treasury. For this they were claimed by Marx and Engels as forerunners of communism. They might equally be claimed among the first modern populists.

Their organizers travelled the countryside winning over villagers. They injected a levelling spirit into a time marked by aggressive attempts on the part of Germanic princes to consolidate their rule and by the imposition of new forms of taxation on peasants aggrieved at the loss of their customary access to the commons for food, pasture, and firewood. They looked forward to a time, as one pamphleteer-printer put it, when "the cities will be humbled," "nobility of birth will pass away," and the rural villages will become "rich in property and people."[2] Some of them supported and joined in the peasants' uprising of 1525. When it was brutally suppressed—Martin Luther's blunt counsel to the nobility having been that the ears of the rebels should be opened with musket balls—the remaining remnant adopted the more separatist position that some had urged from the start. They renounced the sword and, with it, the oath of allegiance demanded by earthly rulers. For at least a generation, they were hunted down by Catholic and Protestant authorities alike as a threat to public order and sound doctrine.

Like the Jews, they fit uneasily into a Europe being carved into distinct territorial states. From Friesland and Gröningen in northern Europe, to the Vistula Delta, to southern Russia, my Mennonite ancestors lived as stateless, migratory peoples at the privilege of rulers who desired them for their agrarian skills and economic prowess. As the age of nationalism filled those states with the glue of fraternity, equality, and popular sovereignty, their privileges and territorial enclaves again became more precarious. As Hannah Arendt has written of the Jewish people in *The Origins of Totalitarianism*, they had "no political tradition or experience"; they were scarcely aware of tensions between state and society; and they had concluded that "authority, and especially high authority, was favorable to them and that lower officials, and especially the common people, were dangerous."[3]

My ancestors' diaries respectfully record the visits of monarchs: of Friedrich William IV of Prussia passing through a village en route to his coronation, then returning in 1845 to inspect the floodwaters retreating after a dam had burst[4]; of the Russian empress and her daughter, stepping from their boat on their journey down the Dniepr River to the songs of schoolchildren ("The Lord's angel go with them"[5]); of the Russian Crown Prince Nicholas, for whom a parade route in Ekaterinoslav in 1863 was lit spectacularly by Bengal lanterns; of King George VI speaking by radio from Regina in 1939 as the Royal Couple toured Canada ("They are...ordained by God and it is wrong not to honour them."[6]). Between 1798 and 1800, my paternal ancestor David Epp was part of the delegation that negotiated with imperial officials in St. Petersburg for two years on the Charter of Privileges that defined the terms of Mennonite settlement in Russia.

He eventually gained a personal audience with Paul I and brought home the charter with the emperor's signature. His descendants were among its keepers, anxious that its most crucial clause—the exemption from military service—should not be annulled by future czars, who, as a consequence, had to be petitioned in the most loyal terms. His preacher grandson Jacob, my great-great-grandfather, led in prayers of thanksgiving and protection for "our beloved" Alexander II after news arrived of an assassin's unsuccessful attempt on his life in Paris.[7] My maternal great-great-grandfather Martin Klaassen was also among those chosen to travel to St. Petersburg to seek reassurances when the imperial court appeared to lean politically with the first breezes of popular nationalism. It is a matter of no small family pride that his detailed drawing of an estate hung in the Winter Palace. He was an unflinching advocate of the divine right of kings. His son, Jacob, once he had settled in Canada in mid-life after a long sojourn in the United States, could transfer his earthly loyalty to an English king, and to a constitutionally benign rather than an authoritarian one at that. By then, the latter were an endangered species, and the former were not undeserving of sympathy: "for even a King cannot always do as he likes."[8]

The other king to whom my ancestors affixed their loyalty in Canada was the Liberal prime minister, William Lyon Mackenzie King. Some of my Epp ancestors had adapted quickly and enthusiastically to the Liberals' frontier partisanship after their arrival among the earliest homesteaders in the Eigenheim district west of Rosthern, Saskatchewan, in the early 1890s. They were swept up, no doubt, in the deliberate recruitment of community leaders in German-speaking immigrant communities; at election time, the children of one of them reportedly "ran about the yard waving the good old Union Jack and calling out—'Vote Liberal.'"[9] While my maternal ancestors were much more politically reserved, they were connected even more tightly to King by kinship. Jacob Klaassen worked closely with his brother-in-law David Toews in the organization that brought thousands of Mennonite refugees from the Soviet Union in the 1920s. In this cause, Toews's personal relations with King were a matter of mutual benefit, to say nothing of local legend, especially once King was forced to contest a by-election in 1926 in the Prince

Albert constituency to return to the House of Commons. According to King's famous diary, Toews was the first to congratulate him on his victory—he had carried the polls where my family would have voted by almost 100 percent—and to assure King that "people voted for me not only for political reasons but because they 'loved' me. It was a very beautiful beginning in my new relationship—I should like above all else to be of real service to these pioneers of western Canada."[10] When King returned to Rosthern in 1928 to lay the cornerstone for a new post office, Jacob Klaassen attended with his two youngest sons. He followed the prime minister's entourage to a picnic at the Dominion Experimental Farm, where he "had the honour of shaking his hand. He gives a very favourable impression."[11]

So it is that I have inherited almost—*almost*—nothing except proximity to connect me to the history of agrarian radicalism in the West. No connection to the populist campaign across the Great Plains in the 1890s. No connection to the Farmers' Union or then the Socialist Party that swept parts of the Oklahoma countryside in the second decade of the twentieth century on a peculiar mix of rural grievance and holiness religion.[12] Not to the great cause of the Wheat Pool in Saskatchewan. Certainly not to the Co-operative Commonwealth Federation as it built a movement that eventually formed a government. Not even to the woolly cause of Social Credit, which was imported unsuccessfully from Alberta during the Great Depression. Though his neighbours were interested—some voted for the local Social Credit candidate in the 1938 provincial election—my great-grandfather Jacob Klaassen would not be fooled by this movement. He would not be reassured by its radio-preacher leader or shaken from his general dislike of political campaigns for the way they aroused popular passions, when all he desired was the opportunity to live in peace: "Premier Aberhardt [*sic*] is speaking in Rosthern today. That'll be a real con job. The poor people, they insist on being deceived."[13] He declined, he said, to vote at all.

Though my settler-ancestors lived on this continent by much the same practical community creed of mutuality and local autonomy; though they, too, knew how many meetings it took to run a mutual telephone company or school board or doctor's co-operative; though they faced the same economic hardships, their attitude towards agrarian-populist movements seems to have been sceptical, indifferent, even hostile. Those were the responses that came most readily to them from the well-trained Old World reflexes of self-preservation and principled separation. Those are the responses that still demand a hearing in the inner dialogue of a political life. As a matter of personal inheritance, they ask to be understood. And in their relation to the testing-ground of immigrant experience—settlement, war, Depression—they shed their own light on the mass movements that shaped prairie societies at an earlier stage. They temper my admiration with reminders of the truth identified by the U.S. historian Catherine Stock: that agrarian radicalism has always been a two-sided coin[14]—the defence of small producers and their communities being never completely free of the dangers of vigilantism, or the need of scapegoats.

II

It is unusual and even impolitic, as I have had to learn, to live in North America with a vivid historical sense of identity that is shaped by events stretching back five centuries and across an ocean. As a result, I am not convinced of the familiar claim that history is always written by the victors, that it represents an act of power that secures their ideological hold on the popular imagination—that it matters that much to them. Perhaps it does. But stories, told and retold, have been the lifeblood and the glue that binds those minority communities vanquished to the margins of modern nation-states.

By the late 1520s, the wildfire of armed peasant uprisings throughout southern Germany had been crushed. The millenialist utopia of Münster had ended in a chaotic, suicidal bloodbath—the Jonestown, Guyana of its time—that enabled secular and ecclesiastical authorities to paint all theological dissenters with the same dangerous colours. For the next decade, militias would keep a suspicious watch in the cities of Europe for signs of similar unrest. While most of the earliest leaders among the so-called Anabaptist theological radicals were inclined from the outset to renounce violence, on the model of a "defenseless" Christ, they consolidated this position under conditions of relentless persecution. They retreated from the idea of a Christian society. Instead, they essentially accepted

Luther's refashioning of the medieval notion of two kingdoms: that of the sword, of law, divinely ordained to restrain evil in the world; and that of the spirit, of grace, of inward freedom. But where Luther imagined that Christians lived in both kingdoms and could rightly serve as magistrate, soldier or hangman for the sake of order, the radicals determined that they should live apart as a voluntary, un-coerced community of believers according to the higher norms of the spiritual kingdom. The Schleitheim Confession, adopted at a council in Switzerland in 1527, renounced all use of the sword by Christians whether to punish sin among them or to protect the good. It was outside the perfection of Christ. The Confession also declared that the baptism of infants was the "highest and chief abomination of the pope."[15]

There was nothing timid or expedient about this political retreat and theological consolidation. There was no greater crime within reach of the Holy Roman Empire than to call into question the Church's sacrament of baptism or to re-baptize an adult in mockery of it. When Lutheran theologians presented their own confessional document to Emperor Charles V at Augsburg in 1530, at a council summoned to find common ground for alliance with the princes of northern Europe against the advancing Turk, it stood in full conform-ity on the baptism question. Moreover, its fighting-creed preamble began with the threat of "that most atrocious, hereditary, and ancient enemy of the Christian name and religion," and expressed the senti-ment that "we all are under one Christ and do battle under Him." There was no question that Christians could stand in legal judgment and serve as soldiers in a just war.[16] In effect, the document pointedly named the heresies and the heretics on whom the sword of Lutheran and Catholic authorities alike would be turned with a righteous vengeance and a fresh intensity in subsequent years. On this much they agreed. Forgetting for a moment the gulags, the police-states, and the juntas of recent political history, it is hard to imagine that it should matter so much to coerce a confession or consent to right doctrine by means of tongue-screw or fire; or that it should matter so much to some to withhold without wavering the words—only words—that the authorities, for sake of their own twisted con-sciences, seemed to need to hear. So there were many martyrs.

Martyr stories, in turn, reinforced and shaped the identity of those who took the name Mennonite after the Dutch-Frisian priest Menno Simons. Tellingly, the martyrologies they collected and published were restricted to persons who had been killed for purely "spiritual" reasons—that is, without a hint of sedition or rebellion.[17] In keeping with their two-kingdom theology, they "emphasized even more the purity and the withdrawn character of the biblical church."[18] In subsequent centuries, those who would correct waywardness in the community would return to the martyr stories and the model of the suffering, defenseless, true church. In 1873, my maternal great-great-grandfather, a schoolteacher, delivered his own such prophetic manuscript to a publisher in Prussia.[19]

III

My paternal ancestors settled in 1894 in the North-West Territories, in the district whose church and school would bear the name Eigenheim. They were among the first Europeans there. Now four generations are buried in the church cemetery. My Epp ancestors had come for an uncomplicated mix of reasons. Land was one—the chance to farm in a part of the world the Canadian government had helped them to imagine with its boosterish promotions. The fragile status of young men's exemption from military service was another. Though they were among the first Mennonites in the North West to settle on dispersed homestead quarter-sections, rather than the traditional village model, they brought with them communal practices of mutual aid from their semi-autonomous German-language settlements in Russia. They had experience with municipal and school governance. And, since in their new country they were part of a community that constituted a clear majority of the local population, it was not so great a leap into public life: the school board, the agricultural society, a grain elevator co-operative, all within the first decade of arrival.[20] The novel next step, for a few, was an active and seemingly exhilarating involvement in the provincial and federal Liberal Party. The point of connection was Gerhard Ens, homesteader, entrepreneur, immigration promoter for Clifford Sifton and the first Member of the Legislative Assembly for Rosthern constituency elected after the creation of the province of Saskatchewan in 1905. Ens shared their

Russian Mennonite background and low German dialect. Over time he managed to distance himself from the church without severing his connections with the Mennonite community, for whom he became an important political intermediary. The benefit was mutual. Ens was the sort of local notable who quickly became a valuable player in the Liberal Party's winning strategy to attract ethnic voters—this at a time when the Conservative and Provincial Rights parties upheld a fundamentally British, Protestant view of the country, resisting separate schools and immigration from Central and Eastern Europe, and when a social democratic stalwart such as J.S. Woodsworth was warning of the "strangers within our gates," who cancelled out the votes of "the most intelligent Canadians.... Peoples emerging from serfdom, accustomed to despotism, untrained in the principles of representative government, without patriotism—such peoples are utterly unfit to be trusted with the ballot."[21] The Liberal Party used the resources of the state, federal and provincial, to identify ethnic populations, gerrymander constituency boundaries, pad voters' lists and subsidize "foreign-language" newspapers.[22] A more charitable interpretation is that the Liberal Party was singularly open to non-British immigrants, for whom participation conferred an acceptance of their status as citizens. In Eigenheim, it is not clear how much to attribute to recruitment and propaganda as opposed to desire and ideological affinity. In either case, during these early years the district became a party stronghold. In three provincial and two federal elections after 1905 and prior to 1917, Liberal candidates' share of the vote ranged from 89 to 96 percent.[23]

My maternal ancestors—Klaassens and Jantzens—had come to Nebraska and then to Oklahoma beginning in 1894. They were among the survivors who had abandoned a horrific and humbling wagon-train sojourn from their village near the Volga to the volatile Russian frontier region that is now Uzbekistan and Turkmenistan. It was horrific because of the death toll along the desert and mountain roads, and then the banditry; there was no peace at the end of the road. It was humbling, perhaps embarrassing, because it had been motivated not just by genuine fears about the introduction of compulsory military service and by the prospect of a place to farm free of such obligations, but also by family loyalties and, in varying measures, by the captivating, chiliastic dream of moving east to meet the Lord on his imminent return to earth.[24] In Oklahoma, the cluster of Trek people kept mostly to themselves. Their experience reinforced a dread of disorder and a centuries-old disposition to work hard, avoid notice, ask little of government save basic protection, and be prepared to move if necessary. Electorally, Mennonites on the Great Plains inclined strongly towards the muscular, militarily adventurist presidency of Theodore Roosevelt[25]—a puzzle apart from the historic preference for the security of strong rulers. I suspect that Jacob Klaassen was more determinedly apolitical than that, though not for lack of interest in world affairs, and that he withheld his vote from all sides.

In less familiar ways, however, the world had begun to close in again. Early in the twentieth century, Oklahoma was convulsed by an unusual radicalism—agrarian, sometimes Christian and, in the end, explicitly socialist. What was a rural-based movement had emerged from the economic hardships and political frustrations of smallholders and tenants: first the Farmers' Union, which built co-operatives and learned to exercise collective leverage by withholding crops from market, especially cotton, until an established floor price was paid; and then the Socialist Party, which resisted the patronizing, centralizing guidance of the midwestern industrial unionists and eastern intellectuals, proposed democratic reforms, and eschewed land nationalization in favour of redistribution from landlords to those who actually farmed it. The same Washita County where my great-grandparents had settled was a particular hotbed of agitation. It was home to the speaker and pamphleteer S.O. Daws as well as the newspaper *Sword of Truth*, a feisty organ of small-producer radicalism: "The banker, the money shark, the merchant, the petty grafter, ...the courthouse ring, their slaves, such as clerks, deputies, stenographers, etc., are waiting for the harvest of the farmer. They are of the class that produces not. They get their living out of the sweat and toil of the farmer, the working class."[26] The *Sword* had staked out a strong position particularly on the issue that generated a divisive, three-day debate in a schoolhouse and then in county newspapers in 1912: did socialism threaten to undermine the Christian faith, and with it the family and allegiance to country?[27] For its part, the *Sword* published a "socialist prayer." It asked God to "permeate our souls with divine discontent and righteous rebellion," "strengthen within us the spirit of revolt," and then to "hasten the day" when the "Great Revolution shall come to free men and women from their fetters and enable them to be kind and noble and human."[28] In neighbouring Beckham County, the Socialists elected a state representative in 1914, much to the horror of the establishment Democrats in the towns. As late as 1916, Socialist Party presidential candidate Eugene Debs polled one in six votes in the state, and a much larger proportion in some counties. My great-grandfather's autobiographical writings, however, are silent about all this political and theological agitation. Likewise they make no mention of the more ominous notices posted around the county seat of Cordell in late summer 1916 ("We mean business!"). They warned landlords not to charge more than one-third of a crop share, lest they find their houses and barns burned, their fields seeded to worthless grass, and warned renters they would be "looked after" if they accepted less than their due.[29] My great-grandfather's own father had not been so sanguine about the aborted European revolutions of 1848 and their implications for world history.[30] But by 1916 Jacob Klaassen would have been watching other, more familiar clouds on the horizon. Unsettling clouds. At the height of his prosperity as a farmer, the United States declared war—"and the undisturbed life that we had enjoyed was over."[31]

In Mennonite history, at least once the time of martyrs had passed and the authorities' preoccupation with heresy was sublimated to *raison d'etat*, it was war that defined, tested and endangered a separate people. It was war, too, that made the modern state. The European state-system emerged on the battlefield, out of the dissolution of Christendom, as ambitious princes and other political entrepreneurs shook off medieval moral constraints, adopted new weaponry and raised standing armies—which necessitated the search for new revenue streams and the imposition of new taxes on unwilling subjects—so that they could consolidate control of territory against their rivals within and without.[32] The dictates of survival and expansion left little else for the state to do. Mennonites' most common response to the shifting geography of war was flight. They migrated from the cities and became more pronouncedly rural. Outside of places like Amsterdam, those who would not take up arms or swear oaths of loyalty often were not welcome to live within city walls or to work in certain guild occupations. They also migrated towards the geopolitical periphery, towards whatever relative toleration they could negotiate: for my ancestors, the Vistula Delta and then southern Russia; for others, Quaker-founded Pennsylvania. But the periphery never remained peripheral for long. There was no place to live clean of entanglement in the territorial aspirations, the mercantilist requirements or the military affairs of states. Consequently there was no escape from the practical dilemmas of everyday lived experience: whether Mennonite shareholders in the Dutch East India Company could accept the prize of ship and cargo captured from the enemy Portuguese[33]; whether to shelter troops; whether to hide young men whose height made them strikingly desirable for service in the palace guard of Frederick the Great; whether to marry the Swedish officer whose regiment was dispersed in defeat; whether to make cash payments in lieu of military participation. As European states learned to bend to the pressures of popular nationalism in the 19th century and turn patriotic sentiment to advantage in mobilizing "the nation in arms," war shone a harsher spotlight on the Mennonites' negotiated exemptions. It marked them as outsiders—fair game for popular resentment. It introduced a confusing new political complexity. It shifted the heaviest burdens of conscience and conflicted belonging to the young men of the community. And it presented new dilemmas: whether to buy war bonds; whether to accept conscription into alternative medical or forestry corps, or else face imprisonment. Even if Mennonites had been so inclined, there were no broader pacifist movements prior to the romance-gone-sour experience of the First World War with which they might have made common political cause.

In Western Canada, the war and the attendant conscription crisis proved to be a major watershed. For farmers, events during the war represented a final blow to the credibility of Conservative and Liberal parties and the spark for third-party agrarian political movements. For German-speaking, pacifist Mennonites, the war was no less crucial. A minority enlisted, or encouraged their sons to do so. The majority clung to an 1873 federal order-in-council that they interpreted as an exemption from military service, raised money for the Red Cross and Victory Bonds, and otherwise withdrew in the face of an increasingly hostile outside world.[34] The attack on the "Mennonite menace" came from several sides: Protestant churches, media, farm organizations and politicians.[35] When the Borden government introduced conscription in 1917, the Mennonite response followed a traditional pattern: a delegation of church leaders went to Ottawa to seek assurances that their exemption would be respected. That same year, however, in response to public pressure, Parliament passed the *Wartime Elections Act*, which disenfranchised broad categories of Canadians: conscientious objectors, naturalized "enemy aliens," and all Mennonites and Doukhobors who did not enlist. Only a few Liberal members objected.[36] As the war neared an end, Mennonite leaders in Saskatchewan petitioned the governor-general to stop the harassment of their communities:

> We are accused of fraud. We are referred to by leaders of our fellow citizens from public platforms as outlawed parasites. We cannot even cast a vote in our protection. Any one can afford to slight or insult us or to assault or neglect us. We are not outlaws in the sense of disobedience to constituted authority.... Parasites we are not. We are earning our bread by honest labour, and if we mistake not, our labour has assisted materially in advancing the material welfare of our country. We do not depend for our living on the sustenance or efforts of others. We do not require any one to shed his blood for us. We would rather die ourselves or languish in prison or leave our home and again settle in some wilderness, the same as our forefathers have done, than to require a sacrifice of any kind by any one on our behalf.[37]

In the U.S., entry into the war and the passage of the *Conscription Act* in 1917 had been accompanied by "a veritable orgy of anti-immigrant hysteria." Whatever the military merits of conscription, it fit President Woodrow Wilson's underlying purpose to "mold a new nation" freed of hyphenated Americans. He had signalled as much already: "There are citizens of the United States, I blush to admit,

born under other flags, but welcomed under our generous naturaliz-
ation laws to the full freedom and opportunity of America, who have
poured the poison of disloyalty into the very arteries of our national
life.... The hand of our power should close over them at once."[38] In
Oklahoma, the population had become increasingly polarized in the
months leading up to the declaration of war. The German-language
press had campaigned for U.S. neutrality, but the major daily newspapers had sided squarely with Wilson in his attacks on "hyphen-
ism" and enemies within. Still, the first response to conscription
was widespread opposition especially among farm people. The
initial number of draft registrants was relatively low. In parts of the
state the so-called Green Corn Rebellion—a fascinating, loose anti-
war alliance of disaffected tenant farmers, syndicalists, German-
Americans, blacks and Seminole Indians—provoked mass arrests,
newspaper hysteria, and at least one ill-fated shoot-out with U.S.
troops.[39] Ambivalent about the rebellion, and the war, the Socialists
were implicated nonetheless in the fallout. The war and the subsequent uprising embarrassed the state establishment and provided a
pretext for civic leaders to suppress all manner of discontent under
the semi-official banner of the Oklahoma Council of Defense. The
Council, whose purpose was to promote the war effort, eventually
enlisted one million Oklahomans in local volunteer committees in
a broad spectrum of activities: from selling bonds, making speeches
and distributing anti-German pamphlets, to producing a loyalty
card, pressing municipalities to pass anti-sedition laws and iden-
tifying dissenters. The local committees operated at only a slight
distance from the vigilante mobs that tarred and feathered opponents, painted their homes and businesses yellow, burned German-
speaking churches and forced German-speaking newspapers to
close.[40] Disloyalty displaced rent-gouging as the target of mob justice with astonishing speed and, since it had the tacit approval of the
authorities, much greater effectiveness. The dream of one nation
indivisible prevailed. In Washita County, the committee shut down
a church college in Cordell whose students, faculty, and board were
judged to be disloyal. It cancelled a talk in nearby Bessie by a leader
of the populist Non-Partisan League, after which a farmer who pro-
tested the action was dragged from his house at night and tarred.[41]

An insufficiently patriotic newspaper editor was shot on the court-house steps.

The same county courthouse in Cordell was the registration site for young men aged 21 to 30—Mennonites included—in June 1917. The local draft board was antagonistic. There were no historic exemptions in the U.S. to which to appeal, and a delegation to Washington was rebuffed. By September Jacob Klaassen's nephew John received notice to report to Camp Travis in Texas. While Jacob and his brother, like their father before them, wondered whether Mennonites had "forgotten the history of our fathers," since they could not arrive at a clear position on the war, those lessons had been imprinted on their own sons. John was one of a group of Mennonite and Quaker conscientious objectors in camp who refused from the start to wear army uniforms and then, since it could be construed as support of the war effort, refused their assigned work in the kitchen and barn. He was among those who remained undeterred by four days in the unprotected sun of the stockade. He was court-martialed to 25 years' hard labour at Fort Leavenworth in Kansas. Within months he was dead—the stated cause was pneumonia—and shipped home in a coffin, his body dressed in uniform.[42] It is hard to imagine that it should matter so much to the state that a Mennonite boy in Texas should wear khaki, or that it should matter so much to him to refuse. Jacob's two oldest sons, one of them my grandfather, did not wait for the draft board to determine their futures. They left hurriedly for Canada under cover of darkness. Having been preceded by a family reputation for plain-spoken honesty, they were coached across the line by an acquaintance in Montana. In Moose Jaw my grandfather was taken from the train, lacking the citizenship papers his brother carried, to spend a lonely night in the local jail. He was transferred to a military prison in Regina until his identification had arrived and his uncle, David Toews, who had drafted the petition to the governor-general, could intercede on his behalf. He kept a skeletal diary on the God, King and Country letterhead provided for him.

In 1919, Western Canada was only a sanctuary in relative terms. If anything, the popular and political backlash grew as veterans returned home, or didn't, and as economic conditions worsened. The fact that Mennonite farmers had prospered during the war years while making relatively few apparent sacrifices was a flash-point of resentment. Mennonites became the target of considerable verbal and occasional physical abuse against slackers.[43] The most drastic political response to public pressure came in British Columbia, where the legislature voted to disenfranchise Mennonites, Doukhobors and all other individual conscientious objectors; the legislation was not repealed until 1948.[44] Also in 1919, the federal Conservative government issued an order-in-council prohibiting the immigration of Mennonites and members of other pacifist religious groups into Canada. Farm organizations announced support for the ban. In the House of Commons, Mennonites were denounced as "cattle." Wildly exaggerated estimates of the number who had entered Canada from in the U.S. in the late stages of the war were circulated as proof of the growing menace to the freedom for which the country's young men had just died.

The order-in-council and the public hysteria surrounding it might have been inconsequential but for the fact that revolution and a murderous civil war in Russia had created a desperate situation for Mennonites in the German-speaking enclaves in that country. The prospect of another 100,000 knocking at Canada's gates was not lost on the political debate. Mennonite leaders reverted to the time-worn practice of a direct petition to the authorities; there was no other political option. Their delegation's only success was in securing a commitment in 1921 from the opposition leader, Mackenzie King, that he would rescind the order-in-council if his party were to be returned to office—as happened later that year. King, in typical fashion and timing, fulfilled his commitment quietly, not publishing the change in the *Canada Gazette* for fear of arousing public antagonism.[45] It was enough to ensure that "western Mennonites would again be Liberal for at least another generation."[46]

In the years between the world wars, immigration dominated the agenda of Mennonite relations with the state. The issue also reinforced the war-time sense of a people set apart, having a distinct set of interests that were best advanced not through party-political activity but rather through direct representation by leaders to government. Though the franchise was reinstated, voter turnout in Mennonite polls was nowhere near pre-war levels. In 1923 the first trainload of refugees from Russia disembarked the train at Rosthern—an event still remembered with great emotion. During the next six years about 30,000 Mennonites would be resettled in Canada through an enormous organizational effort that required ongoing negotiation with government authorities on two continents and the co-operation of the Canadian Pacific Railway in a large transportation loan.

While public resentment abated, it never disappeared. This was especially the case on the agrarian-populist political left. In Alberta, where the United Farmers of Alberta had formed a government in 1921, the arrival of Russian Mennonite refugees in the southern part of the province provoked a backlash. Among the leaders was Norman Priestley, the United Church minister who was to become a UFA vice-president and then national secretary of the Co-operative Commonwealth Federation in the 1930s. The UFA local sponsored a meeting to stop Mennonites' expansion in the area and protest the permission given them to teach German and religion on Saturdays in a public schoolhouse. The fact that some colonists had bought CPR land under a special deferred-payment system meant to boost sugar-beet production in the new irrigation districts created resentment among those who thought it gave Mennonite farmers an unfair advantage.[47] E.J. Garland, the Progressive member of parliament for Bow River, later part of the Ginger Group, complained in the Commons about the "iniquitous" system that benefited the CPR and threatened community life, since Mennonites were "unassimilable," took "no interest in the welfare of the district," avoided political meetings, and neither voted nor shared in the "responsibilities of citizenship."[48] The CPR, of course, was a prime agrarian target. The gap between southern Alberta Mennonite immigrants and their neighbours was never marked so vividly as it was at a special church service of thanksgiving in Coaldale in 1937, with 700 people present, among them CPR President Sir Edward Beatty. As one historian has put it: "One of the biggest of the 'Fifty Big Shots' then so vehemently denounced by Social Credit and socialist orators" was welcomed not with hostility but with celebration and gratitude.[49] The *Lethbridge Herald* gave the event front-page coverage, and seized the opportunity to lecture the discontented among its readers in an editorial:

We are hearing so much these days about 'soulless corporations' and the 'fifty big shots' that it is refreshing to read the story of the presentations of addresses by the Mennonite community of Coaldale.... That they should have made the opportunity to express their thanks to one of the so-called 'big corporations' shows how greatly they appreciate the freedom under which they are living today after having lived all their lives under autocratic governments of one kind or another in Russia.[50]

Whether or not Mennonite farmers had learned from experience to attach themselves to their neighbour's grievances over rail cars and freight rates, their exodus left them with other debts to settle.

In Saskatchewan, hostility from the left was associated principally with George Williams, president of the United Farmers of Canada (Saskatchewan Section) and later the leader of the provincial CCF. Williams was not known to mince words. He disdained pacifists—on this issue he was sharply at odds with Woodsworth—and promoted an immigration quota system that would guarantee places for more desirable British migrants. For Williams this was a compromise position. In 1931, on his return from a UFC-sponsored trip to the Soviet Union, he wrote a series of highly favourable articles for the *Regina Leader-Post*. The articles launched an acrimonious debate waged over several months in newspaper columns and from public platforms. David Toews, chairman of the Mennonite Board of Colonization, among his many roles, responded with a letter to the *Saskatoon Star-Phoenix* challenging Williams's observations and raising the issue of religious persecution.[51] Provoked, Williams intimated to a large audience at Saskatoon's venerable Third Avenue United Church that, "on good authority," Toews had received a commission for his immigration work and that some of the Mennonites who had arrived during the 1920s were collecting municipal relief despite prior assurances that they would not become a public burden. He also characterized Mennonites as having been *kulaks*—landed gentry—in Russia, a label that suited some but not most of the recent immigrants.[52]

By 1931, however, the immigration window had already been shut tight for two years in response to mounting public pressure from various directions: not just the Orange Order and Legion, but farm organizations, labour unions fearing downward pressure on wages, provincial governments in Alberta and Saskatchewan, and a new grassroots organization that had burst onto the prairie landscape— the Ku Klux Klan. In Saskatchewan, the Conservatives had broken the Liberal stranglehold on provincial office with a 1929 campaign to "Canadianize" immigrants, for which they received the Klan's quiet support.[53] The Conservative platform fit well enough with that of the agrarian-based Progressive Party, whose activists shared the same pro-British sympathies and dislike of the Liberals' historic lock on the ethnic and Catholic vote, and whose five seats propped up its minority government for five years. Indeed, there is some evidence on the prairies of overlapping membership between the farmers' movement and the Klan; certainly there were parallel concerns about immigrants from Central and Eastern Europe. In Alberta, the 1929 UFA convention passed a resolution opposing the entry into Canada of the last, desperate Mennonites who had made their way to Moscow and who instead were dispatched to Siberian locations when the two provincial governments informed Ottawa they would not accept them.[54] There was no question in Saskatchewan: "[T]he admission of Mennonites from Russia, though not Catholics, would have antagonized the very people who had so recently voted for the Conservatives."[55]

IV

In his classic study of the rise of the CCF in Saskatchewan, *Agrarian Socialism* [1950], the American scholar Seymour Martin Lipset identified Catholics and Mennonites as most identifiably resistant to the new politics and most loyal to the Liberals. Of the latter group, he wrote: "Many of them are refugees from the Russian Revolution and identify the CCF with the hated communism of Russia from which they escaped. The largely Mennonite constituency of Rosthern is the strongest anti-CCF seat in the province."[56] Lipset's talent for stating the obvious should not go unrecognized. Close analysis of the 1930s and 1940s suggests that rural receptivity to the CCF often had less to do with class position, farm size and economic circumstances than with religion and ethnicity—especially as the movement clarified its position on land ownership at the urging of its own farmer members. In the 1934 provincial election that returned the Liberals resoundingly to office, the Rosthern constituency showed the lowest dollar-per-acre return of any that elected government MLAs. Indeed, the highest overall dollar return was in a constituency that elected a CCF (Farmer-Labour Group) member.[57] In Rosthern, the poll-by-poll results show no surprises except a record-high voter turnout. In 1921 and 1925, the Liberal had won by acclamation. In 1929, the Conservative challenger had made a respectable showing. In 1934, the Liberal margin was restored to its historic proportions; the Farmer-Labour candidate registered only scattered interest. In 1938 the CCF concentrated its resources strategically and did not run a candidate in Rosthern.

There are multiple reasons for Lipset's observation, in addition to the Liberal record on immigration and the agrarian left's recent flirtation with nativism. One was the CCF's vulnerability on the socialism question, notwithstanding a series of careful shifts in policy, and the Liberals' ability to exploit that vulnerability in Mennonite communities whose members had taken in refugees from Soviet communism, experienced it first-hand, or in either case still were receiving grim letters about remaining family members who had been sent into Stalinist exile.[58] The long-time Liberal MLA for Rosthern, John Ulrich, was notorious within CCF circles for playing on the fear of communism.[59] Walter Tucker, MP for Rosthern from 1935 to 1948, continued to warn against CCF plans for land collectivization long after the party had abandoned any talk of public ownership except in the natural resource and utilities sectors. A campaign advertisement in the area's weekly newspaper—"Let's keep socialism out of Saskatchewan!"—ended with this sombre warning: "Don't let them fool you. It's your home, your farm, your business, your money."[60] It would be patronizing to assume that such partisan caricatures necessarily hit the mark with a politically unsophisticated audience. That said, typically the only non-religious publications in area Mennonite homes in the 1930s were either practical farm journals or the weekly newspaper, The Valley News,[61] which had a long history of Liberal owner-editors whose political affiliations spilled naturally onto the news pages. There were few subscribers to the CCF paper, the *Saskatchewan Commonwealth*. Arguably, Mennonites were less likely to judge party policy for themselves, take note of its denunciations of communism or, later, learn that several CCF members of parliament had spoken as forcefully in their defence as Tucker in war-time debates over the status of the Mennonite exemption from military service.[62]

A second reason was theological. The formative influence of the social gospel on the CCF would have generated caution for Mennonites unaccustomed to the hope of building the New Jerusalem on earth. Though their Gospel had its own serious moral implications, such society-wide reformism and language would have been as unfamiliar as English.[63] Moreover, many Mennonites in the newness of North America were attracted contrarily to the print, radio and tent-meeting voices associated with the major alternative Christian movement of the early twentieth century: fundamentalism. This alternative was not a tight fit either, with its emphasis on individual salvation, its disregard of the doctrine of non-resistance and its tendency to reduce social ethics to a catalogue of personal vices to be avoided. Nonetheless its more selective engagement in the political realm would have seemed purer, less threatening, more respectful of authority and realistic about sin. At the very least, fundamentalism—not the social gospel—became the lightning-rod focus of denominational debate for and against.

A third reason had to do with the contrasting organizational character of the Liberals and CCF. The former represented a classic example of what political scientists call a brokerage party, aggregating and juggling the interests of diverse groups of voters sufficient to be electorally competitive. This model asked little more of Mennonites than to vote on election day; they did not need to become "political." Their bishop, David Toews, could speak for them directly to the prime minister. The CCF, in contrast, fashioned itself as a popular movement. In its early years policy was made at delegate conventions through a rigorous, broad-based process of membership input; sometimes to their chagrin, its leaders did not have the same free hand. To join the CCF, the UFA at its height or even Social Credit initially in Alberta, was to accept not just the need for sweeping social-economic change, but also the obligation of active involvement in party affairs: meetings, study groups and membership recruitment. In some ways it appeared as a rival *gemeinde* or church community; it asked too much.

For all that, the results of war-time federal and provincial elections suggest caution against any deterministic reading of history. In 1940, the federal CCF ran a Saskatoon lawyer, Peter Makaroff, a Doukhobor well-known in the area. He was also a pacifist who sided with J.S. Woodsworth in the pitched battles that divided the party over how to respond to the war against Nazi Germany. Without any apparent prior indications of a shift in voter support, Makaroff received 5,456 votes—more than 40 percent of votes cast, and three times the CCF vote in 1935—against Tucker's 6,612. In the predominantly Mennonite polls combined, he received one of every three votes; in a few he won a clear majority. "All this was accomplished," he wrote,

> in a war-time election and in the face of incessant charges of 'Socialism' and 'Russian Communism' against the CCF, and constant denunciation of its candidate as a 'pacifist.' 'A vote for Makaroff is a vote for Stalin and Hitler,' was the battle charge at every Liberal meeting.... Had we had another two weeks to go we would have easily won, .... demonstrating that no constituency in Saskatchewan is too difficult for the CCF to conquer as the harvest is ripe and awaits only the reaper.[64]

In 1944, in the provincial election that produced the surprise of a CCF government, the party's candidate in Rosthern ran a strong second. He won several of the Mennonite polls west of town—Tiefengrund for one—and trailed the Liberal, a Mennonite, by only 49 votes to 39 in Eigenheim. In each case, however, the result represented an electoral high-water mark. When Premier T.C. Douglas campaigned in Rosthern in the 1952 election, which the CCF would win overwhelmingly, he acknowledged that he was in unfamiliar territory and made an odd, almost plaintive pitch: "We need you to come and help us—not for our sake but for your sake, so that we can form a new society."[65]

V

There is no simple or even dialectical resolution of the stories that are bred in the bone and those that I have learned from the agrarian history of the North American plains. At least I will not attempt one. There is an historical irony to be developed, though it would require some care, about how a distinct settler people so disposed to communal life should have come to feel comfortable with party-political options most congenial to market forces—arguably, the most powerful of modernity's individualizing solvents. There is probably some introspective work to do about deep filial inheritances: the sense of holding back, wary of the crowd, never feeling entirely at home in the world, as if it could turn hostile yet again in another clarifying, dividing flash of military escalation and patriotic fervour. My interest, however, lies elsewhere, in the ambivalent character of populist politics and political belonging.

Catherine Stock argues convincingly that those who would "recover a usable Populist past"—as I have tried to do against a prevalent rural fatalism and loss of effective political agency—cannot ignore its "sour side." Looking back from the perspective of the Oklahoma City bombing to a decade in which rural militia movements had proliferated in the context of farm crisis, she writes:

> [T]he roots of violence, racism, and hatred can be and
> have been nourished in the same soil and from the same
> experiences that generated rural movements for democracy
> and equality. In many places and at many times in the
> American past, the best and worst, the most forgiving and
> most vengeful, the most egalitarian and most authoritarian,
> the brightest and darkest visions of American life were
> alive in the same men's souls, nurtured at the same dinner
> tables, learned in the same schools, and preached from the
> same pulpits.[66]

I do not mean to conflate American and Canadian experience. Between them there is a difference in degree—both best and worst. The same may be true of Saskatchewan and Alberta. In the latter province, where a creative and robust agrarian populism was a spent political force by the time the CCF was elected in Saskatchewan, two Mennonite churches in the Vauxhall district would be torched on a spring night in 1940 in a resurgence of indiscriminate anti-German sentiment.

What of this sour side? What complex susceptibilities come to light? Historically, agrarian populism has been characterized by a disturbing plasticity. The repeated experience of such capacious political energy being co-opted, redirected to other targets and simplified in its analysis to the identification of villains who are made fair game for vigilantism, is a sober caution to those who would invoke the people in an angry cause. Poor white farmers in the *post-bellum* South who joined the multi-racial Populist campaigns of the 1890s would be enlisted later into the rough politics of racial segregation, lynch-mobs and burning crosses by propagandists for the wealthy "bourbon interests." The energy that was rallied for economic justice in rural Oklahoma would be turned against slackers and then non-whites. In this way North American agrarian populism shares in what Charles Taylor describes as a new kind of modern politics, first enacted in the terrors of the French Revolution, in which a taste for direct action was joined to black-and-white moralism. The result was that "every misfortune had a malevolent cause."[67] Just as the cohesion of the people seemed to require an enemy, the frustration of political action seemed to require traitors, outside agitators or conspirators. In Social Credit's first term in Alberta after 1935, the failure to implement the promised reforms suggested to some the hand of Jewish finance.

A second susceptibility is the temptation to regard difference as dangerous and to flatten out diversity in the name of an equality that is defined simply as sameness. No slackers. No hyphenated citizens. No bloc settlements. If the best of agrarian populism on the North American prairies is associated historically with a democratic, egalitarian politics, it also stands in a more problematic line reaching back to the 18th-century philosopher Jean-Jacques Rousseau's essay *The Social Contract*. From that lineage the populists inherited not just a healthy suspicion of political representation. They also absorbed two other important assumptions found in Rousseau. One is the idea that there exists a single "people" with a common will that can be determined if particular or selfish interests are set aside. The other is that a high degree of cultural uniformity is required to sustain a society in which citizens live under the laws they make for themselves. The current contention over the status of Muslim enclaves in Western liberal democracies reprises the issues identified around German-speaking immigrant settlements in North America in the First World War. If citizenship is the most important, most inclusive category of belonging in diverse societies, what common values, obligations and education does it require? How much difference, or indifference, can the public square accommodate? In what sense is the political sphere the "highest"? These are difficult questions that continue to strike at the intersection of democratic and pluralistic principles—and most acutely in the immigrant experience.

My ancestors chose the pluralist Canada, the one that promised an undisturbed, side-by-side home for diverse peoples. For my great-grandfather Jacob Klaassen in Oklahoma, the fact that Canada made room for French-speaking Quebecers was no small reassurance that it could make room for him too. He was unprepared for the radical democratic Canada, or the egalitarian Canada, or the war-fighting Canada, whose champions shared the same polity. He had no political instincts, only reservations. People like him are among the vulnerable and bewildered when, in times of crisis, the populist dream of unity comes crashing to the fore. A singular identity ("patriot," "Canadian,") can displace all others, invite a heightened sense of belonging for most, and draw the lines of exclusion against others. I cannot be a democratic absolutist.[68]

At the same time, reflecting on my family's aloof political history, I feel the opposing tug of Hannah Arendt's critical account of a world in which the public realm has largely lost its place and speech its power, but in which human beings can still exercise the miracle of freedom by acting together to create something new.[69] Political freedom, she proposed, consisted of this generative power. She associated it with a kind of joy. It was nothing like the right to be left alone. For Arendt, those who put themselves outside this public realm and the company of equals by their commitment to an exclusive, eternal truth, however noble, were consigned as a result to an acute kind of human alone-ness.

My grandfather Diedrich Epp was not a wealthy farmer even by Depression standards, not by comparison to others in his district— especially his in-laws, the comparison that counted most. His land was poor, his family was large, the times were unrelentingly difficult. My grandfather shared a name with his uncle, the free-thinker in the Eigenheim community, who had little use for sermons on Sunday morning but who was heavily involved in Liberal politics in the early years. He had once met the premier, Walter Scott, at a banquet.

My grandfather, it turns out, was a bit of a free-thinker in his own way. Against the mighty tide of his community and family, he once told me, he leaned CCF. Not only that—and I must trust his word and my memory on this—at a time when farmers voted publicly with their grain, when good Liberals hauled to the United Grain Growers' elevator to avoid the taint of socialism, Diedrich Epp dared to haul his wagon to the Wheat Pool instead.

Seven

# We Are All Treaty People
## History, Reconciliation, and the "Settler Problem"

*To have no history is to face only natural obstacles and one's own limitations.*

Sheldon Wolin, *The Presence of the Past*

I

In an Ottawa stateroom in January 1998, elders and chiefs present, the Canadian government made a "solemn offer of reconciliation" to aboriginal peoples. The offer was read by the minister of Indian Affairs—not the prime minister, as some noted—as part of a long-awaited response to the five-volume report of the Royal Commission on Aboriginal Peoples (RCAP), that had been appointed following the armed standoff between Canadian troops and Mohawk warriors at Oka. The government's offer accepted the Commission's historical outline of the relationship between aboriginal and non-aboriginal peoples in what is now Canada: first, separate worlds; then, contact and co-operation; displacement and assimilation; and, finally (hopefully), renewal and respect. "Sadly," it said,

> our history with respect to the treatment of Aboriginal people is not something in which we can take pride. Attitudes of racial and cultural superiority led to a suppression of Aboriginal culture and values. As a country, we are burdened by past actions that resulted in weakening the identity of Aboriginal peoples, suppressing their languages and cultures, and outlawing spiritual practices. We must recognize the impact

of these actions on the once self-sustaining nations that were disaggregated, disrupted, limited or even destroyed by the dispossession of traditional territory, by the relocation of Aboriginal people, and by some provisions of the *Indian Act*.[1]

The minister, Jane Stewart, on behalf of her government, assured those who had assembled that "we have listened and we have heard," that "the days of paternalism and disrespect are behind us," and that a commitment to a new relationship meant "coming to terms with the impact of our past actions and attitudes...History cannot be changed, but it must be understood in a way that reflects that people today are living out the legacy of decisions made in a different time."[2] The most tangible expression of reconciliation announced that day was a monetary one: a $350 million fund for community-based healing projects to deal with the particular legacy of physical and sexual abuse at residential schools.

The government's statement of regret and its commitment to change had been encouraged by RCAP. Its report, optimistic and ambitious, with more than 400 recommendations, had begun with the assertion that a "great cleansing of the wounds of the past" was necessary before the work of reconciliation could begin and before it was possible to "embrace a shared future," to "complete" the Canadian federation.[3] For the recent past—roughly the early 19th century to the 1960s, with its cultural triumphalism, its "battering ram" of the *Indian Act*, and its residential schools—was filled with "evidence of the capacity of democratic populations to tolerate moral enormities in their midst."[4] It could be forgiven but not forgotten. Still, the RCAP report held out as a realistic goal a new relationship based on mutual recognition, respect, and sharing, and a "just accommodation" of aboriginal political and cultural aspirations within Canadian institutions. That goal was reiterated in the government's carefully-crafted response as a matter of "building a true partnership."

Subsequent events, however, quickly made the solemn offer of reconciliation seem less a beginning than a high-water mark from which Ottawa has retreated awkwardly. Whether Canadians generally were more than vaguely aware of the offer at the time it was made, or shared its sentiments, or can recall it now, is an open question. In any case, backlash has become the political order of the day. BACKLASH is the word shouted from the cover of *Report Magazine,* whose inflammatory interpretation of a series of recent Supreme Court decisions was couched in terms of "public outrage over the reverse racism of the Indian rights industry" and a country "on the edge of anarchy."[5] In the province of British Columbia, which has become the focus of land-claims litigation and treaty negotiations in the absence of any historic "extinguishment" of aboriginal title, the extremist forecasts of radio talk-show hosts and the inferences of headline writers (e.g., *The Vancouver Sun*: "BC Indian chiefs lay claim to entire province, resources"[6]) strike an all-too-responsive chord. Attuned to the prevailing political winds, the federal government gave virtually no public defence of the Nisga'a treaty to which it was a signatory, through all the public controversy that ensued, and apparently has lost interest in more treaty negotiations; the B.C. government, elected by a landslide in 2001, followed through with a promised referendum on the entire treaty process. On the other side of Canada, in New Brunswick, violent confrontations followed judicial decisions about the status of historic treaty rights to fish and cut timber—the courts, as one analyst put it, having been left "by political default" to define the formal relationship between aboriginal and non-aboriginal peoples. In the coffee shops, meanwhile, "words of bigotry and fury resonate across a part of the country better known for tranquility and a powerful sense of community."[7] The federal government's role was a reactive and, again, largely a passive one, at least until the conflict had escalated to incendiary wharf-side hostilities. No wonder that an increasing number of Canadians tell pollsters that relations with aboriginal peoples are deteriorating.[8]

All of this is grist for those skeptics who, at the time of the offer of reconciliation, dismissed it as part of a world-wide fashion for apologies, reflecting both the new advice in crisis management literature that previously would have counselled stonewalling and the "gimme-a-hug political culture of the late 1990s, where empathy and symbolic gestures so often substitute for real action."[9] Limited-liability guilt-management on behalf of Canadians is one plausible characterization of federal policy.[10] But Ottawa's caution also reflects the marked political-ideological shift since the early 1990s, when the federal and all ten provincial governments could still sign on to an omnibus constitutional accord that, while ultimately unsuccessful when put to Canadians, included among its many provisions the recognition of an "inherent right of self-government" for aboriginal peoples. That constitutional window has closed decisively. By the end of the decade, moreover, those who imagined themselves outside the so-called aboriginal rights orthodoxy could claim the respectable sponsorship of a major newspaper (the *National Post*), the Official Opposition in the House of Commons, and academics such as Tom Flanagan, a former Reform Party research director, whose book-length response to the RCAP report, *First Nations? Second Thoughts*, was published to widespread acclaim in policy circles. By the logic of his argument, the entire enterprise of reconciliation is not only a misguided and dangerous one, politically and economically, because it encourages the "orthodoxy" that would turn the country into a "multinational state embracing an archipelago of aboriginal nations that own a third of Canada's land mass." More germane to my purposes, reconciliation becomes unnecessary if Flanagan's premises are accepted. Aboriginal peoples ("Siberian-Canadians"), his book argued, are mere descendants of prior waves of immigrants; they did not constitute sovereign political states, only kinship groupings or "tribes"; European colonization of North America was both inevitable, owing to an advanced technological civilization, and justifiable, owing to the availability of uncultivated lands; "land-surrender treaties" mean no more than what they say; the assimilation of aboriginal individuals into the mainstream should be encouraged for their own well-being.[11] There is, in short, no ruptured relationship, only a natural succession. There is no enduring cultural difference worth preserving or mediating politically. Certainly, to follow Flanagan, there is nothing for which to make amends.

Such is the landscape on which the question of reconciliation is now encountered. At the same time, aboriginal peoples, their traditions, and especially their status and rights are the subject of unprecedented attention, if not understanding; and the resulting body of writing is too large to canvas profitably here, but large enough, it is safe to say, to command its own section of any quality bookstore. There are Supreme Court decisions sold inside stylish covers.[12] There are collections of legal essays on complex topics like aboriginal title. There are manifestoes by aboriginal intellectuals,[13] declarations by political bodies like the Grand Council of the Crees,[14] and biographies of aboriginal leaders. There are abstract policy studies with their rehearsed menu of identity categories: "First Nations," Indian, Metis, Inuit, "C-31," "non-status," "equal Canadians," "citizens plus."[15] There is fresh scholarship from across the humanities and social sciences. There are guides to native sites and spiritualities, some in German translation for the tourists, bearing out Peter Nabokov's warning about "sentimentalizing and fossilizing" cultures, and his suspicion that "were there not Indians we would have somehow come around to inventing them, as a utopian antithesis to so much that alienated us."[16] There are, in addition, the relentless fragments of daily media coverage of court cases, blockades, corruption allegations, and leadership struggles.

The politics of that landscape are complex and highly charged. Aboriginal assertions cut to the heart of the most basic political questions in this settler country—questions having to do with identities, histories, and imagined communities. They invite strong emotions: anger, fear, confusion, evasion, weariness, even hope of all kinds. They divide real aboriginal communities along lines of generation and gender, "traditionalist" and "accommodationist," "elites," "grassroots," and "warriors." They transform aboriginal rights critics into opportunistic, latter-day champions of fisheries conservation or the welfare of reserve residents (whom they will never meet) against alleged band council nepotism and profligacy. Those assertions prod a federal government, stung periodically by international human rights publicity while promoting Canada as the best place in the world in which to live, to recycle old policies that would safely contain the meaning of self-government, without seeming to reject it, and to drag its feet where it might instead negotiate, in hopes that the courts will decide an issue first and absorb the political fall-out.

There are many dilemmas of reconciliation that might be explored in this context. An obvious one is the role of legal determination and monetary compensation in coming to terms, say, with historical grievances about land or residential school abuses. Beneath this, however, there are subtler, deeper, more elusive reconciliations or cultural divides that are very much at play: between liberal-individual and tribal-communal identities, between venerative and instrumental attitudes to language, between oral and written histories, between covenantal and contractual understandings of treaties. The Supreme Court in its *Delgamuukw* decision saw itself as attempting precisely such a reconciliation. But that raises a second fundamental question: Whose work is reconciliation? Judges? Ministers of Indian Affairs? Aboriginal negotiators? Or does it extend far beyond them?

I have begun with a long introduction because the subject itself is a sprawling and intimidating one. Moreover, the nature of the subject makes it important to position myself inside it. For I will long remember the sharp, protective question asked by a bright Anishinabe student, whose professor had shown her a conference paper I had written about historical and contemporary aboriginal diplomatic activity, and ultimately about the disciplinary presumptions in the field of international relations that had rendered it invisible.[17] "Why," she asked, "are you writing about this?" The same question could be asked fairly of this paper, and indeed of the entire literature which takes the aboriginal as its subject. My interest here lies in rethinking the relationship, so that instead of posing the question about reconciliation as a matter of what "they" want—recognition, compensation, land—and what "we" can live with, the subject under closest scrutiny becomes "ourselves." In other words, the subject is not the "Indian problem" but the "settler problem." This might be said to be work left mostly untouched by RCAP's five volumes.

In this spirit, I want to explore two related interpretive claims. One is that solemn offers of reconciliation, however sincere, however eloquent, are still framed within a liberal, settler political culture, fundamentally Lockean in its philosophical fragments: forward-looking, suspicious of history, or, more likely, indifferent to it, and incorporating into its imagined social contract an almost-willful amnesia about whatever might be divisive. Reconciliation to a liberal society may turn out to mean only the ability of strangers to live together in pursuit of individual projects.

The second claim is more straight-forward, and at least as contentious. It is that while an offer may be spoken in Ottawa by a minister of the Crown, on behalf of all Canadians, the burdens, the opportunities, or, more neutrally, the imperatives of reconciliation are not distributed equally. Treaty rights, land claims, or self-government are scarcely abstract issues in places where non-aboriginal communities, struggling to survive against the decline of traditional economic sectors—fishing, logging, farming—are understandably threatened by negotiations or court judgments that require them to share access to dwindling resources and available livelihoods. This is the reality to which *Report Magazine* and the radio fear-merchants play so skillfully. But it is a reality all the same: in northwestern British Columbia around Nisga'a territory; in Burnt Church, New Brunswick; in prairie towns like Punnichy, Saskatchewan, where it is not uncommon for residents to buy up adjacent lots and tear down the houses to pre-empt the possibility of Indian renters from the nearby reserve moving in next door.[18] In such places, mostly rural, interdependence is a difficult but almost inescapable challenge. The casual racism of everyday speech is shocking to outsiders. Reconciliation, in turn, is a task to be taken up without the cover of scholarship or the luxury of geographical distance. But it is in such places, places where not one but two working human cultures—aboriginal and settler have been dispatched to the dustbin of history by the proponents of the new economy, that words of reconciliation must ring true and people must be enlisted in new relationships. Dauntingly pessimistic as this might sound, there is promise here as well, but it lies in breaking free of Lockean myths and thinking anew about history and inherited obligations.

II

"In the beginning," wrote John Locke, the 17th-century English political philosopher, in his *Second Treatise of Government*, "all the world was America."[19] In other words, in what amounted to a political creation myth, embellished with a crude anthropology to suit European imaginations, America was a blank slate—the primordial void out of which the institutions of private property and limited government were established by means of consent, and painted with adjectives such as "wild," "wasted," and "wretched." While Locke had also written a colonial constitution for the Carolinas, he had, of course, never visited the Americas. All the same, he was certain that its peoples lacked real government and the efficient, productive cultivation of land that justified ownership of what had been given to humankind in common for sake of preservation. Like other social contract theorists, beginning with Thomas Hobbes, Locke's political philosophy relied more centrally than is often recognized on the "alterity" of the aboriginal. His association of liberty with property and of property, in the first instance, with appropriation from nature—by the mixing of one's labour—was singularly attractive in colonial America. At the very least, it provided intellectual comfort to those who had traversed an ocean for the prospect of freehold title and were determined never to be tenants again.[20] Locke's conception of natural property as an extension of the labouring self allowed even the "wild Indian" ownership of "the fruit or venison which nourishes him." But, he claimed, neglecting all the aboriginal assistance that settlers received in growing suitable crops, cultivation of the earth was the "chief matter of property." The Lockean standard of "civilization" rested on relative efficiencies in the use of land: "For I ask whether the wild woods and uncultivated waste of America left to Nature, without any improvement, tillage or husbandry, a thousand acres will yield the needy and wretched inhabitants as many conveniences of life as ten acres equally fertile land doe [sic] in Devonshire where they are well cultivated."[21]

The practical consequence of Locke's argument was plainly drawn in the 18th century by the eminent European diplomatist Emmerich Vattel. His *Law of Nations* began from the familiar contractarian premise that the earth once belonged to all in common, but that at some stage of population growth cultivation was required of every nation as a matter of natural duty, since hunting or herding were no longer sufficient, and for that reason, morally justifiable. "Those who still pursue this idle mode of life occupy more land than they would have need of under a system of honest labour, and they may not complain if other more industrious Nations, too confined at home, should come and occupy part of their lands." Vattel made clear his disapproval of the Spanish "usurpation." By contrast, the colonization of North America—whose "vast tracts of land" were only "roamed over," rather than inhabited, by "small numbers" of "wandering tribes"—could be considered "entirely lawful." Those tribes had "no right" to keep it to themselves: "provided sufficient land were left to the Indians, others might, without injustice to them, settle in certain parts of a region, the whole of which the Indians were unable to occupy." It was not against nature, he concluded, to confine them within narrower bounds.[22]

Vattel is more commonly remembered for his insistence that membership in international society was exclusive to sovereign states on the (emergent) European model. This, too, was a position rooted in contractarian premises and, in particular, in Locke's concern to distinguish political commonwealths from families and political authority from the sort of patriarchal justifications for absolutist kingship that had gained a following in his day. Locke again drew those distinctions through the counter-example of the American tribes. While admitting his ignorance as to the political arrangements of these "little independent societies," the logic of his argument required that they remained in a state of nature, lacking proper government, that is, founded on the consent of individuals for the limited purpose of preserving their lives and property.

These intellectual positions can scarcely be relegated, like museum pieces, to the status of ideological curios. For one thing, they continue to resonate in everyday speech, for example, in the familiar claim that settlement of the Canadian prairies should be insulated from moral and political scrutiny on the grounds that "there was nothing here before we came" and "we made something of it." This is the story reflected in countless community and family histories of the homesteading era. Doubtless the same could be said of northern miners and loggers. Indeed, the Lockean myth has been renewed in successive generations of immigrants, who came to this "new" world to escape an impoverished or oppressive past, to live as equals, and to wrest a future from an unforgiving environment through hard work. There is enough experiential truth in all of this to sustain it in what is now an overwhelmingly urban country. In a famous essay, "In Defence of North America," George Grant once called it the "primal" spirit of a society that, uniquely, "has no history (truly its own) from before the age of progress" and that in its "conquering relation to place has left its mark within us."[23] But, as

Flanagan's book demonstrates, Locke and Vattel also still constitute the intellectual bedrock for a coherent, and powerful, contrary position on such contemporary subjects as treaties, land claims, and aboriginal rights in general. As he puts it, they stand on the civilized side of a fundamental divide, which is marked by (1) the extension of rule by "organized states" over "stateless societies," and (2) the displacement of hunter-gatherers by cultivators, such that the European entry into North America and Australia was "the last act of a great drama—the spread of agriculture around the world."[24] So much for what RCAP's *Report* characterizes as the era of dispossession and assimilation.

Flanagan's simple dichotomies are a tempting target in themselves, even if their purpose is acknowledged to be primarily a polemical one. They disregard examples of aboriginal cultivation and resource management and, ironically, diminish at the same time the status of the cattle ranchers whose "winning of the open range" is so important to the mythology of the North American West. They discount aboriginal modes of governance, as well as the influence of aboriginal practices such as federalism on the American colonists. And they misconstrue the centralized state and agrarian communities as partners in progress. The reality of early-modern Europe, much less Stalinist Russia, post-colonial Africa, or even the Canadian West, suggests a much more conflict-ridden relationship over the loss of autonomy and the extraction of wealth from the periphery.[25] A close reader of Flanagan's book could register other quibbles, for example, at the way he dismisses the idea that historic treaties involving European states and aboriginal polities could imply meaningful diplomatic relationships among rough equals—on the linguistic conceit and the relatively recent international legal doctrine that only sovereign states could be signatories of such agreements. Even as recent a compendium as the *Consolidated Treaty Series, 1648–1918*, would tell a more complicated story about recognition within international society. So would the U.S. government's commissioning of a report as late as 1918 to answer the "question of the aborigines" in international law—a report whose conclusions Flanagan cites as proof of his position rather than as evidence of contestation. And so would the now-forgotten diplomatic campaign of 1923–24 to prevent

Iroquois admittance to the League of Nations, at a point when the matter of membership for Canada and the other so-called white settler dominions of the British Empire had not been settled.[26]

To pursue such a line of criticism, however, is to miss what is most revealing about Flanagan's argument: namely, a mode of reasoning that is conceptual not historical. In this fundamental sense it mirrors the work of the classic English social-contract theorists. That work betrays little of its own time. It founds its arguments about political authority and the pre-eminence of the individual on abstract claims about nature. It begins (in the case of Hobbes) from a concern, not unlike Flanagan's, to confine the meaning of language against political dispute. And it resorts (in the case of Locke) to a crude evolutionism of property and government as if to preclude any other arrangements. In this mode of political reasoning, the past is problematic, even dangerous.

In the first place, the past is dangerous as the domain of unavenged grievances and, partly for that reason, of partial solidarities nourished by memory. This is manifestly clear in Hobbes, who invites his readers, not to *remember* the destruction of the English civil war, but to *calculate as a logical possibility* that life would be "nasty, brutish, and short" in the absence of the order provided by strong government. Michael Ignatieff has restated Hobbes's position most forcefully in recent years in the context of extreme nationalism, genocide, and "truth-commission" proceedings. "All nations," he writes, "depend on forgetting: on forging myths of unity and identity that allow a society to forget its founding crimes, its hidden injuries and divisions, its unhealed wounds." What reconciliation requires is for people to "awake from history," to recognize that inherited identities are not fate, and to reject the "nationalist fiction" for the "liberal fiction," in which individuals are recognized as "simple, equal units of one indivisible humanity."[27] When my students read Ignatieff, they have no trouble situating his arguments about Yugoslavia, Rwanda, and South Africa in a Canadian context. With what seems relief, they seize on and amplify it: the past is past; we could never agree on what happened; worse, appeals to history would "put us into a defensive mode" as the "inheritors of our ancestor's sins," while locking aboriginal peoples into a victim identity; government policy should not be based on "retribution" for past actions; what's more important is to find practical ways out of the cycle of poverty. And so on. Their reactions are common enough. Alan Cairns has registered a similar warning to steer clear of the "divisive legacy of history" in his recent book, *Citizens Plus*: "[T]he past identities that separated us from each other survive in memory and are reinforced by politics and policies that both feed on and provide sustenance to difference."[28] If the past is problematic as the domain of grievance and partial solidarities, however, and if awaking from it is crucial to reconciliation, it follows—almost perversely—that by far the greatest work falls to aboriginal peoples. It is up to "them" both *to forget* and *to accept* the loss of historically constituted identities, and, by doing so, to release settlers' descendants from a vague sense of inter-generational guilt. That way "we" will not complain when tax dollars are spent prudently and transitionally on the practical task of improving quality of life.

For polemicists such as Flanagan, the past appears problematic in another more intriguing way as well. Arguably, more troubling than any remembered injustices—which, in the last resort, can be chalked up to the inevitable march of civilization—are historical claims about successful coexistence, which might then bear on the contemporary understanding of treaties or else recommend the recognition of aboriginal "nations" within a renovated Canadian federation. Even the memory of reciprocity apparently is dangerous. Indeed, the RCAP report's treatment of this side of the historic relationship may be its most valuable contribution simply because it rehearses a history that Canadians have either forgotten, or, more likely, never been taught. Certainly it flies in the face of the myth of North America as a blank slate, as *terra nullius*, before the Europeans arrived, and the complementary myth of conquest that received such a resounding backhanded boost in 1992 during the denunciations of the Columbus centenary. History tells a more complicated tale. Out of necessity or principle, the British Crown engaged in extensive diplomatic relations with aboriginal peoples from first contact. As its 18th-century conflict with France carried across the Atlantic, it negotiated treaties of peace, alliance, trade, and coexistence with Mikmaq and Iroquois— negotiations conducted in aboriginal languages, according to elaborate tribal protocols, and, arguably, bearing out confederal relations of "living kinship" (or "many families living in one house") into which the stranger could be adopted.[29] In 1763, the Crown issued a proclamation recognizing Indian nationhood, territory, and rights in land that could only be extinguished with consent—the basis of recent claims in British Columbia and the North. In the 1870s, it made real concessions in treaties signed on the Canadian prairies so that land could be opened quickly for settlement at a fraction of the cost the U.S. was spending on its "Indian wars." In a very real way, most Canadians exercise a treaty right simply by living where they do. On the prairies we are all treaty people.

So why is there no more volcanic an issue in Canadian society than treaty rights? It is not a sufficient answer to point to political and media presentation of aboriginal demands as unreasonable, unending, and likely to bankrupt the country. Canadians are not simply passive recipients. They live in a political culture in which a certain idea of equality has gained a powerful foothold—fed by such different sources as the U.S. civil rights movement, the adoption of a Charter of Rights and Freedoms, and the reaction against the proposed "distinct" constitutional status of Quebec in Canada. Tribal identities are a puzzle, if not an anathema, in liberal societies; they make conflicting demands of well-intentioned people who, with reason, understand the struggle for non-discrimination as a significant one. But surely another part of the reason is the mark left by the myth of *terra nullius*. Imbued with that myth, Canadians can live more comfortably, forgetfully, with the dirty little secret that the treaties were a one-time land swindle than with the possibility that they might mean something in perpetuity. They do not want to know that aboriginal peoples had their own understandings of treaty-making as a form of sharing. Some of them would be outraged by James Tully's claim that "Canada is founded on an act of sharing that is almost unimaginable in its generosity"—not only land, but food, agricultural techniques, practical knowledge, and trade routes.[30] Certainly they would not accept his conclusion that a postcolonial relationship might be built out of the memory of that sharing. Instead, they clamour for "closure," for "final settlements." They want no more surprises. Though they often identify themselves as conservatives, curiously, they recognize no inherited obligations.

This kind of anti- or post-mnemonic society, writes the political theorist Sheldon Wolin, can again be traced back to social-contract theory in ways that are pertinent to my own analysis. Contract theory holds out the possibility of a fresh, voluntary start. Its "sacrament of innocence," he argues, so attractive and culturally formative in North America, offers "absolution from the foolishness of our fathers and mothers" and, in every generation, "soothes us with the knowledge that we were not there." It posits memoryless, dehistoricized—but equal—persons. When set over against the ambiguous legacy of an expansionist history filled with economic opportunity and social mobility for immigrants, "the function of social contract thinking becomes clear: to relieve individuals and societies of the burden of the past by erasing the ambiguities." It understands that for a certain kind of political society to operate, "some things had to be forgotten"—Ignatieff's point precisely—or at least not "publicly recalled." It assumes that "it is possible to talk intelligibly about the most fundamental principles of a political society as though neither the society nor the individuals in it had a history."[31]

Over against the contractarian tradition, Wolin proposes the idea of a birthright, derived from the biblical story of the brothers Esau and Jacob, in which the latter, the younger, disguises himself in order to acquire his father's blessing. A birthright assumes that "we come into the world preceded by an inheritance" that is collective, that extends over time, that we can disavow but do not choose, and that comes with "accumulated burdens" as well as benefits: a name, debts, obligations, quarrels: "When we accept a birthright, we accept what has been done in our name." We also accept an obligation to use that inheritance, "take care of it, pass it on, and, hopefully, improve it." In this way, a birthright is not a fixed entity. Its meaning in any generation—Wolin has in mind the American Constitution, but we might substitute the treaty relationship between Crown and aboriginal peoples—needs interpretation; as such it is subject to dispute, revision, and renewal, the work by which we "make it our own."[32]

Significantly, the story of Esau and Jacob ends with a dramatic reconciliation. After a long estrangement, it is the usurper Jacob who takes the initiative and returns, though fearing for his life, to face his brother, with whom he is bound—like it or not—in a common history that cannot be denied except at the expense of one's own identity.[33] Nor can its moral imperatives be resisted indefinitely. There must be a facing-up. The relationship between aboriginal peoples and settlers, I suggest, constitutes an equally powerful common history, inherited, not chosen, whose birthright we can either disavow, because its burdens seem too great, or else make our own through respectful initiatives.

III

I am a fourth-generation settler on the Canadian prairies, on Treaty Six land, one who wonders what it means to live here and what I must know in order to do so. My father's family homesteaded in 1894 in the rural district trustingly named *Eigenheim*, literally, home of one's own. That same December, my grandfather was born. Not far away, in 1897, Almighty Voice, the Cree who had been arrested for illegally butchering a cow and then escaped the Duck Lake jail, was killed by a barrage of bullets and cannon fire in what the *Canadian Encyclopedia* calls the "last battle between whites and Indians" in North America. In 1918 my mother's family came to the same district and farmed near the corner of Beardy's Reserve. They had left behind a homestead in Oklahoma that had been claimed also in 1894 when Indian Territory was opened up in the great land rush, among the patchwork of allotments chosen by Cheyenne, some of whom had survived the massacre upstream on the Washita River at the hands of General Custer's Seventh Cavalry. I am, in other words, a product of Indian policy on both sides of the border. My story cannot be told apart from those of Cree and Cheyenne. When I was a child, especially in the first years after my maternal grandfather's death, we picnicked and I ran along the reconstructed pallisades at Fort Carlton, due north of Eigenheim, where Treaty Six was first negotiated and signed late in the summer of 1876. Sixty years later, in 1936, while my great-uncle's family had turned inward in mourning at the death of a wife and mother, still in her 30s, thousands of people, including the governor-general, passed by the farm in a cloud of vehicles to the same site to mark the treaty's diamond anniversary. She was buried, meanwhile, at the country-church cemetery where all my ancestors who died in Canada are buried. If there is sacred ground for me anywhere on this earth, ground that signifies sacrifices made and remembered, it is there.

I have lived most of my life on Treaty Six land. I grew up in a small town in the southeast corner of that vast tract of 120,000 square miles, though I would have no significant contact with aboriginal people before brief stints in young adulthood as a daily newspaper journalist and a government bureaucrat. I now live and teach on the western side of the treaty area. I have driven across it, west to east and back, so that its terrain has become familiar.

I have taught introductory politics to Cree students at a cultural college housed in a former residential school, filled with peep holes and bad memories, where I once brought a group of uncomfortable non-aboriginal students for a joint session on "self-government" that was a spectacular failure, a mismatch of those who had no sense of themselves as historical beings and those who did. I returned to the same building some years later to struggle as the solitary *moniyaw* in a Cree-language class. I have brought my children to a pow-wow in the community, after which my daughter confessed surprise that "there were so many of them," having received an impression in her elementary school curriculum of the demise of a people. I have attended a wake for a suicide. I have heard horrific accounts of local political intimidation and hopes to bring about change whether through ballot-boxes or building occupations. I have sat quietly at a morning meeting—Regis and Kathy Lee on the large-screen TV at one end of the room—while skeptical elders debated a proposal to derive a contemporary watchdog on band government from the traditional concept of "whipman," thereby demonstrating both the richness of Cree as a language of public affairs and, whenever they reverted to an English word such as "rights," its limits. I write beneath an eagle's feather for no other reason than that it was a gift from a friend, an elder in the making, whom I had seen through a degree.

I am not sentimental either about real, existing reserve communities, though they contain much more cultural vitality than is commonly imagined, or else about the prospects of racial harmony "if we could only get to know each other." Even in a self-selected university environment, I am disabused regularly of the latter notion. The class I teach on aboriginal political issues in alternate years, typically a mix of non-aboriginal and aboriginal students, is easily the most difficult on my plate, the most likely to leave me with an unshakable sense of inadequacy, but also, because so much seemingly is at stake, the most likely to produce honest human encounters—the life-changing kind. This is the class I bring to the top of Driedmeat Hill to talk about treaty-making with an eyeful of land in every direction. This is the class from which I learned to venture the unlikely idea that rural and aboriginal peoples on the Canadian prairies might actually be well placed to understand each other—this after a non-aboriginal student shattered stereotypes on all sides by describing what was for her an inseparable interconnection of personal identity with the land on which her Ukrainian family had farmed for three generations. She did not have to disavow her own settler-cultivator ancestors in order to understand dispossession. Quite the contrary. It is not too strong to say that she feared such a loss for herself.

IV

For the Canadian government to face up formally to its "past actions and attitudes" is no small thing. Simple acknowledgement is an essential step in any process of reconciliation. This is so even if it is possible to wonder about the government's commitment to what it began, its careful confession of general but not specific wrongs, its willingness to say what without really asking why, or its tendency to portray the Crown as the sole active agent in the history of dispossession. Moreover, this is so even if most Canadians paid no attention to the offer. The offer remains a significant point of reference. While, as Ignatieff writes, the most gifted political leaders may "give their societies permission to say the unsayable, to think the unthinkable, to give rise to gestures of reconciliation that people, individually, cannot imagine,"[34] the effect of broad-brush government statements should be neither exaggerated nor minimized. Canadians do experience their history as a burden, only selectively available to them. Aboriginal communities live its legacy in brokenness and suspicion, most of it, indeed, directed internally. To offer reconciliation is to state for the record that a relationship has been ruptured and that the resulting estrangement needs to be overcome short of aboriginal disappearance into mainstream society.

The most meaningful work of reconciliation, however, will lie in small, face-to-face initiatives for which the imperative is greatest where communities exist in close proximity. In a qualified way, I take Alan Cairns's point, though on a local and regional level, not a national one, that "those who share space together must share more than space" and that relations between them must be politically rather than legally mediated.[35] Paul Tennant has proposed something more germane in the land claims hot-house of British Columbia: namely, creative strategies for bilateral local diplomacy between municipalities and First Nations—"the art and practice of neighborliness"—based on mutual respect, "co-equality," common goals, and regularized channels of communication.[36] Such initiatives might readily be extended to schools and relevant community organizations. What they require is yet another kind of historical acknowledgement, not of wrongs, but of the sheer survival of aboriginal communities with a degree of cultural continuity despite decades of government policy to the contrary. In other words, that means coming to terms with the reality of coexistence and of difference that must somehow be bridged by the practical work of understanding.

For me, the most familiar setting for such imperatives is the rural prairies—not only specific communities but also the province of Saskatchewan, given the estimates that aboriginal people, Indian and Metis, will account for between one-third and one-half of its population within the next half century. Such a scenario must surely raise doubts for those policy "realists" who are confident that the future is on their side by force of numbers, if nothing else, and who dismiss talk of mutual respect in political relations as belonging to some prior century when rough parity prevailed. In Saskatchewan, rough parity *is* the future. Correspondingly, the dilemmas of reconciliation have as much to do with the future as the past; they are real enough. The province is not a wealthy one. Its economic core, agriculture, is in trouble. Its population is aging. Its tax base is not expanding enough to meet the demands for services, especially in health care, a problem which is exacerbated by the fact that status Indians are exempted from taxation on on-reserve and related income and, until recently, from provincial sales tax on purchases anywhere. Needless to say, taxation is already a political lightning rod for a range of resentments.[37]

Saskatchewan, however, provides only the most politically concentrated setting for what is a wider phenomenon across the rural prairies (and, indeed, rural Australia). I am certain that the position I am venturing will seem incredulous to many of the people who live there. For good reason: across North America, farmers have been the means and justification of colonial expansion, rivals for land, and symbols of a very different, proprietary and instrumental, relation to it. They are, after all, Locke's producers. Agrarian-populist culture, moreover, still ascribes honour and shame in relation to hard work and visible prosperity, and if that culture is hard on its own members, especially during times of financial stress, it is no less forgiving of "lazy" aboriginal neighbours who appear to disregard the code altogether.[38] Its politics eschew pity and "welfare." It is readily aroused on grounds of equality over issues like aboriginal hunting rights and, of late, the way in which Indians seem more successful than farm groups at prying money out of Ottawa. As one farmer told a radio talk-show, "we had our own treaty"—the "Crow" statutory grain transport rate—"and we had it taken away."

Not only that, as the rural economy contracts to fewer and fewer service centres, rural communities are characterized by a dramatically different demographic trajectory than that of aboriginal communities. Their populations are declining or, at best, stable, and aging at that. They are threatened by the consolidation of schools and medical care in larger towns (while, on adjacent reserves, new facilities may be under construction) and by the erosion of meaningful local authority (while the talk in aboriginal circles is about self-government and co-management of resources). These differences are easy to draw. But they represent only part of the picture. And, increasingly, what come to the fore may be the similarities, the common challenges, and the interdependencies between them. Rural and reserve-based aboriginal communities, which are, of course, generally rural as well, are each significantly dependent on government transfers—including pensions and a few professional incomes—and on the infusions of money that come with treaty land entitlement deals. Each lives with the fact that their brightest young people will leave for higher education and likely not return. Each is confronted with the limited opportunities of a global economy, where investment concentrates in cities, and where the rural places most desperate for employment bid against each other to absorb in a concentrated form the social and environmental messes of low-wage manufacturing, garbage dumps, toxic (even nuclear) waste, tire incineration, pulp mills, and massive hog barns. While the romanticized images of the pioneer, the rancher, or the costumed Indian are appropriated for big-city summer fairs and the festivities surrounding world-class sporting events, rural and aboriginal people are now routinely perceived as parasites on the public purse. In the scolding phrase that is heard increasingly, they are unwilling to "move to where the jobs are." Government strategies will ease more farmers off the land; from time to time, though not so explicitly as in the U.S., that has been a policy goal for aboriginal people too. In the new political economy, "the good citizen...is one who is mobile, who is willing to tear up all roots and follow the promptings of the job market."[39]

To portray rural and aboriginal communities merely as partners in hardship and grievance—enjoined in a futile fight against some inevitable tide of history—would leave an overly pessimistic impression. There are also cultural correspondences that can be bridges for coexistence; without them, there would be no basis of understanding from which to deal with what are now flashpoints. For the most part, that common ground is still unappreciated and unexplored. On occasion, though, it appears in flashes of recognition, as in the classroom incident described above, or in the case of another student from redneck ranching country, who was shocked to discover that of all the essays generated from a conference on a contentious piece of federal conservation legislation, the one that rang truest to his situation was by an aboriginal speaker. A provisional list of cultural correspondences might well include an understanding of the importance of multi-generational family identity—of inheritance—rooted in land and community, shaping something other than the "portable self" of urban modernity; and a relationship to nature as something other than playground or object. I do not want to make too great a claim for this brief list; it is distilled from conversations, mostly untested, and the risk in suggesting it at all is that it can be translated into another set of stereotypes that substitute for the complexity of real communities. But there is something to it. It constitutes part of the common ground for treaty *peoples* whose inheritance is filled with mixed blessings, and includes obligations of memory and relationship on all sides. It can nourish tentative steps in the "art and practice of neighborliness," in *miyowicehtowin* (good relations) and *witaskiwin* (living together on the land).[40]

Author's note: This essay first appeared in Carol Prager and Trudy Govier, eds., *Dilemmas of Reconciliation: Cases and Concepts* (Waterloo: Wilfrid Laurier University Press, 2003). It is reprinted with permission.

Eight

# What is the Farm Crisis?
## *Seven Short Commentaries*

*Ill fares the land, to hastening ills a prey.*
*Where wealth accumulates, and men decay;*
*Princes and lords may flourish, or may fade;*
*A breath can make them, as a breath has made;*
*But a bold peasantry, their country's pride,*
*When once destroyed, can never be supplied.*

Oliver Goldsmith, "The Deserted Village," 1770

*... I went through this process of really beating up on myself as the farm manager, that somehow it was my fault that the farm is going the direction that it is. I think that I am a good manager. And I think that my friends and neighbours who are struggling all around—it's a testament to their willpower that they're still out there... I am frustrated and angry with the fact that we've been put out on the chopping block by ourselves, 'cause that's how we feel... We're spinning our wheels to try to stay in an industry that we're very passionate about and it seems like that kind of passion is being, in a way, used against us. You know, yeah, there will always be food produced, but there doesn't seem to be the concern about who will be producing it.*

Eldon Funk, grain farmer, Laird, Saskatchewan

*One often hears the statement that agriculture is changing and we must adapt to the changes. Few persons who repeat the statement really understand the magnitude of the changes and the implications of them for agriculture and the long-term sustainability of the food system.*

William Heffernan, University of Missouri

There is a stretch of highway southeast of Rosetown, Saskatchewan, past Milden and the Conquest turn-off, then south to Macrorie, and across the Gardiner Dam—that monument to the mastery of water built in the 1960s—to places like Loreburn and Davidson, where the truth of the new prairie grainbelt comes clear. The pavement is patched, potholed, and sometimes given up to gravel. There are few other vehicles on the road save the tandem-trucks that must be approached with caution because of their size and their capricious capacity to spin a rock through a windshield. They are doing the work that railroads once did, hauling grain to concrete terminals clustered at strategic points in a contracting economy. There are few farms along the road. The towns have a diminishing, desolate look about them. The experience is altogether shocking—there is no other word for it—though it is hardly peculiar to this particular route. A similar experience awaits those who venture out, memories alert, from any of the major cities in which most prairie people now live, and into the new outback that stretches from southwestern Manitoba into parts of eastern Alberta.

There is little here to warrant the shiny optimism of the federal government's promotional mail-outs in the mid-1990s, when the last vestiges of the Crow Rate were phased out, leaving farmers to absorb the full shock of grain transportation costs. In return, they were told to expect prosperity: an efficient rail system, new value-added pro-cessing, and "new potential for farm families and rural commun-ities." Now it is not too dramatic to say that the future of this historic, export grain-growing region is in the balance—though it evidently matters less to governments, to the national economy, or to most people in what is now a very urbanized country, indeed, a very urban-ized West. In many places it may already be too late. The region is emptying out of farm people: a drop of 20,000 in the last Statistics Canada labour-force report. It is filled, at the same time, with more than its share of anger, shame, confusion, desperation, and lost hope—the currency of a good deal of rural speech.

This is my world. I grew up in it and now teach at a small univer-sity campus at its western edge. It is also the world from which many of my students come. What is there to say to them about a world in which, as one student describes it, his mother works at three part-time nursing jobs at hospitals, each an hour apart, on bad roads, to keep a farm going? What is there to say on the day the cattle-liners come for the last time? What is there to say about a world in which a father has deliberately minimized his son's exposure to farming for fear he'll get "hooked on it" and want to return, a world in which smart, hard-working people cannot imagine a long-term future for themselves in a vocation they love and cannot afford themselves the self-respect of recommending it to their children? What do you say to your farm friends who, come spring seeding time, say that for the first time there is no joy left in it? What do you say to old men who are reduced to tears by news that the Wheat Pool built by their fathers has been dissolved by a corporate merger? What do you say to farm people, as someone who ought to know something about politics, that will explain why their provincial government is so anxious for foreign investors to build a massive hog-barn complex in their district, whatever the social and environmental consequences, whatever their determined opposition? What do you say about this world to a parliamentary committee, big-city newspaper readers or national radio listeners when the opportunity arises? What is the farm crisis?

The short essays that follow are responses to that crisis drawn from a decade of engagement with farm and rural issues. They have been revised only slightly to minimize overlap and dated references. While they reflect the immediate circumstances that gave rise to them, including successive years of negative net farm income on the prairies, they also aim at a truth that is deeper, sharper, than any temporary shift in the accounting trend-lines. As the first essay argues, the farm crisis is not merely about income. As wheat prices reached record levels in the winter of 2008 and biofuel promoters promised a limitless demand for grains, cornstalks, grasses and anything else that could grow in a field, urban Canada could be tempted into imagining that the farm crisis was over.[1] The rise in prices was an important life-line for many producers. But it was true only for the grain sector. Even then, it came with a parallel rise in fertilizer and fuel costs, as well as a new round of speculation in farm land that pushed prices skyward. What had not been reversed was either farmers' structural position within a global food economy or the recent policy inclination across the prairies to treat the rural as a resource plantation from which transient people extract wealth for distant investors.

I    WHAT IS THE FARM CRISIS? (1999)[2]

The phrase "farm crisis" is back on the lips of politicians and media commentators. Indeed, the two words have been joined so frequently they might as well be a single word. For all that, the farm crisis is commonly misrepresented and misunderstood as being primarily about cash flow and commodity prices, or drought, especially when it typically is followed by a third word—bailout. Suffice to say the farm crisis is not merely about short-term net income.

In the new outback, the farm crisis is about rural communities where rail-lines are abandoned and grain elevators come down, where tax bases shrink, where retail stores and government services like hospitals, schools, and post offices are consolidated in larger centres. Populations age and decline. People who have given volunteer energy to the work of building community wear out, retreat into the isolation of hard work, or move away.

The farm crisis is about the lack of leadership that can speak for a fractured agricultural community to a wider audience. It is about coming to terms with the national political irrelevance of the prairie farm vote, and with urban-rural tensions ripe for political manipulation in every western province.

The farm crisis is about fears for the future of what is good work—work that feeds people, engages parents meaningfully with their children and grandchildren, and requires multiple skills. Now farm people talk about the prospect of becoming "bio-serfs" under contract to one of a handful of seed-chemical conglomerates. They work great distances off the farm to subsidize their operations (in vulnerable rural professions like nursing), and risk Revenue Canada reclassification as hobbyists for their trouble. They constitute one of the oldest occupational groups in the country. Many of them are eating up retirement equity, postponing what eventually will be a make-or-break generational transfer. In that sense, too, the crisis is about the immense psychological burden of keeping a third- or fourth-generation family farm that is not merely a business, but a physical, historical anchor of home and identity.

The farm crisis, finally, is about an acute sense of abandonment by governments, which are no longer willing—or perhaps able—to play the role of balancer on behalf of disadvantaged regions or economic sectors. For roughly the first century after Confederation, the Canadian government took a direct interest in the development of prairie agricultural settlement. That was *the* National Policy. The government negotiated treaties involving real concessions to Cree, Blackfoot, and other First Nations people. It surveyed land, promoted immigration, underwrote the cost of railroad construction, established dominion experimental farms to assist immigrant farmers and built post offices in all the villages built up around grain delivery points. It did all this as if a governmental presence mattered across a vast rural territory. Much of that has changed radically in the last three decades.

The federal government, for example, is now considering whether to yield the last traces of regulatory authority over railroads that have already made it clear that grain is a commodity like any other, and not a high business priority at that. Farmers already pay several billions more per year than they once did to ship their grain; they have seen few of the promised productivity gains from deregulation. Even in Alberta one hears the rally cry: "Remember the Crow."

The same government has seemed all too willing to play free trade "boy scout" with western grain, reducing subsidies far ahead of schedule without any assurances that competitors will follow. It has also virtually surrendered agricultural research to the private sector and given enthusiastic support—including legal protection—to the so-called biotechnological revolution, helping to create a situation in which seed diversity is dangerously limited and ambivalent farmers are caught in the crossfire of consumer boycotts and plant breeders' rights. They speak wistfully of the not-for-profit innovation that once came from the federally supported experimental farms.

Make no mistake: there is an urgent need for the right kind of graduated, farm-cash infusion—even if the largest beneficiaries might well be creditors. At the same time, when politicians and urban voters hear what sounds like yet another demand for a bailout, they should understand how much the public safety net has been withdrawn from the farm economy. Whatever the perception,

Ottawa's financial support for farmers has dropped steadily and sub-stantially since the 1980s—as much as any funding envelope in this era of belt-tightening.

To the extent that the farm crisis is about community and leader-ship, the primary responsibility lies, of course, with farm people. But government policy can help or hinder them. These days, farm people can be forgiven their envy at the European Union's political commit-ment to farm populations and to food security despite the trade dif-ficulties it sometimes causes. They want a similar recognition of the importance of family farm-based agriculture.

At the very least, they deserve not to be written off as the sacrificial lambs of deficit reduction and trade liberalization.


II    AGRICULTURE WITHOUT FARMERS (2001)[3]

In 1970, *National Geographic* published an illustration of what it called the "farm of the future"—drawn with the help of U.S. govern-ment agronomists.

The "farm" is directed from the control-tower bubble of a Jetson's-style house. Its vista is spectacularly clean. A remote-operated com-bine glides on tracks over a ten-mile-long wheatfield. Fruits and vege-tables ripen in climate-controlled domes. High-rise cattle pens are attached to feed mills and a packing plant, while, according to the comforting caption, a "side drain flushes wastes to be broken down for fertilizer."

There are, significantly, no farmers in the picture, no school buses, no clues of community life. It is unclear who works on this farm besides the control-tower operator. It is unclear who owns it—who *could* own it—though, safe to say, this is not the family farm maligned of late by national newspaper columnists like Terence Corcoran and Lawrence Solomon.[4]

The dream of revolutionizing agriculture, in other words, is hardly new.

These days, a refined version of the dream is being floated by the federal agriculture department, caught between farmers' demands, trade agreements, and urban taxpayers. It matches the dreams of bankers, "life-science" companies, their university research part-ners, and select farm groups; and it has been foisted uncritically on newspaper readers across the country in a supplement paid for by "Canada's agri-food sector."[5]

This brave new world is seductive enough. Canada can have safe, subsidy-free, premium-brand agriculture to compete in global niche markets. Equipped with the latest technology, those farmers who are "diversified," "innovative," market-savvy, and big enough to be credit-worthy, will flourish.

The demise of rural communities is sad, of course, but who can afford to be sentimental?

The farm people I know—real innovators—are sceptical of this dream, and hard-pressed to locate themselves or their children inside it. But if the dream is meant for them, it is only to discourage.

The real targets for enlistment in the revolution are consumers. For them, the demands are modest, the message reassuring: you will have your cake and, genetically modified or not, be able to eat it too. Affordably. That's all you need to know. Evidently Canadian readers could be spared serious analysis of the implications of this revolution in the countryside. No mention of agribusiness concentration and convergence across grain, meat, and bio-chemical sectors—even in the shadow of a merger deal that spells the end for the last surviving prairie wheat pool. No mention of the profit and patent-protection strategies of the seed and chemical companies. The newspaper features equated new technologies such as global positioning with producer power, when their effect is as likely to diminish farmers' skills and allow more decisions to be made off-farm. They also recycled stereotypes of mounting subsidies for grain farmers when abandonment is nearer the truth—beginning with the abolition of the Crow freight rate. Government policy has shifted decisively from producers to products, which, reliably and cheaply available, can attract "value-added" processors. Witness governments' plans to dramatically expand cattle and pig production even as small producers are displaced.

Critical analysis like this is common in farm conversations. Of course it's not only farm people who have an interest in who owns the economy, who has access to its technologies or is made redundant by them, and what kind of livelihood and community that economy affords. These issues are universal. It's just that in rural Canada you can already see the future.

"Are you ready"—slight dramatic pause—"for the future of agriculture?"

That's the question being asked on commercial radio, in the sooth-ing baritone of your favourite uncle, in the weeks before spring seed-ing. What follows is a pitch to farmers to become a "technologic-ally advanced partner" of the largest corporate player in agricultural biotechnology, Monsanto, the manufacturer of both the herbicide Roundup and the canola that is genetically engineered to resist it.

In a very real sense, farmers are on the front lines of the biotechno-logical revolution as they weigh the promise of slightly lower costs and slightly higher yields against a contractual strait-jacket that forbids them from saving seeds for the following year and gives the company intrusive rights of inspection against any such copyright infringement. More than half the canola grown on the prairies is already Roundup Ready. The high-powered advertising campaigns aimed at what must be tiny fractions of radio and prime-time television audiences, as well as the vigorous legal defence of "plant-breeders' rights" against indi-vidual farmers, make it clear that big money is at stake.

Farmers caught in a prolonged cash squeeze are left unfairly on their own to wrestle with the ethical and environmental implications of this brave new world of genetic manipulation. Above all, many of them are downright afraid of a future in which they lose what's left of their jealously-guarded sense of independence and become, in effect, "bio-serfs," or low-margin contract workers—their subordin-ation to one or a handful of seed-and-herbicide conglomerates ensured by the obscene prospect of a "terminator gene" that prevents regeneration.

Small pockets of resistance are forming, but farmers' power is lim-ited. In any case, the issue is too big to be left to them. All of us should be asking whether we are ready for this future, and why there has been so little public debate about it in this country.

Tellingly, the Canadian government had a virtual free hand on this issue at international talks in Colombia in 1999. On behalf of the United States and a small group of countries, it took the diplomatic lead in scuttling a draft convention to regulate trade in genetically modified seed, livestock, and food products. This story was scarcely reported by the mainstream Canadian media, and it prompted no opposition outrage in Parliament—nothing to compare to the case in Britain, for example, of cross-pollination from a Monsanto experimental plot that was front-page news and a political scandal for the Labour government.

Certainly prairie farmers bear the risk of losing international markets in Europe and Asia due to heightened consumer sensitivity abroad about all North American canola. The battle that has raged in the World Trade Organization over Europe's attempts even to label food as genetically modified will only intensify over any such so-called "protectionist barriers" to "free trade."

The GMO issue is too easily framed around the periodic bouts of consumer panic about food health—concerns on which the corporate biotech revolutionaries are best able to defend themselves. There are also political, economic, and social questions to be addressed, about who has access to biotechnology, on what terms, and who sets its priorities. Can the biotechnological revolution in agriculture be interrupted by serious scrutiny in the name of the public good, or will the pacifier of cheap food for an increasingly urban population, the faith in technology as progress, and the dull weight of laissez-faire ideology prevail?

IV    MEAT (2000)[7]

When our family drove through Garden City, Kansas, on a summer vacation, it was hard to miss either the message painted on a roadside silo—EAT BEEF—STAY SLIM—or the smell of feedlots across an entire county. For all that, we had no idea we had come so close to the leading edge of the North American meat industry.

Garden City, whatever its name, is no Eden. A small city located in the sparsely populated high plains of western Kansas, it is home to two major packing plants employing some 4,000 workers and surrounded by some of the largest intensive livestock operations in the United States. Garden City is also home to the social and environmental challenges that come with the packing industry's relocation from large urban centres, close to markets, to small cities and towns, close to a concentrated supply of cattle and hogs.

The pattern is a familiar one from Kansas to Brooks, Alberta. Companies like IBP/Tyson or Cargill, which now control a large share of meat processing in North America, descend on a community, extract local tax concessions where possible, promise jobs, and end up relying on transient labour for what is hard, dangerous, high-turnover work. The human consequences are left to volunteer-run organizations, social service agencies, schools and police forces.

In the year 2000, the new political economy of industrial meat production arrived in east-central Alberta with all of the familiar conflicts over economic futures. In the County of Flagstaff, Taiwan Sugar Co. was issued a municipal permit to build a 7,200-sow hog barn complex that, at peak capacity, would have been the third-largest city in the province in raw-sewage equivalent terms. In places like Flagstaff, where populations have declined and grown older, and where prospects seem limited, the promise of even a few jobs at modest wages can be a powerful consideration for municipal politicians.

The most vocal opponents aren't genteel acreage owners who dislike the smell of manure. They're farm people who worry about environmental and community impact and, deep down, about their own future as small producers in a world of intensive livestock operations and preferential market access to packing plants based on volume or even corporate cross-ownership. The Flagstaff residents forced a rancorous appeal hearing. They packed the hall. They sold sandwiches and pie at lunch to offset their legal bills. They risked irreparable rifts with some of their neighbours. They sat uncomfortably while their "emotionalism" was discounted and an opposing lawyer—who would never have to return—urged the appeal board to "face the fact" that the family farm was dead. When the board upheld the permit by split decision, the residents took their campaign into wider political, media and legal forums. Eventually the company abandoned the project and left the province without paying its court-ordered costs to the residents.

In one deeply divided rural community after another, across all three prairie provinces, municipal councils have struggled with this kind of development application. They have neither the technical expertise nor the fiscal resources to evaluate them; and, if they impose conditions on approval, as Flagstaff attempted, they could not realistically enforce them.

Provincial governments, having courted both producers and large-scale processors, are caught in the difficult position of being both promoters and environmental regulators of intensive livestock operations. In Saskatchewan, the difficulty has been compounded because of the province's equity share in the home-grown company Big Sky Pork. The next logical step has been for governments, anxious to protect their reputations as safe havens for investment, to limit the powers of municipal authorities and, as rural people suspect, the possibility of saying no to developments that would have a tremendous impact on their local communities. Those same people are puzzled at why they have been left on their own to defend their interests. Isn't that what governments are for?

Outside of Manitoba, where the industry is concentrated, the hog-barn bubble burst quickly across the prairies. The irony in some communities is that successful opposition will have saved potential local investors from the kind of substantial losses sustained in places where barn complexes now stand empty. But the challenge of building a resilient economic base remains. And desperate rural communities are still susceptible to the next dubious job-creation schemes: strawboard manufacturing, tire incineration, big-city landfills, coal-fired power plants or factory farms.

Location, it turns out, still matters in the global economy. Some places reflect the clean prosperity of the new knowledge industries. Others—mostly out of sight, out of mind—are at risk of absorbing in a concentrated form the messes left by large-scale, export-oriented resource development, by a throw-away society and by a food industry that delivers affordable products to consumers safely removed from their source.

Tough choice, indeed, for rural communities, if choice is the right word for it.


V    THE PROMISE OF LOCAL GOVERNMENT (2002)[8]

If there was ever a golden age when election to a rural municipal council meant a bit of local prestige, a big-city convention, and, after council meetings, entry into an old-boys' club whose backroom currency was a bottle or a pouch of sunflower seeds, all in exchange for keeping the roads gravelled and the weeds under control, those days are gone.

The real world of municipal politics across the prairies is now shaped by the economic challenges of a wealth-extracting global economy.

It is shaped by the struggle to maintain services as cost-cutting provincial governments scale back grants, restrict local tax powers, and abandon decades of public investment in infrastructure. Rural municipalities face new, unavoidable concerns about water quality. Their roads bear some of the brunt of changes to the grain-transportation system.

Rural municipalities are caught in the culture clash that comes with residential subdivisions. In at least one Alberta county, a ban on the operation of combines after 9 p.m. has been debated.

Rural municipalities are also caught in the middle of land-use conflicts that will intensify as messy, divisive developments are promoted for what look like "empty" spaces. Not only do such developments strain local resources. Often enough, rural councillors are caught between the fierce opposition of local residents, provincial pressure, and their own resignation to the realism of imperfect choices especially where populations are declining, tax bases are shrinking, and economic options seem limited.

Those hard choices may, in fact, be temporary ones, as transient investors move on and as meaningful local authority is eroded on a range of land-use and other legislative fronts. The result is that many of the decisions affecting rural communities are made by people who don't have to live with the consequences.

All of this is a familiar part of the rural landscape. For rural municipal leaders, though, the sense of being caught in-between also means uncertainty about how to respond politically. On one hand, direct confrontation with provincial governments is hard. It requires overcoming the fear of biting the hand that feeds you, or that at least controls the purse-strings, and it means unlearning a well-established culture of deference. As urban populations grow, rural municipalities have reason not to risk the share they have.

On the other hand, rural communities are being re-politicized through an array of *ad hoc* organizations formed around the single purpose of saving something (like a local school), stopping something (like industrial hog barns or oil-field flooding) or filling in the gaps left by governments (like monitoring air-quality in sour-gas regions). These organizations are often unpolished. They face steep learning curves about politics, law, science, and statistical methods. But they embody a sharp understanding that rural communities must look out for themselves. Right or wrong, their members sometimes see municipal governments either as captive local agents of the province or as irrelevant. In effect, they lay claim to community leadership.

All of which is to say that the life of a municipal councillor is a difficult one: more pressure, less real power.

From another angle, however, municipal councillors might be well-placed at a critical time to change the political landscape. They represent a distinct set of interests which do not necessarily coincide with the "public interest" as determined at a provincial level. If they understand that, they need not be deferential or intimidated. They will learn to articulate those interests in the face of policy agendas increasingly focussed on the needs of cities. They will resist the conception of rural places as mere resource plantations or dumping grounds. They will be interested in economic development that is genuinely sustainable because it makes communities resilient—a better rural word than competitive. They will engage in intensive land-use planning with whatever powers are left to them.

If municipal councillors understand that they represent distinct interests, they will learn to share expertise and facilities with neighbouring jurisdictions. They will co-operate within watersheds. They will come to understand those *ad hoc* community-defence organizations not as rivals or troublemakers, but as potential partners, filled with people committed to living where they are. They will not be afraid of public consultation and debate; for no one else is in a better position to reinvigorate and channel local democratic energies—and democracy is nothing if it is not local.

Rural municipal councillors are really the last remnant of that vibrant democratic society of local office-holders built across the prairies by farm people in the first third of the twentieth century. They are the last representatives of the great dignity invested in local governance. But the history of what has happened to municipal authority in subsequent generations should make them wary of a certain historical truth. It might be stated in this way: whenever provincial politicians promise to save the people from politics, as William Aberhart did in 1935, it turns out they mean less *local* politics; and whenever provincial politicians promise to give the people "less government," it turns out they mean less *local* government.

The emerging political divide lies not between traditional parties, Wendell Berry writes, but between futures organized around the needs of either the local community or the global economy. What he calls the "party of local community" has the strength of rootedness; it is mostly unorganized; its members are only becoming aware of each other and the challenges they face. But this party has room for a broad spectrum of community-minded people. Rural municipal councillors worthy of their heritage ought to be among its leaders.

VI   THE SPACES IN-BETWEEN (2004)[9]

On those rare occasions when I am in a glass-and-steel downtown business district, like that in Vancouver, where so much prairie grain historically has come to port, I cannot shake the thought that the vertical architectural landscape around me represents the sedimented wealth and labour of rural people: farmers, loggers, fishers, miners. Suffice to say there are no buildings as impressive as this in Daysland, Alberta. I have the same reaction on my grandparents' behalf when I am in the historic grain district north of Portage and Main in Winnipeg. It is as if the economic, political and social topography of Canada has been tilted so that, by force of something as natural and irresistible as gravity, people and wealth trickle downhill into the major cities. And, if that visual image is helpful, I would add that the slope has steepened and the trickle has become a torrent in recent years.

Major cities are now the subject of a sophisticated and energetic policy debate in Canada. Cities are presented as the competitive nodal points of the global economy, and home to the creative class. They have managed in recent years to establish a united front to make the case for reinvestment in urban infrastructure and a place at the national political table. A major national newspaper columnist has encouraged the federal government to understand Canada "correctly—as a country of cities strung together by countryside."

My role in this debate is to ask: what about the spaces in-between? What about rural Canada? I do not want to get tangled at the outset in a definitional exercise about what is rural. The polarities of "urban" and "rural" say little about the great variation within each category, or the routine ways in which people live, work, play and shop across them. Modern means of communication—with the possible exception of broadband—do not stop at the last suburban street.

But those who demand a new deal for cities know the difference. And they know where the weight of numbers lies. To no one's surprise, the 2001 census confirmed that Canada is now a very urban country—one of the most urban in the world. Four of five Canadians live in centres of 10,000 or more, and most of those in four major metropolitan corridors. In addition, the fastest rates of population growth outside of cities belong to the bedroom communities that ring them, in good Canadian fashion, like doughnuts.

Rural Canada, taken as a whole, presents a distinct set of policy challenges. Its demographic and economic trajectories are different than those of cities. Rural populations typically are declining or stable, and older than the national average. They are ethnically less diverse, apart from the fact that in many parts of the country aboriginal people also live in rural settings. Rural Canadians are less likely to have a university degree; their children are still less likely to proceed to post-secondary education—evidence, perhaps, of a rustic suspicion of pointy-headed professors but, without doubt, of the very real financial costs and cultural dislocations of having to leave home to go to school.

Across Canada, too, except in semi-rural pockets of resource or recreational development, there is a widening urban-rural income gap. In the large census district in east-central Alberta in which I live, per-capita income is less than two-thirds what it is in Calgary; it would be even lower if the two largest centres, in which retail investment and public services have been consolidated, were removed. Its population and economic indicators, hidden in provincial aggregates, have more in common with western Saskatchewan. Pensions are a leading source of income in many of its communities. I have taken to calling this the "other Alberta," out beyond the Edmonton-Calgary corridor, the mountain parks and the resource boom-towns of Fort McMurray and Grande Prairie. But there are at least two British Columbias, two Newfoundlands, and so on.

Rural Canada can still be differentiated by its resource-based economies, which is to say two things. First, while not all of those sectors necessarily have been export-oriented, they have been subjected to intense global price pressures in recent years as a result of trade liberalization *and* to the most dubious protectionist measures (for example, softwood lumber, beef, potatoes). Second, while those sectors and those who worked in them—especially farming and fishing—might once have been romanticized as the heart of the country, they are now widely viewed as parasitic on the public purse. They are subsidy industries.

One other distinguishing feature of rural Canada is the extent to which its communities are subject to decisions made elsewhere—provincial and national capitals, corporate headquarters—by people who scarcely know them and certainly do not have to live with the consequences. Rural people have suffered repeated losses of local authority around land-use, taxation, education and health care. They live in monstrously large electoral constituencies. Consequently their political responses are often fragmented and frustrated; their alienation from mainstream politics is real, though it does not serve them well. While there are many commonalities of position and experience between Nakusp, British Columbia, Viking, Alberta, and the fishing villages of northern New Brunswick, there has been no co-ordinated effort, for example, from rural municipalities to match the new cities' agenda.

What would a new deal for rural Canada look like? In short, it would affirm the importance of rural communities—vibrant, resilient, attractive ones—for reasons that are still nationally compelling. It would commit national and provincial governments to think differently about health-care delivery, small schools, child care and aging in place. It would commit them to support the arts in rural places. It would also commit them to the renewal of basic transportation infrastructure—for people as well as commodities—in places where it's not just crumbling, it's disappeared. A new deal for rural Canada would involve tax-sheltered community-reinvestment options to keep local capital in local circulation as an alternative to the frenzied pooling of retirement savings in the hands of metropolitan-based fund managers. It would place a high priority on the kind of food security that is achieved not through high-tech screening but through a decentralized economy with room for many small-scale producers and processors. It would respect rural people as partners in resource conservation, whether endangered species or watersheds, rather than as potential threats. Not least, that new deal would return a sense of citizenship and political participation to rural Canadians, and return meaningful decisions about their communities and futures closer to home.

VII    WHAT IS AT STAKE? (2003, 2005)[10]

The challenges facing farm-based communities like Viking, Alberta are experienced most powerfully and personally in the loss of neighbours. But there have been other losses as well.

One is the continuing loss of wealth out of your community. Let's be clear: there is still money being made here in farming. Lots of it. This is not like the east-coast cod fishery where the cod disappears. The problem is that the money doesn't stay around long. Producers operate at the most vulnerable end of a highly-concentrated, vertically-integrated, continentally- and globally-organized food system— one that is dominated by a small number of corporate food-chain clusters across the seed/chemical, grains, and livestock sectors. Your role in this system, in competition with producers around the world, is to supply the cheap raw materials for the big processors' "value-added" activity. You bear the weight of downward price pressures. You are vulnerable to the entry of cheaper imports—Ukrainian feed barley or U.S. corn. You live with a disproportionate share of the risk when something goes wrong in this system; remember BSE—just one cow in northern Alberta. And you lack market power in either grain or livestock. In this room there are only "little guys." You are all small operators. None of you can negotiate toe-to-toe with Monsanto or Cargill or Archer Daniels Midland.

That may sound overly pessimistic. After all, we are told that agriculture has grown to be a $7.4-billion industry in Alberta, and that the value of Canadian agri-food exports has grown from about $2 billion to almost $30 billion a year over the past three decades—especially after the U.S.-Canada free trade agreement came into effect. What you don't hear is that return to producers, adjusted for inflation, has flat-lined since the 1970s. Your share is diminishing. So then you are told that new technologies—biotechnology and computerization—will give you that important competitive edge. But when gross farm revenues are charted against net farm income since World War II, with the progressive introduction of tractors and combines, electrification, chemicals, GMO crops and now global positioning systems, the pattern is always the same. There is a short-term boost in net income at the onset of new technologies, followed by longer-term decline, while at the same time gross farm income steadily increases. In other words, more money passes *through* your hands and out of your community with every technological "advance." Input costs, machinery costs, and bank-credit costs all rise in what are thinly-disguised strategies of profit maximization. More than that, many new technologies displace the farm knowledge that is shared within a community with knowledge that is embedded in computer chips or biotechnological patents. This is a highly extractive economy.[11]

The other thing you have lost is some of the self-confidence and taken-for-granted purpose that once came with what you do. This is a moment to remember how experimental, how radical, and how successful your grandparents were in building local and larger institutions in rural Alberta—co-operatives, a wheat pool, credit unions, municipal governments, school boards, and a political movement that governed the province for 14 years. They did all this because, not unlike you, they needed to defend themselves and their communities from economic exploitation and political indifference. No one else would do it for them. And they needed to give themselves dignity as farm people.

It's also a time to think hard about what it means to be rural. When I did interviews for a national radio documentary and asked thoughtful rural people what was at stake in the countryside, I repeatedly heard reference to culture—a way of life, a good one, distinct from but somehow important to the well-being of the larger society. The same people often struggled, however, to articulate what they meant. It was new to them to have to explain who they were as members of a minority culture and to do so in a language that would be understood.

Here's what I think you instinctively know and value:

*Independence*: Farm people enjoy working for themselves. They have a long memory of their ancestors' struggles to free themselves from feudalism, which sometimes comes out when they declare that they do not want to be "bio-serfs" to a seed-and-chemical company either. Real independence is not easy. It requires members of a household to have multiple, practical skills in order to be free in a practical sense.

*Neighbourliness*: Farm people know that they are dependent on each other and obliged to help out when asked. They know that there is no sense surviving economically without neighbours. But think about how so much farm work now happens in isolation on larger machinery; the change in grain transportation, for example, means that the conversations in the elevator line-up no longer happen.

*Good work*: Farm people know that they are engaged in good work. It feeds people. It gives meaningful responsibility to children and engages them with parents and grandparents. It requires creativity and competence at many skills. It joins mind and body, indoors and outdoors.

*Rootedness*: Farm people are "placed" people with stubborn attachments. Their identities are invested in known places that they do not easily abandon. In this sense, too, they are radically counter-cultural. The dominant message from economists and politicians is that they should simply relocate for sake of employment.

*Nature*: Farm people know that it is possible to know, respect, and love "nature"—a piece of land, a landscape, animals—not just as a playground preserved from human activity, but as a place of livelihood. This is distinct from the perspective common among urban environmentalists, but it has a richness of its own.

*Mystery and gratitude*: Farm people know that land is a gift and food is a miracle; they are not just commodities. A kernel of wheat is a thing of wonder. There is something sacred in the everyday.

*Community*: Farm people know that a community is a complex association of people who, despite their differences, must live together, who must sometimes rely on each other, who cannot avoid each other at the rink, the church, or the post office, and must live, successfully or not, with the reputations they make—for as long as a lifetime. There is no anonymity in rural communities. This may sound stifling to some. Certainly it takes skill and grace to do well. But a real community is a place in which you can be an active member, not a stranger; not everyone has such an opportunity.

What else do farm people instinctively know? You know that the most sustainable rural economy and community and environment is one in which ownership is dispersed, not concentrated in the hands of a few. You know that too much absentee ownership is a dangerous thing. You know that the fundamental decisions that affect a community should be made by those who will have to live with the consequences. You know that Main Street is a social, cultural and economic meeting-place—much more than a big-box parking lot.

I don't want to romanticize rural culture or communities. That's not fair to anyone. One of the dark sides of rural communities is the damage that is done to people by the kind of honour-and-shame mentality that can operate in a place precisely because people are known, their family histories inherited and their apparent success or failure a matter of public conversation. But my purpose is to suggest what it is you value. It adds up to a distinctive culture that contains critical resources but also some hard questions for you. If you value practical independence, neighbours, good work, and diverse, multi-generational communities of people, how will those values be reflected in the choices you make?

Looking to the near future, it is not a settled question who will own the countryside, live in it, produce food or have access to farm knowledge. What is fundamentally at stake for everyone is this: a society that loses the collective, practical skills to produce food—not just manage inputs or manipulate futures markets—is in that measure less free. It is therefore more vulnerable to the dangerous weaknesses of what is now a highly concentrated, hydrocarbon-based, long-distance food system. For that reason, it matters that large numbers of skilled farmers see no future at farming. It matters that farm land is taken out of production; that farm knowledge is increasingly privatized in computer chips, biotechnological patents, and global positioning systems; that Western Canada is becoming merely a residual supply region for the North American food-processing industry; and that, even when a BSE crisis temporarily closes the border and interrupts that trajectory, there is still no intelligent discussion in this country about anything that resembles food policy. The sustainable food system of the future will be a more regional one in many respects. It will require more processing points not fewer—this is the best security against all imaginable threats—and likewise more skilled producers, who are equipped with enough market power, cultural respect and environmental responsibility to grow food in ways that reflect what, at best, they know and value.

Nine

# Two Albertas
## *Rural and Urban Trajectories*

*If you look at the face of the new West, it is an urban face.*
Roger Gibbins, president, Canada West Foundation [1]

*If the city-state cannot be the core of new political boundaries, then can it be the core of a new self-understanding and a way of seeing the region in which the local designation of Calgarian, for example, is more important than the designation of Albertan?*
George Melnyk [2]

I

At the start of a new millennium, the *Calgary Herald* published what it declared to be a tongue-in-cheek commemorative supplement casting ahead to the year 2025. In that bright near-future, Calgary was rich and self-reliant. It was the "perfect model" of the city-state, emerging with its "global sinews" out of the plodding, "old-style" political jurisdictions of countries and provinces—all of them "hollow inside, weak and irrelevant" in a borderless, high-technology economy. Calgary's income levels were the highest in North America, rivalling those of Zurich. Its economy had been freed from reliance on oil and gas production by the petroleum industry's visionary reinvestment of profits extracted from Alberta's hinterlands in cleaner, sustainable energy sources. Calgary's population was somewhat older, though, of course, still especially vigorous. It was said to be distinctly Eurasian. [3]

Most strikingly, that population lived in splendid, self-imposed isolation behind an electronic wall, as safe as possible from cyber-criminals, crazed Montana terrorists, Third World refugees and the riff-raff from Vancouver and Edmonton "who come banging at our gates every time there is a wave of unemployment, or an earthquake, or a change of government." The electronic wall controlled the entry and departure of residents, each fitted with the "minor inconvenience" of identity chips; visitor access was restricted to those worthy of a temporary implant. Poverty seemingly had been abolished or else banished outside.

The *Herald* was equally silent on whether the peasants still left in rural Alberta would ever be allowed through those gates. It made no reference, in or out, to the Tsuu T'ina First Nation. It said little about real as opposed to virtual geography. It was unclear whether greater Calgary—a "city with big dreams and ambitions"—had incorporated the Rockies and the recreational property along the Eastern Slopes to which its more prosperous residents had grown accustomed to retreating a generation earlier. It did refer to a second Winter Olympics. And while it noted approvingly that Calgary had successfully distanced itself from the "Cow Town and ten-gallon hat image" of the first Olympics in 1988, it nonetheless also boasted that the Stampede was "still the world's richest rodeo." Presumably in 2025 this would mean that bull-riders, steer-wrestlers and barrel-racers, bearing their temporary chip-implants and after competing for automatic-deposit prize purses, would then be escorted out of town in their trucks and trailers along a designated mud-and-manure corridor nowhere near, say, the venerable Ranchmen's Club.

Futuristic projections tend to disclose more about the world in which they originate than the one that they envision. That much is certainly true of the *Herald's* 10-page supplement, which, tongue-in-cheek or not, would have been a forgettable piece of millennial hubris, save for the sense in which it reflected real fault-lines—political, economic, cultural—that were already close to the surface of a not-so-monolithic Alberta. To some extent, these fault-lines have been there for a century. The *Herald* and its big-city sister, the *Edmonton Journal*, historically have sometimes posed as sober guardians of the public interest against the succession of wild-eyed populist movements that coalesced in the countryside against bankers, railroads, manufacturers and lawyers, and that were once powerful enough to elect governments. Alberta society has never been so homogeneous, or so rural, as some explanations of its peculiar pattern of single-party political dominance have assumed.[4] Rural-urban tensions are not new either. In 1948, for example, an initiative for a single, publicly-owned electrical utility, which rural voters generally favoured, was rejected by the narrowest of margins in a province-wide plebiscite, thanks mostly to a long-remembered three-to-one "no" from Calgary. Indeed, Alberta's latest political dynasty has been built on a complex, sometimes delicate, coalition of urban and rural interests ever since the Progressive Conservatives formed a government in 1971—a coalition made easier to manage by the ability to spread the benefits of abundant energy royalties over potential conflicts.

There was a new triumphalism, all the same, in the *Herald*'s crystal ball-gazing, and with it an undercurrent of impatience. That triumphalism was rooted in the changing material realities of population and economic power in what had become a very urban province. By the close of the 1990s, impatience and resentment could be heard, for example, in demands from Alberta's major cities that they be granted significant legislative and fiscal autonomy, in order to position themselves competitively in a global economy and put in place the infrastructure to accommodate growth: why should their fuel taxes subsidize rural secondary highways when they had freeways to build?[5] The same tone could be heard from national radio panellists eager to differentiate Calgary, a diverse, cosmopolitan and tolerant metropolitan enclave, from the backward parts of Alberta.[6] Not least, it could be heard in the controversy over a provincial electoral map that challenged the principle of representation by population by preserving more seats in rural Alberta than numbers alone warranted. The future, like it or not, belonged to the cities.

This essay takes the year 1996 as the immediate subject for a series of reflections about the changing relationship between urban and rural. More precisely, it marks the emergence of what might be called two Albertas with starkly divergent spatial geographies and prospects. The first, concentrated in the Highway 2 corridor linking Calgary and Edmonton, and also including the northern resource boom-towns of Fort McMurray and Grande Prairie, was the Alberta reflected in cock-sure provincial self-images and in a series of dynamic economic and demographic indicators; in 1996, according to Statistics Canada, its fast-growing population was also younger and better-educated than that of any other province. The other Alberta, spatially "outer Alberta," was hidden statistically in provincial aggregates. It was increasingly "other" in at least two senses of the term. First, it *was* different. In some respects it resembled Saskatchewan more than Calgary. Its population was at best stable or declining, certainly older, far less likely to have completed a university degree, and, in most communities, whiter. Its per-capita income in some regions was less than two-thirds of what it was inside the Highway 2 corridor, and much more reliant on government transfers, including pensions. Its communities lived on the defensive, struggling to maintain schools, hospitals and other public services in the face of population losses and government cuts. And, partly as a consequence, this other Alberta had come to be understood by outside policy-makers and investors not so much as a place of settled human community but as a resource plantation, a transportation corridor or merely as empty space upon which to project large-scale industrial or recreational developments. Second, this other Alberta was an unfamiliar world. It contained no mountains or mega-malls as day-trip destinations. Too often, it was encountered only through the distance of caricatures—romantic, red-necked, even racist portrayals—against which the sophisticated and forward-looking Alberta would define itself, or from which it would aspire to be unshackled.

In reality, of course, it would have been no simple task to draw a clear line between urban and rural. The latter was the site of acreage subdivisions, bedroom communities, championship golf courses and factory farms; there was no single rural landscape. Moreover, rural people routinely worked, shopped and played in cities. Conversely, and paradoxically, Alberta's cities continued to draw mythic cultural significance from the rural—albeit the historic rural or the ersatz rural—even as they became increasingly disconnected from the working countryside and resentful of its residual political power. There was no other formative story to replace it. So Calgarians newly arrived from Vancouver or Houston, who would not think to venture further east into the countryside than 30 miles to Strathmore, joined without irony in the pageantry of white Stetsons at Stampede Week each summer, while provincial politicians clad in denim flipped flapjacks. So Edmontonians bought Wranglers and straw bales for party atmosphere when the Canadian Finals Rodeo and the annual Farm Fair came to town in November.[7] So Albertans bought more pickup trucks per capita than other Canadians, and parked many of them in suburban cul-de-sacs and downtown parking lots.[8] In August 1996 they packed arena venues for three nights each in Calgary and Edmonton to hear new-country, faux-cowboy singer Garth Brooks. They proclaimed an affinity for wide-open spaces but lived in sprawling suburban developments carved out of what used to be farm and ranch land. The maverick mythology persisted, but also obscured and disconnected. What did it mean to be an urban prairie province? And what did it mean to live in the "other Alberta," no longer at the centre, subject to decisions made elsewhere and to the powerful forces of change that those decision-makers imposed on the countryside?

II

The choice of 1996 as the year to mark a longer historical trajectory is not as arbitrary as it might seem. That year the federal government phased out the last vestiges of the historic Crow's Nest Pass freight rate, leaving prairie grain farmers fully exposed to the cost of rail transportation—save for a substantial one-time payment—and thereafter less likely to grow wheat for export. At the same time, grain companies continued their consolidation of the prairie elevator system. In 1996, the census provided a benchmark against which to measure the population effects in rural communities of restructuring and cuts to public infrastructure. It also recorded a sharp rise in the number of cattle and calves in Alberta, from 4.7 million in 1991 to almost six million in 1996—a faster growth rate than for people in the same period.[9]

In 1996 public hearings began into the proposed Luscar coal mine just outside Jasper National Park. The same year, in those parts of rural Alberta dotted with flare-stacks and criss-crossed by pipelines, serious land-use conflict had begun to emerge in response to accelerated oil and gas development and the partial deregulation of the energy industry. It was in 1996 that the soon-to-be controversial, larger-than-life Wiebo Ludwig had a 4-by-8 foot plywood sign posted outside his family's Trickle Creek farm in the northwest Peace region: "BEWARE of the mounting anger of the local residents! ABANDON any thought of further gas and oil exploration in this area!—LAISSEZ-FAIRE—."[10] The pace of industrial change belied any simple framing of the rural as bucolic and constant.

The Crow Rate had been critical to the settlement of the prairie West for agriculture. It began as an 1897 agreement between the federal government and the Canadian Pacific Railway, giving the latter a cash subsidy to extend its track into the rich mining regions of south-eastern British Columbia in exchange for reduced freight rates, "in perpetuity," on eastbound grain and westbound settlers' effects. The agreement was suspended during World War I, then reinstated by statute in the mid-1920s for grain and unprocessed grain products such as flour. This victory against the railways represented prairie farmers' collective political strength and, given their distance from ports, sustained the kind of high-volume, export-grain agriculture that lay at the economic heart of the National Policy. In some circles still, it is not uncommon to hear farmers recall the Crow as "our treaty," now "broken," parallel to those negotiated with the Cree and the Blackfoot in setting the basic terms of communal existence and livelihood on the prairies. But the Crow was contentious from the start. By the 1960s and 1970s it was a target of mounting criticism from those who argued either that it locked the prairies into the role of shipping raw materials and jobs outside the region, or that it gave the railways little incentive to improve service to farmers. The Alberta government was prominent among the critics. In the sharply-polarized debate that waged throughout the countryside when the repeal of the Crow was before Parliament in the early 1980s, it dangled visions of value-added food-processing prosperity in front of grain producers. In a publication subtitled *Freedom to Choose*, the government also pointed to the salutary effects of market discipline, proposing that no improvement in the farm economy "can occur until farmers face the impact of paying full transportation costs."[11]

The *Western Grain Transportation Act*, which took effect in 1984, had replaced fixed statutory freight-rates with a direct subsidy to the railways for hauling prairie grain. The subsidy amounted to between $500 million and $720 million annually. But this policy compromise was short-lived. In 1995 the federal Liberal government pushed through Parliament what it called "necessary and urgent" changes to grain transportation. It did so on the pretext of deficit reduction, fairness to other farm sectors, and compliance with new international trade rules. At the same time it promised a more efficient rail system, economic diversification and "new potential for farm families and rural communities" as a result of grain transportation reform.[12] To compensate for an expected decline in land values and to soften the blow politically, the federal government made a one-time, $1.6-billion payout to prairie farmers calculated on a formula that accounted for acreage, historic yields and distance from port. Alberta farmers' share was $435 million. This payout, combined with a short-term spike in grain prices, produced the last great infusion of cash into farm communities.[13] In some cases that money enabled farmers to pay off bank loans, perhaps buy a recreational vehicle and retire honourably to the nearest full-service town. It also fed another round of large-machinery capitalization and land consolidation into bigger farms that could rationalize such purchases.

The payout masked any immediate negative impact. But freight rates doubled in 1996, and have continued to rise to the point where almost a billion dollars a year is extracted from the rural prairie economy in additional shipping charges—not including the cost of trucking grain from the farm to more distant elevators. Secondary roads have taken a pounding. Export-grain production has virtually disappeared as a viable activity in the more remote Peace River region. In Alberta, more so than in Saskatchewan or Manitoba, crop diversity has actually diminished.[14]

The primary result of grain transportation reform was to reinforce the rapid expansion of the livestock industry, the flagship of provincial agriculture policy. At one level, that expansion was evident in cattle feedlots—as large as 100,000 head—concentrated especially along the Oldman River near Lethbridge. It was also evident in new or enlarged slaughter facilities in Brooks and High River, owned by

U.S.-based agribusiness corporations IBP Tyson Foods and Cargill respectively.[15] At the bottom end of this so-called value chain, grain farmers were likelier to grow feed barley, oats and hay for regional livestock consumption.[16] More of them developed cow-calf herds to supplement their income and get in on what seemed to be the one agricultural sector with a future. Indeed, the 1996 Census of Agriculture registered a statistic that ran counter to the long, if gradual, historical trend: a small increase in the number of farmers in Alberta.[17] By itself, however, the figure was somewhat misleading. These farmers were older on average than in 1991, and more of them worked off the farm, typically in construction, the oil patch, trucking, nursing and service industries in the nearest town. Still, 1996 was a relative high-water mark in numbers and net income. Five years later the Census of Agriculture reported a nine-percent reduction in the total number of Alberta farms, a hollowing out of the midsized, family-operated sector, and an acceleration of the patterns of aging, off-farm work and outright exit from the industry. According to Statistics Canada's labour force surveys, the number of Albertans employed primarily in agriculture declined by more than 10 percent annually in the years between 1998 and 2001.[18] All this was in motion *before* the events that provided fleeting national media images of a farm crisis: prolonged summer droughts and the discovery in May 2003 of a cow with bovine spongiform encephalopathy in northern Alberta.

The restructuring of grain transportation in the mid-1990s does not by itself account for the troubles in agriculture. After all, Ontario stands next to Alberta and Saskatchewan in the number of farmers lost later in the same decade. The Alberta labour-force figures are partly also a measure of the industrial scale of farm machinery, available off-farm work and, in areas such as the Highway 2 corridor, residential and recreational developments that effectively crowded out agriculture and pushed land values out of reach. Nonetheless, the redistribution of people and wealth that followed the loss of the Crow hit hardest at what was once Alberta's grainbelt: the eastern side of the province, the south and the Peace region in the north. As a government MLA task force would concede in 2004, those parts of the province had not shared in the so-called Alberta Advantage.[19]

Internal government studies, reluctantly made public, showed a province of striking regional disparities.[20] The large census districts in eastern Alberta containing Hanna and Stettler experienced population decline. Those census districts with substantial farm and/or aboriginal communities—around Fort Macleod, Slave Lake, St. Paul, Camrose, Lloydminster and Hanna—showed per-capita incomes far below the provincial average, even though they all contained pockets of significant oil and gas or other resource activity. Depending on the measure, census districts or economic regions around Medicine Hat, Athabasca and Drumheller were also out of step with the official Alberta. The disparities would have been much greater had the comparative macro-units been subdivided to distinguish between the countryside and the relatively prosperous regional centres named in this paragraph, in which retail trade and government services have been consolidated. Homestead communities with such storied names as Foremost, Cereal, Empress, Delia, Cremona, Alliance, Coronation, Lougheed, Mirror, Viking, Dewberry, Two Hills, Vilna, Waskatenau and Valleyview recorded population losses in 1996. So did larger towns like Pincher Creek, Bonnyville and Peace River. The same was true for rural municipalities far from the prospect of acreage subdivisions for urban commuters: Forty Mile, Acadia, Starland, Flagstaff, Paintearth, Minburn, Vermilion River, Smoky River.

Already in 1996, and certainly throughout the rest of the decade, the sense of emptying-out in this "other Alberta" fed a political economy of extraction and desperate local choices. The agri-food industry flourished in the form of packing plants and potato-chip factories, but the overall net return to primary producers was no greater when adjusted for inflation; in some commodity sectors, it was much lower than it had been in the mid-1970s. Profit margins narrowed. The common response—to compensate with volume—required bigger machinery, more land, more credit, more costly chemical inputs and the willingness to adopt new genetically-engineered seed varieties on the promise of higher yields. Money was still being made out of farming, but most of it slipped quickly out of local circulation. It was extracted wealth: the growing gap between gross and net returns. In a very real sense, individual survival strategies undermined community futures.

At the same time, rural Alberta was confronted with a harsher face of government than it had known for more than a generation. The so-called Klein Revolution's commitment to spending cuts, tax cuts, deficit reduction and privatization exemplified a much wider "neo-liberal" shift among the liberal democracies. The purpose of government was not to balance opportunities or defend key sectors of the economy; instead it was to create an attractive climate for mobile investment dollars in a competitive global economy. There was no more of the talk of "province-building" that had led Peter Lougheed's Progressive Conservative government to invest directly in an energy company, an airline, rail cars and west coast port facilities in the 1970s. There was no more relocation of government offices to smaller centres outside of Alberta's capital city, Edmonton. There was no more public commitment to ensuring that the quality of life in rural Alberta was equivalent to that in the cities. The trademark Alberta Advantage denoted a low-tax regime that gave a wide berth to market forces. Fiscal powers were concentrated provincially at the expense of municipal taxing authority. Large regional school and hospital districts were created—again at the expense of local control—with the effect of distancing the provincial government from the impact of cuts and narrowly casting individual board members as defenders of their community's facilities against others. Hospitals that had been over-built, sometimes for political reasons, in the Lougheed era were closed or else converted to long-term care centres for aging rural populations. School closures throughout eastern Alberta reflected but also hastened depopulation. Good professional jobs were lost. Local women who often held such jobs in hospitals, schools and social services were forced to patch together part-time work at greater distances. They spent more time as informal caregivers to aging parents. They had less time and energy for the community-building roles that they customarily had played in local volunteer organizations. Their children spent more time travelling on school buses on secondary roads that were subject to punishing new levels of traffic, mostly tandem grain-trucks and oil-service trucks, and that municipalities, absorbing cuts to transportation grants, were hard-pressed to maintain. On top of all this, the government's most lucrative new revenue source, video lottery terminals, elbowed aside community charities and extracted millions of dollars for the provincial treasury, a fraction of which was returned in well-publicized cheque presentations.[21] In 1996 rural people and municipal politicians clung to pre-election hints that the revolutionary phase of spending cuts had ended and that "reinvestment" in public infrastructure and services would soon begin.

The point was not forgotten, after all, that much of Alberta's resource wealth was extracted from beneath the countryside and that rural people lived disproportionately with the inconveniences—and sometimes serious risks—of an energy industry that benefited the whole province far too much to be curtailed. The public interest dictated development. But there had always been an ambivalence in the relationship between rural people and the energy industry. On one hand, farmers and ranchers depended on oil and gas development for off-farm work, lease revenues and municipal taxes to maintain a level of services for which they would not otherwise have wanted to pay.[22] All this was particularly true given the economic pressures of the 1990s. On the other hand, they farmed around pump-jacks, well-sites and battery stations, and above a network of pipelines that, laid end to end, would have stretched two-thirds of the way to the moon. They were sometimes left with contaminated soil, fractured water tables and diminished property values. Some of them resented that oil money had weakened an older spirit of neighbourliness in their communities. Some became increasingly convinced that hydrogen-sulphide emissions from sour-gas flares were detrimental to the health of their families and livestock. And some, who carried with them files thick with the documents of unresolved personal grievances against a particular oil company, were convinced that they knew where political power ultimately lay in Alberta. All this was particularly true in the 1990s given the changing nature of both the oil and gas industry and its public regulator.

During the first half of the decade, the provincial government had absorbed the Energy Resources Conservation Board into the Alberta Energy and Utilities Board. The new agency was given a mandate that included "discovery, development, and delivery," but not conservation; it streamlined the application process and, as a result, reduced the scope for public participation in decisions about development applications; and, by both ideological conviction and the practical effect of government staffing cuts, it leaned heavily in the direction of industry self-regulation.[23] This at a time when sour-gas and conventional oil-patch activity had intensified. For one thing, there was money to be made: the reduced royalty rates introduced by the Getty government in the late 1980s to kick-start the industry remained essentially in place even as world prices for oil bounced back from under $10 to over $30 a barrel. For another, the Alberta oil patch, once the domain of a small number of large players, now involved more than a thousand small companies operating on their own slim margins. Needing to generate revenues from every well, they were less inclined to appease landowners; and they were often harder to trace when well sites were abandoned prior to proper reclamation.

In the 1996–97 fiscal year, provincial revenues from royalties and sale of subsurface leases jumped more than 30 percent to $4.3 billion.[24] The industry drilled 7,500 new wells, produced 942,000 barrels of oil (nine-tenths of it exported) and 52 trillion cubic feet of natural gas, and generated $25 billion in revenues.[25] In support of this activity, it also continued to cut seismic lines through back-country forests. Industrial development on this scale could not coexist easily with other land uses. By 1996 the province's much-touted Special Places initiative for wilderness preservation had already been scaled back radically to allow "multiple use" so as not to "sterilize" designated areas from economic activity.[26] Family-farm agriculture, meanwhile, had become a tolerated land use so long as it did not interfere with, or was willing to live beside, large-scale energy resource developments. Most farmers made their own peace with the industry. A few of their neighbours, however, initiated lawsuits and regulatory challenges in response to the practice of gas flaring.[27] In 1996 a scientific study, funded jointly by governments and industry, raised cautious questions about the efficiency of flaring in consuming harmful gases prior to dispersal downwind.[28] It would be a number of years before the provincial government would be prodded to conduct further studies and strike a policy compromise between the interests of two of its strongest constituencies: petroleum and cattle producers.

In mid-January 1996 Premier Ralph Klein took a conspicuous drive down Highway 21. His calendar had been cleared for this road-trip when he backed out of a Team Canada trade mission to India, Pakistan, Indonesia and Malaysia. In places like Three Hills, Mirror and Bashaw, the premier told listeners that he was suffering from "dome disease"—an affliction caused by too much time in the provincial legislature—and needed to talk directly with those he had taken to calling "severely normal Albertans."[29] Indeed, he was beset by charges first raised in the legislature that his wife Colleen had purchased shares in a Calgary-based software company, Multi-Corp, at below market value, with no money down, and that some of his closest political advisors had invested in the same company about the same time Klein was promoting it while on a trip to Asia. Multi-Corp's share prices skyrocketed soon after he had officially opened its Hong Kong office. When Colleen Klein sold her $10,000 investment after the first of two investigations by the province's ethics commissioner, she made a profit of over $50,000—all of which she donated to a charity. Klein's biographer later called the lingering controversy a political "near-death experience," one in which the premier's man-of-the-people image was tarnished.[30]

Not that rural Alberta was necessarily such a safe place for the premier that January. While people on the street might have been willing to forgive the complexities of Multi-Corp—"they [Klein's critics] can find faults with everyone," one bystander said—Klein nonetheless carried other potential liabilities with him. Reports of his late-night lifestyle had never endeared him to those so-called social conservatives who expected political leaders to model a higher personal morality. A goodly number of them lived in towns like Three Hills. That was part of it. More importantly, having posed as the defender of rural hospitals to win the leadership of his party against Nancy Betkowski in 1992, and then to win an election against Laurence Decore's deficit-fighting Liberals in 1993, Klein could not assume that political amnesia would overcome people's everyday experience with the health care system. In Bashaw, where the town's hospital had been reduced to three active-treatment beds, he heard that emergency services were unavailable weekends and evenings and that dialysis patients had to drive to Wetaskiwin for treatment. He was scolded by an eighty-three-year-old woman in a hospital bed who threatened to withhold her vote next election if the cuts didn't stop. Still, the premier pronounced himself satisfied: "They're still calling me Ralph, and that's important."[31]

Rural Alberta in 1996 was a place of contradictions, not just tensions and ambivalences. This was especially true of its politics. If anything, its notorious electoral allegiance to the Progressive Conservatives was solidified during the same decade in which the provincial government's actual presence in rural communities receded as a consequence of budget cuts and centralization. The party would sweep rural Alberta in the 1997 election; once again, serious discontent would dissipate when ballots were cast. The puzzling voting patterns in the countryside—low turnout rates aside— begged for an explanation.

The fact that rural Albertans were enlisted with relatively little protest in the initial stages of the Klein Revolution owed something to the cultural residues of an older, agrarian antagonism against debt as a form, plain and simple, of captivity to the banks. It also owed something to a resonance between rural notions of self-reliance, rooted in practical experience, and the effective neo-liberal ideological campaigns of the 1990s to scale back the public sector. This resonance was partial nonetheless. It did not capture the consistent, contrary demands that had come for over a century from rural Alberta for government involvement to counter-balance the distortions of the marketplace or compensate for its limits: state-owned packing plants and grain elevators in the 1910s,[32] debt relief and lend-lease programs for land in the 1930s, public electricity in the 1940s, seniors' lodges in the 1950s, hospitals and fuel subsidies in the 1970s. For that matter, the Klein government's privatization and deregulation initiatives in health care, highway maintenance and then electricity neither originated nor found significant support in rural Alberta. Quite the contrary. It was incorrect to ascribe a free-market ideological reflex to the countryside; the puzzle of entrenched voting patterns ran deeper than that.

What has characterized rural Alberta's relationship to the provincial government for two generations is a powerful patron-client exchange that has no close parallel elsewhere in Canada.[33] This relationship is based on the patron's generous provision of public services and the client's support—even indifferent support—at election time. The chief currency of this relationship has been oil and gas revenue. Since the 1950s, it has given provincial governments the fiscal capacity to spend generously compared to other provinces, without having to resort to high levels of taxation.[34] The political bargain has been a defensible one in rural Alberta. The advantages have been tangible enough. The costs have been harder to calculate or even identify, but surely include an increase in the province's leverage over its supplicant municipalities, a gradual loss of the political skills needed for independent community self-defence and a deepening of the mentality in which, as an *Edmonton Journal* guest columnist from the village of Warspite observed in 1996, rural Albertans "have learned that it is better to be a friend of government than an enemy."[35]

The new face of government in the 1990s might have been expected to dislodge this mentality more than it actually did. After all, the patron essentially suspended the old exchange relationship. Rural populations were left increasingly to fend for themselves, with less community-level control of their futures, while new private sector capital investment poured into Calgary and the Highway 2 corridor. The situation might have called for a radical rethinking of old assumptions and a sharper political-economic analysis. Instead, one common response was to make a more desperate, fawning appeal for the favour of the premier as patron. What was the alternative? This kind of response could be found in countless letters written directly to the premier, like that from a small landowner in the Peace region who had exhausted his bank account and all avenues of bureaucratic-regulatory appeal in his fight for proper reclamation of an oil-company well site. The letter began: "I would like to thank you for being our premier. I am proud of having you represent this province. I have voted progressive conservative [*sic*] all my life"—as if that should have offered some special protection—"and I was very satisfied when you cut the debt." The three-page letter ended with a plea for the premier's personal intervention and advice on "how I can get justice in this case."[36]

In the 1990s the heated politics of electoral boundary review were deeply enmeshed with the pattern of patron-client exchange in Alberta. One thing the patron *was* still willing to do for rural Alberta was defend its level of representation in the legislature, notwithstanding the demographic shifts noted in this essay. Without doubt, this defence of an important political base, one that included Klein's imagined every-couple, Martha and Henry in Rimbey, had something to do with the interests of the premier's party and the rural MLAs in his caucus. But it was a politically tricky defence all the same. It risked a backlash from across the ideological spectrum. Already in 1992, two prominent members of Calgary's circle of conservative academics had described Alberta's electoral districts as "grossly malapportioned"—at variance with judicial requirements for the fair and effective representation of all citizens. The authors challenged the "accepted norm" of "rural over-representation," along with the standard arguments about the difficulty of serving vast constituencies, and they urged a speedy "reapportionment revolution" to achieve real representation by population.[37]

The 1993 provincial election, Klein's first as premier, was held under legal challenge within constituencies that were established by a committee of government MLAs and then approved by the legislature. Opposition members had refused to participate in the process on the principle that politicians should not set their own boundaries. The committee's task had been framed by a Supreme Court judgment in 1989 that proposed a maximum deviation of 25 percent above or below the average constituency population as the standard for relative equality of voting power. Two of the committee's members, including the chair Bob Bogle (Taber-Warner), represented ridings with less than half the population of the largest Calgary ridings. While the Alberta Court of Appeal in 1994 stopped short of invalidating the election results—that would have created a "political crisis"—it made it clear that another boundaries review was required before the next election, one that was less partisan, more in keeping with the principle of relative equality, "if Alberta wishes to call itself a democracy."[38] That review was completed in 1996. It resulted in a modest redistribution of one seat each to Calgary and Edmonton, though the premier mused publicly that those cities did not need to have more MLAs than they had municipal councillors.[39] The new boundaries preserved two large northern ridings, under special provisions of the law, at much more than a 25 percent variance, and consistently created urban ridings with more people than the average constituency population and rural ridings with less. Nonetheless, the report met with fresh rural resistance and threats of legal challenge. As one *Edmonton Journal* reporter was told on a rare foray outside the capital: "You can't just keep deleting the number of MLAs from the country and expect the country to carry on."[40]

On democratic principles, there was something indefensible about rural arguments against any further loss of ridings to the cities. Boundaries widely seen as unfair would cast a sense of illegitimacy over provincial elections and reinforce the city-state, go-it-alone tendencies already stirring in Calgary. At the same time, the arguments bespoke a genuine fear of declining political influence. Who imagined that population trends would be reversed? Beneath this fear was a crisis of political agency in rural Alberta that had multiple sources, only one of which was the dependency bred by a long history of patron-client relations. The issue of effective representation, to use the Supreme Court's words, took on its own urgent complexion outside the cities as community-level authority was eroded in significant ways in the 1990s. The displacement of meaningful decisions in education, health care and social services either to the province or to a profusion of new regional authorities—each with a set of different boundaries—frustrated the efforts of rural Albertans to form effective political communities of influence in order to defend their interests. For that matter, vast provincial constituencies *were* difficult to represent; and, geographically stable or not, they made it almost impossible for candidates to mount serious challenges at election time without benefit of name recognition or media coverage across scattered small communities. In all these ways, democracy was at risk in the other Alberta too.

IV

"City" and "country," the cultural theorist Raymond Williams once wrote, are each dynamic historical realities in themselves and in their relationship one to the other. Neither is fixed in time. Calgary is no

longer the working-class railroad city of the 1930s; the rural countryside has been industrialized. And yet, Williams argued, each is
marked by persistent, polar-opposite identities that could be traced
through several centuries of English literature: the city with the
future, with human achievement and machines, civilizing influence
and opportunity, but also moral decay, noise and crime; the country
with the past, with a "natural way of life," innocence and quiet, but
also limitation, ignorance and backwardness. These powerful images
could not be dismissed simply as illusions, even if they did not necessarily reflect the complex reality of people's lives in either setting.
Instead, he asked: What kind of experiences did these images interpret? What else did they mean? For what deeper impulses were they
a kind of ideological shorthand? And why did they recur in periods
of particular stress?[41]

Certainly these persistent polar images were alive in Alberta in
the 1990s. They could be heard in farm kitchens with a distinctly
defensive inflection. They also infused the bold triumphalism of
the *Calgary Herald's* futurists and the countless commentaries—
resentful or patronizing—that illustrated how rural people could not
count on a sympathetic treatment in the mass media. What stresses
helped to generate them? What contradictions? What cultural, if not
economic, anxieties?

One of the most thoughtful attempts at framing the contradictions around questions of identity came from Calgary-based writer
George Melnyk. In a series of essays published as *New Moon at
Batoche: Reflections on the Urban Prairie*, Melnyk asked: "Why must
the prairie city be at odds with prairie identity? Why must it be considered out of place when it is in place?"[42] This was especially so
when the countryside had been so thoroughly industrialized and
when two out of three prairie residents—even more in Alberta—
lived in cities. Melnyk then argued:

> The continuing self-image of the region is one of endless
> prairie fields or grasslands with their icons of farmers and
> cowboys holding us in its sway. The reason for this is obvious.
> The wheat farmer and cattle rancher are icons because they
> reflect the distinguishing feature of the region—its prairie

geography and a livelihood tied to it—while the Western
Canadian urban reality is viewed as the same as that of
other cities.[43]

Compared to the Metis buffalo hunter or the sunburnt farmer
on his tractor, images of the Western city are almost an
afterthought that expresses some kind of inauthenticity in
relation to the region.[44]

Melnyk's argument was no lament. It was aimed at the sense of
inferiority and inauthenticity that constituted the "vise of an urban
denying identity" and inhibited the emergence of a city-state region-
alism more in keeping with the new "digital geography." But it was
not clear what new cultural mythology might displace the "glorifica-
tion of agrarian settlement," or who was responsible for achieving
it. Melnyk's urban neighbours, with their apparently impoverished,
at least untroubled, imaginations? Other writers? Or the dwindling
population of rural people, who themselves were not necessarily
well-served by caricatures that stood in reassuringly for the complex reality of their experience and masked their place in a political
economy of extraction? Must they let go of something? Accept their
marginal place?

In *Culture and Truth*, Renato Rosaldo developed the idea of
"imperialist nostalgia," that is, the desire of a dominant coloniz-
ing culture to preserve—and thereby contain—the fragments of a
subordinated culture. It does so for a variety of reasons: mere entertainment; a yearning for what is lost, traditional, primitive, authentic; and, at the same time, a validation of its own succession against
ways of life whose displacement is both deserved and inevitable.
Imperialist nostalgia means that the agents of transformation "long
for the very forms of life they intentionally altered or destroyed."[45]
An obvious example is that of aboriginal peoples, whose communal
identities are carried forward in the names of freeways and suburban neighbourhoods, whose cultural artefacts help to differentiate Canada abroad and whose dancers and drummers are invited
to lend a distinctive (authentic?) flavour to world-class events that
happen in this country. But something like imperialist nostalgia may

also account for the enduring power of rural-based cultural mythologies in what has become a very urban Alberta: the hats, the trucks, the flapjacks and the straw bales. In the 1990s these mythologies continued to give a certain standing, and a limited political claim, to those who resembled their rural subjects: rugged individualists hard at work in wide-open spaces. But they did not confer real political or economic power. If anything, they relieved those who lived comfortably inside the dominant culture, in the inner, urban Alberta, of the need to think hard about their consumption of the rural as recreational playground and resource plantation, or about the forces that made it harder for rural people to stay where they were, make a modest living and imagine that their children could succeed them.

These same mythologies often captivated people in the outer, rural Alberta as well. The idea that there could be a single Alberta story, a single mythology, a single interest, is in large part the legacy, ironically, of agrarian populism's former hegemonic position. In the 1920s, "the people"—that is, *producers*—were imagined as a unity against the plutocratic economic parasites of central Canada. If that kind of radical populism died long ago at the hands of Social Credit, the reflex of unity against all threats to Alberta has been a more enduring, malleable feature of the province's political culture. It has underwritten the pattern of single-party dominance in the legislature. It has provided politicians with an unfailing rallying point against federal encroachments, real or imagined, on Alberta's oil resources. It was the basis for Klein's successful campaign against the "special interests" inside the province who challenged his debt-reduction revolution out of selfish regard for their public-sector salaries. In a crisis, criticism or whining could be dismissed as un-Albertan. But by the mid-1990s this legacy of unity had trapped rural Albertans. Though they lived on the fringes of the official story of prosperity and youthful energy, they were reluctant to complain; surely their struggles were their own fault. Though they suffered the messes of the energy industry, their resistance was left largely to solitary landowners with guns, or to authoritarian figures like Wiebo Ludwig who did not care to fit into communities. And though Calgary's futurists had begun to dream out loud about an unencumbered city-state, rural people could scarcely comprehend it.

The Western writer Wallace Stegner observed that, in little more than a single lifetime, it was possible on the North American prairies to witness the eclipse of two land-based cultures and economies: aboriginal and settler.[46] Though it would be wrong to consign either to the dustbin of history, it is important to mark this eclipse, and to note the curious kinship between the two, however difficult the everyday relations might be in places like Wetaskiwin, Gleichen or Cardston. Each culture has been displaced from the centre save for ceremonial occasions, when a distinctive dash of colour and history is required. But by 1996 there were signs of flourishing cultural renewal in aboriginal communities alongside the well-documented social problems. In rural farm-based communities, alongside the anxiety that could not be ameliorated entirely by the bravado of niche markets and value-added processing, there were also signs of hope in the form of energetic, small-scale cultural projects. One was the award-winning conversion of a Wheat Pool elevator into a museum in Paradise Valley.[47] In other words, rural people began telling their own stories—sentimental ones, sometimes, but balanced by the realism of the particular and the complexity of local memory.

Such tangible story-telling collaborations helped to strengthen the sinews of rural community life, draw people out of the isolation of hard work and restore self-respect. For stories "are places to live, inside the imagination. We know a lot of them, and we're in trouble when we don't know which one is ours. Or when the one we inhabit doesn't work any more, and we stick with it anyway."[48] This was Melnyk's point too. In rural Alberta, the link between small efforts at cultural renewal and a capacity for effective representation could be observed in the feisty local self-defence initiatives—to save or to stop something—that increasingly became a part of the rural political landscape by the end of the decade, around issues like schools, hog-barns or oil-field flooding. In each case, new activists identified what was at stake in the other Alberta: community survival. Perhaps the only advantage that rural people enjoyed in the telling of their own stories to fit their own contemporary circumstances was a stubborn attachment to place that, at its best, was more than instrumental, more than merely consumptive. In a global economy based on transient dollars and workers, it was downright radical in its potential.

In 1996, though, that advantage was scarcely recognized as such, and would have been thin comfort to those who saw the need for a new story in rural Alberta. They were still few in number, disconnected, and likely to be discounted by their neighbours if their talk got too political.

Author's note: This essay could not have been written without the research assistance of Stefan Epp and the many conversations I have been fortunate to have had with students and with friends from places like Kingman, Daysland, Viking, Czar, Provost, Paradise Valley, Benalto, St. Paul, Thorsby, Coaldale, Foremost, Valleyview, Debolt, and Valhalla Centre. I am grateful to all of them, and hope that I have done their worlds justice. I have also benefited from comments on an earlier draft from Cody McCarroll and Robert Nichols, both of them promising young scholars firmly grounded in rural Alberta.

Ten

# A University at Home in the Rural

*But before we plow an unfamiliar patch*
*It is well to be informed about the winds,*
*About the variations in the sky,*
*The Native traits and habits of the place*
*What each locale permits, and what denies.*

Virgil, *The Georgics*

*It requires a great deal of courage to be parochial.*

Patrick Kavanagh, "The Parish and the Universe" [1]

I

In July 2004 the private undergraduate college at which I'd taught for
more than a decade, enduring enough financial stress and vocational
doubt to understand the farm crisis almost as an insider, became a
campus of the University of Alberta. I was appointed acting dean and
then the first dean. The "transition," as it became known, required
the negotiated blessing of the church owners—no easy thing, given
nine decades of educational history on the same site. More than
that, it required tangible assurances for internal and external audiences, including alumni, that a large, research-intensive university
would respect and enable our campus, Augustana, in the small city of
Camrose, to preserve the commitments to first-rate university teaching and the development of well-rounded students on which it had
built a reputation. To their credit, the University's senior adminis-
trators glimpsed as much potential in the campus as any of us had
in the creative era, long past, during which my colleagues and I had

been hired from places like Queen's, McGill, UBC, York and Western; they insisted that it should not become a feeder campus or a pale imitation of what happened in Edmonton. But the University, like the provincial government, also introduced an important new word—*rural*—into its stated rationale for Augustana's incorporation into the public post-secondary system: a "strategic link to rural Alberta," the continuation of a "rural-based" campus. In short order "Augustana" and "rural" became conjoined.

The adjective rural, it is fair to say, evoked a measure of disbelief and discomfort on campus. Though our students come disproportionately from small prairie and northern communities, recruited to what is promoted as a safer, friendlier, human-scale campus, those same rural students know that Camrose—population 16,000—is not really rural; for there is nothing like its full line of fast-food franchises and big-box retailers, let alone traffic lights, back home. And though our professors are prepared to endure the designation "rural" for tactical reasons, assuming it can release new sources of government funding, some of them wear it warily, concerned that it might diminish them in academic circles or bear some hidden implications for their own teaching and research. They had not thought of themselves as rural before.

This wariness is neither surprising nor difficult to understand. Apart from its prettiest places, now often colonized as recreational property, rural is increasingly unfamiliar territory. Almost everywhere in the world, it is the subject of degrading, mostly unchallenged cultural caricatures. Rural is inferior, red-necked, backward. On network television it is fair game for ridicule: a backdrop for a third-rate celebrity's flirtation with the simple life, or else a recruiting ground for reality-show "hillbillies" whose habitation of a Beverly Hills mansion promised a fresh, funny programming angle.[2] At a slightly more elevated level, sociologist Richard Florida's popular book, *The Rise of the Creative Class*, gives a social-scientific gloss to the idea that thinkers, artists, creators—engines of the new knowledge economy—will flock to the most tolerant and progressive of big cities, determining which of them flourishes into the future; rural communities are nowhere on his map.[3] Even the late Jane Jacobs, an admirable thinker on many subjects, identifies the city almost exclusively as the site of

intellectual, cultural and economic life.[4] In step, think-tank economists advise governments to reallocate public resources to major
cities where most people now live, abandoning "dependent" rural
communities to "find their natural level,"[5] and lecture rural people,
especially in hard-pressed resource sectors, simply to relocate.

The idea of a long, irreversible transition from traditional to
modern societies, from rural to urban, simple to complex, is not just
an organizing principle of western social science; it is our common
cultural conceit. In economics it is somehow "natural"—like the law
of gravity, and not a consequence of political and social choices—
that wealth, like rain, though it falls everywhere, should flow downhill in widening streams and ultimately pool in the major financial capitals of the world. The educational parallel of this naturalis-
tic, gravitational fallacy is that intelligence, even when it falls in the
remotest rural highlands, must also be refined and pooled on metropolitan campuses.[6] Indeed, in the great 20th-century migration to the
cities, the university has served as an important transmission belt
from rural childhoods to urban professional careers.[7]

Whether it can be retooled to serve a contrary purpose, that
is, to help reverse the flow of people and knowledge, is part of the
counter-cultural challenge for a campus—my own—that is close
enough to the rural, if not directly in it, to be able to see and experience it through our students. While it is not unusual in the United
States to find major state universities and leading liberal arts colleges
in smaller centres, Camrose is the smallest Canadian city west of
Lennoxville, Quebec, with a conventional public university campus.
Geographically it is what I have called a border city between two
Albertas: one relatively young, urban, prosperous; the other, aging,
rural, hanging on—almost fatalistic about losing its young people
and attracting young professionals even as health care and schools
are consolidated in larger centres. What is the university to them?
What use is a liberal education? By its location and by its mandate,
the Augustana campus does have a distinct opportunity to define for
itself what it means to be a university genuinely at home in the rural.
This is more than a matter of providing a less intimidating or less
distant point of access to post-secondary education for students. It
is more than local jobs and economic spin-offs. A university at home

in the rural will inflect its professoriate, its curriculum and its business practices with a critical appreciation of its particular place in the world. And it will treat its location not as a ready-made excuse for mediocrity but, quite the contrary, as a reason for its rightfully high aspirations.

II

*The diversity with which we presume to challenge students should include that rarest of all academics, the learned professor at home in a place.*

Eric Zencey, "The Rootless Professors"[8]

The heart of any university, its teaching and research, is its professoriate. And so it stands to reason that in order for a university to be at home in the rural its professors, at least a sufficient number of them, must also be at home there. They must enjoy it. They must appreciate its people, understand its cultural cadences and find satisfaction as scholars in the questions it enables them to ask. But this is not so easily accomplished. It cuts against the deep grain of inherited intellectual and institutional prejudices. The idea that the university should be at home *anywhere* in particular, or that thinking, its core activity, should somehow be rooted in a place—much less a rural place—will be unfamiliar, perhaps oddly threatening.

The University of Wales at Aberystwyth, where I once held an appointment as visiting scholar, is a spectacular case in point. It was built in the 1870s in the shell of an abandoned hotel project in an aspiring Victorian-era seaside town. The funds were raised mostly from small donations in a subscription campaign that involved more than 100,000 Welsh households: farmers, miners, slate-quarry workers, widows and, on University Sundays, non-conformist worshippers at chapels in every valley. This great common undertaking was to be the people's university. Perhaps no school could possibly have lived up to such high expectations. While Aberystwyth achieved prominence after 1919 in the then-new academic field of international politics, which it still holds, despite its relative isolation in the United Kingdom, it also betrayed the strongest hopes of some of its initial subscribers. The flagship University of Wales, for example, did not offer courses in the Welsh language until it was prodded to do so in the 1960s by a resurgence of popular nationalism. Instead, though it is a fine university, it conspired in what it was meant to reverse: the tendency of higher education to alienate students from their communities of origin. As I learned from a long, heated pub conversation, an outsider's question about rootedness could bring to the surface a long-suppressed point of contention among department members.

Often enough, and still, universities are tempted to answer one-sidedly to other imperatives. For one thing the road to academic respectability—whether in curriculum or in faculty hiring—runs most reliably through emulation and sameness. For another, the academy at its most high-minded has imagined that it needed to set itself against or diminish the particular in its pursuit of a higher, larger, more universal or more mobile truth. Clifford Geertz writes that the "fear of particularism," even in his own subject, anthropology, for all its field studies, is almost an "academic neurosis."[9] By contrast, the virtue of generalization and detachment is at least as old as the Greek philosopher Aristotle. In one fragment he proposed that philosophy was not just the greatest of intellectual goods but also the most accessible. Its practitioners needed "no tools or places for their work." They could take it up "wherever in the world" they set their "thought to work," since they did not so much claim a particular home in the world as feel at home in the activity of thinking.[10] The critical power of this ethos has been demonstrated and reinforced over the centuries whenever scholarship has prevailed over narrower national and ecclesiastical prejudices. Contrarily, for example, the submission of too many German universities and professors to the Nazi regime, anxious not to appear "rootless cosmopolitans," constitutes the most sobering lesson in its favour. In his Reith Lectures, the late Edward Said celebrated the exile—actual and metaphoric—as the model intellectual; for the exile, he argued, is least tempted by the "rewards of accommodation, yea-saying, settling in."[11] Indeed, the field of international politics, in which I began my career, may have become an "American social science" after World War II but, paradoxically, its dominant figures were mostly displaced European emigrés. In at least some cases the result was a welcome, if world-weary, theoretical distancing from the patriotic dictates of Cold War politics.[12]

Principled indifference to the particularities of place, of course, is not confined to any single academic discipline or theoretical orientation. It may be one of the few points of intellectual convergence between social scientists who still aspire to generalizable, replicable knowledge and their post-modern critics, whose purpose is precisely to *unsettle*, if not in a strictly geographic sense, then in a way that problematizes all categories of space and belonging. This gives an overwhelmingly placeless orientation to most academic research, both mainstream and critical. It could originate as easily in Aberystwyth or Camrose as in New York; it is probably important to its reception that it be read as having no particular point of origin. The best thinking is not supposed to be bound by its location. But there is a price to be paid for this principled indifference. While it may safeguard scholars in extreme times, it can also prevent them from serving or even noticing the people with whom they share an immediate geography.

The practical realities of tight university job markets, in which faculty positions are filled by competitive national and international searches, only reinforce this powerful disposition. Young professors may have geographic preferences, but, looking for a foothold, hired on the basis of conventional merit criteria, they will tend to accept an appointment wherever it is offered—and then, since academic career mobility is restricted, they may stay there until retirement. Likely it will not be in a rural setting, and less likely still in a part of the world that is familiar to them. The odds in the academic hiring lottery are against it. One historian from rural Arkansas, who eventually did land a job that enabled him to return to live on the family farm, put it this way:

> An acute sense of place most often works at odds with a career in academe.... So most academics simply try to find that good, tenure-track job, wherever it may be, and adapt to the surroundings as best they can. After all, don't we make a living with our minds? What difference does it make where you teach World Civilization or Composition I?... But to some of us our physical surroundings, our place, is integral to our lives as academics and as thinkers.[13]

Such a sense of place and displacement is relatively rare in the university. More prevalent is what Geertz has identified as an "exile from Eden syndrome" among professors in a society that prizes upward mobility. Their unconventional career paths begin "at the perceived heart of things," with graduate education at a small number of elite universities, from which they are cast out to teach, if they are that fortunate, at the perceived fringes.[14] Few of them ever return to teach at the centre; some of the others never get over the fact that they ended up where they are, resent it, and take it out on colleagues, students and the community in which they live.

Professors who are genuinely at home in a place need not be native to it. They should be capable of settling in it and taking up what Zencey, at Goddard College in Vermont, once called a "dual citizenship": not only in the world of books and ideas, "but also in the very real world of watersheds and growing seasons and migratory pathways and food chains and dependency webs." I am well aware, though, that to propose a different ethos or to temper the principled indifference to place is to set out on a unfamiliar intellectual path. The American rural writer and philosopher Wendell Berry, having "abandoned" a position at New York University, as some saw it, for a less prestigious one near his boyhood home in Kentucky, had such a path in mind when he wrote that universities and professors needed a "beloved country," a point of reference *outside* the academy itself, typically, the region or community or neighbourhood in which the university is located.[15] Much as I do not wish to quarrel with Aristotle or Edward Said, my own academic experience has taught me something closer to Berry's position: as a scholar and teacher, I had to be at home where I was. It helped that I could claim a beloved country in the rural prairie West—the world in which I grew up and from which many of my students come. It was in the summer of my greatest despair about my career having reached a premature dead-end in an academic backwater that I read Berry for the first time, but, no less important, discovered the Battle River valley, its high places, its local histories, and learned to pay attention again to the farming communities around me. None of this is a consolation prize. It led to things different and better than I had expected.

III

*We educate the young, from country and city alike, to be*
*urban with urban appetites, skills, minds, dependencies, and*
*expectations.... If the human future will be as much (or more)*
*rural as urban, what will the young need to know in order to*
*build prosperous rural communities in the century ahead?*

David W. Orr, "Re-ruralizing Education," [16]

The Augustana Campus is home to about 1,000 students. They come
from around the world and across Canada, but disproportionately
they come from small cities and rural communities across central and northern Alberta, western Saskatchewan, northern British
Columbia, and the Northwest Territories. A surprising number of
them are first-generation university students. Some come from high
schools with a graduating class of a dozen; they may be the only ones
to go on to university. On balance, they are less worldly, less prepared,
less confident, say, than the students I had taught at Queen's. But
they are more teachable, less ideological, less committed to fixed positions—surprisingly, perhaps, since they come from federal constituencies with some of the largest Conservative voting pluralities anywhere in Canada. They recognize the importance of degree credentials for career purposes, of course, but in my experience they leaven
that sort of common instrumental thinking about university education with a refreshing openness to the possibility that it could change
them in ways they can only vaguely imagine when they start.

Certainly they are aware of the costs. Rural students who, as a
matter of course, must live away from home to attend university are
in a disadvantageous financial position before they pay tuition. This
structural inequality partly explains the great, growing gap between
post-secondary participation rates for rural and urban young adults.[17]
In recent years, the prospect of lucrative oil-patch work for strong,
unskilled young men has only widened that gap. But the cultural
barriers and costs are no less significant. The stories of bright high-
school graduates who return home from university by Christmas,
unable to cope with a large, impersonal campus or adult freedoms,
are familiar in every small town. So are the stories of uncles or
aunts—the smart ones, encouraged to go to school—who lost contact

with home once they went off to university, and who remain the subject of the kind of family talk that tells young people, or spouses, how much is at stake in making the same choice.

For rural students, to go to university is still to risk estrangement. If their openness and respect for education is mixed with a measure of guardedness, it is for good reason. When one of our recent graduates—someone who fits the characterization two paragraphs above— told a faculty retreat that he appreciated the sense of home he found on our campus, he said so in a powerfully revealing way: he was "not made to feel ashamed of where he came from." Evidently he had expected otherwise. It is easy enough to confirm in rural students, at age 18, a sense of backwardness and inferiority about their upbringing. They already suspect as much. For generations, indeed, they have paid much of the price inflicted by professors in exile, who "tend to mistake 'disconnected from locale' for 'educated'"—and "to think of education as little more than an organized assault on the parochial point of view."[18] For their students, it follows that university education is experienced as a kind of "cultural disenfranchisement":

> I came to college knowing plenty about growing seasons and a little something about watersheds and ecology, though I did not yet have those words. I was just coming out of adolescence; rebellion had worn thin my allegiance to home. It did not take someone as intellectually eager, impressionable, and malleable as I was long to grasp the real coin of my new realm and shift my allegiance. When it needed careful attention and nurture, my own knowledge, the wisdom absorbed from the fields and woodlots was scythed out from under me. Enamored of the bookish, heady world opening before me, I would not begin to count my losses for years.[19]

There are plenty of points of estrangement in a student's experience of the university. Many of them are pedagogically important. But the organized assault on parochialism in students is ultimately a destructive one, encouraging their alienation from—rather than their critical appreciation of, and their ability to live in—the worlds they know. The point is not that local pieties and prejudices should never be challenged. It is, rather, that those challenges can only effectively and genuinely happen within the context of a responsible relation to a beloved country and those who inhabit it.[20]

A university at home in the rural will have a curriculum that is inflected with an attentiveness to place, finds pedagogical opportunities near home, and instills in students a critical affection for it. That curriculum by definition cannot be a generic one. Students in Camrose and downtown Toronto ought to experience an education that is differentiated, not by the quality and credentials of their professors, but by the histories, cultures, watersheds, literatures and public-policy challenges that frame those respective settings. Otherwise the thinking that is required of professors and students alike risks becoming dangerously isolated from the local responsibilities that flow from it. This is not an argument about whether to surrender either the historic canons of western civilization or the academic requirements of preparedness in any particular discipline to a more provincial agenda. There need be no such either-or choice. Rather, the argument is about good teaching—the kind that looks for points of recognition and finds a larger historic, cultural or ecological significance in the familiar; the legacies of British imperialism and the spectre of global warming, for example, are no mere abstractions in the post-settler society and the increasingly arid landscapes of east-central Alberta. It is also a matter of hospitality to treat students—regardless of whether they expect it—as themselves rooted in real places, stories and cultures, and, if they are from further away, as capable of learning to love their own and another place through such attentiveness.

A university at home in the rural will have a curriculum that is also inflected with an element of physicality as one legitimate, indeed ancient, means of knowing. Physicality may mean standing in the same Arctic river as one of Sir John Franklin's early expeditions or helping to build a school from adobe brick in a Mexican village. It may mean making music or art. Stretching the conventional bounds of a liberal education, it might also mean at least one opportunity, alongside courses in mathematics, sociology, art history or French literature, to design and make a piece of furniture or clothing, to rebuild a machine, to grow and prepare food. Such manufacture would do more than join head and hands in good work. It would provide a sense of accomplishment and make a counter-cultural statement against the near-complete separation of production and consumption that characterizes late-modern societies. Most of all, it would restore something of the classical ambition and literal definition of a liberal education for a new generation: that is, the preparation of free citizens. People who depend entirely on large-scale, corporate-owned, long-distance systems to deliver food, energy and shelter, and who lack the practical skills to provide any of those basic necessities for themselves, have a more precarious hold on freedom than they know. Those skills, in turn, are worth claiming as the terrain of liberal education. As David Orr has observed in a thoughtful essay:

> re-ruralization will require the adoption of a more liberal liberal arts curriculum, one that includes food, agriculture, land, water, energy, shelter design, wildlife, and forests... [W]e are becoming a food-dumb society, fed by technicians and ignorant of the most basic facts about what we eat (including how unhealthy much of the industrial diet is), with what consequences, and at what true cost to ourselves and others. These are fit subjects for liberal inquiry and, unless approached with great pedagogical dullness, are not inherently any more "vocational" than, say, poetry or chemistry. Such subjects are worthy of admission into the liberal arts curriculum because they are central to life and to the human prospect.[21]

While Orr imagines that all universities could respond creatively to such a challenge—he gives the example of an inner-city gardening and direct-marketing food project sponsored by Rutgers—a university at home in the rural ought to lead in the development of a curriculum that combines elements of practical knowledge, critical reflection and meaningful community engagement.

Finally, the kind of university I have described will resist the presumption that its graduates can only be counted successful—and celebrated in its alumni magazine—if they have a metropolitan mailing address. It will encourage them to live and work in rural places, or at least allow them to imagine a future there. It will prepare graduates to meet the desperate need for professionals in small communities free of the false opposition between education and career. Those graduates, however, will be generalists, not specialists. In other words, they will be prepared for rural practice and for participation in the full life of rural communities—as active, globally aware citizens, readers, coaches, musicians, dramatists. They will have absorbed the benefits of a holistic, on-campus education: encounters with cultural and ideological differences, with ideas, books and the arts, with international opportunities that require a critical mass. They will have learned to think for themselves. And they will have been equipped with the skills—part of the informal curriculum of any worthy university degree—that rural people in Alberta once understood as being foundational to a democratic society and their own collective self-defence: a sense of critical judgment and perspective; the ability to present a position, hear contrary positions and find principled accommodation among them; and the experience of working together with other people to build and sustain the institutional vehicles of community action.

In addition to all this, a university home in the rural will do business in a way that reflects what it knows about regional ecology, culture and political economy. It must be mindful of the fact that in rural places words and deeds must align under close and long-term scrutiny; there is no hiding behind marketing campaigns. Of course a university as employer and purchaser must balance any commitment it makes, say, to local procurement against the responsibility of careful stewardship of public funds. But there is still a balance to be struck, not just more economic efficiency to be squeezed out at the lowest price. A university at home particularly among the agriculture-based communities of the rural West will showcase local food producers at its public events and follow the lead of the University of Toronto, of all places, in mandating that a significant proportion of the food served in its cafeterias come from local producers who can meet its ethical guidelines.[22] In doing so, it will create teaching moments and serve the public interest in encouraging the development of a sustainable, healthier, more regionalized food system.

The university at home in the rural will be a good neighbour. It will understand that it exists in a web of reciprocal regional obligations. It cannot flourish on its own. It has things to contribute out of its institutional capacity and its particular scholarly and artistic strengths. Its campus should not be a fortress. Its doors ought to be open for concerts, plays, literary readings and lectures on topical subjects. Its professors ought to be its public faces in the core communities from which it draws its students. They should be involved, as they are at Augustana, in such things as initiatives to sustain wildlife biodiversity, preserve heritage buildings, write local newspaper columns, establish a French immersion program or perform a concert to help a nearby community—which has hosted our Canadian and Mexican exchange students—raise funds to rebuild the local hockey arena after a fire.

For a university to identify with and serve its region in this way is *not* to limit its curricular, research or recruitment horizons, which are properly national and international. It is *not* to stop thinking—the university's core activity—or to lower expectations. There is no reason to do so. At Augustana, however, it does mean that we take a special satisfaction when our student choristers from places like Camrose and Forestburg—and a director from Castor—take the stage at Carnegie Hall in New York for Mozart's *Requiem*; or small-town students from Tilley and Lac La Biche find a sense of vocation in an ecology field-research course in Costa Rica; or graduates from Thorsby and Athabasca, Daysland and St. Paul, take their place among the brightest professionals and young scholars of their generation—without forgetting or disparaging the places from which they come. Likewise, it means that we have been reminded of the liberating power of education when a farmer returns to school in mid-life to complete a degree and, after graduation, enlists his former professors to give a series of seminars for his neighbours, deepening a relationship between campus and community that, like all rural relationships, is built on face-to-face personal contact. Each of those experiences, those students, those linkages, answers the question of what difference it would make if our campus did not exist where it is.

Contemporary universities are complex organizations. They must balance—and sometimes challenge—the expectations of students, governments, granting agencies and industry. They must encourage the self-directed intellectual energies of professors in diverse academic disciplines while fostering a culture of conversation that resists the fragmentation of the university into silos of specialists. They must gesture appropriately towards "excellence" and "world-class." They do not necessarily succeed at such difficult balances. One provocative critic has suggested that the university now essentially exists in ruins—having succumbed to the "logic of accounting" in every realm of its existence. Conscientious teaching, research and service may still happen, he argues, but without the overarching coherence and purpose, whether political, cultural, linguistic or religious, by which universities once framed those activities.[23]

Set against the complexity of this everyday work, even this sense of institutional crisis, the injunction for universities to be self-consciously at home in the world, wherever they are located, is liable to be dismissed as faddish or peripheral or anachronistic, or else as an attempt to curry political favour. Instead, it ought to be understood as foundational and potentially restorative.

For a university to be at home in the rural, in particular, will require uncommon courage. For its professors to claim a dual citizenship in both the academy and in the complex communities and watersheds that surround their campuses will require integrated lives and a practical, sociable intelligence. Such citizenship, however, will come with its own rare rewards. One is the chance to see from the clarity of the cultural and geographic margins. Another is the chance to claim a beloved country and engage it through relationships built on friendship, meaningful inquiry and a shared sense of larger purpose.

# Notes

## Introduction

1. David G. Smith, "On Discursivity and Neurosis: Conditions of Possibility for (West) Discourse with Others," *Dianoia* 3/4 (Spring 1994): 50–51; reprinted in David G. Smith, *Pedagon: Meditations on Pedagogy and Culture* (Bragg Creek, AB: Makyo Press, 1994).
2. That list includes Wendell Berry, Sharon Butala, Barbara Kingsolver, Peter Mathiessen, M. Scott Momaday, Kathleen Norris, Marilynne Robinson, Wallace Stegner, Guy Vanderhaeghe, Rudy Wiebe and Larry Woiwode—Canadian and American writers who are respectful of words, rural places and rural people.
3. Wallace Stegner, "The Provincial Consciousness," *University of Toronto Quarterly* 43 (1974): 307.
4. Charles Taylor, *Sources of the Self: The Making of the Modern Identity* (Cambridge, MA: Harvard University Press, 1989), chs. 1–2.
5. "Introduction," in Catherine McNicol Stock and Robert D. Johnston, eds., *The Countryside in the Age of the Modern State: Political Histories of Rural America* (Ithaca, NY: Cornell University Press, 2001), 8. Similarly, literary scholar Steven Justice has written that it is important to read "canonical literature from its social outside, from great regions of rural experience and practice." *Writing and Rebellion: England in 1381* (Berkeley: University of California Press, 1994), 5.
6. Statistics Canada, "Farmers Leaving the Land," *The Daily*, 22 February 2002.
7. Robert Kaplan, *An Empire Wilderness: Travels into America's Future* (New York: Random House, 1998).
8. Alasdair MacIntyre, "Politics, Philosophy and the Common Good," in Kelvin Knight, ed., *The MacIntyre Reader* (Notre Dame: University of Notre Dame Press, 1998), 237–38.
9. The word "nostalgia" is commonly used pejoratively to parry criticism of the direction of mainstream agriculture and its negative impact on rural communities. I prefer Trevor Harriott's rehabilitation of the word as form of a yearning "for the time when we were still on speaking terms with our landscapes," *River in a Dry Land: A Prairie Passage* (Toronto: Stoddart, 2001), 3.
10. I first explored this idea in "The Political De-skilling of Rural Communities," in Roger Epp and Dave Whitson, eds., *Writing Off the Rural West: Globalization, Governments, and the Transformation of Rural Communities* (Edmonton: University of Alberta Press, 2001), 301–24.
11. "The Canadian Clearances: Hour 2–The New Rural Activism," CBC Radio One, *Ideas*, first broadcast September 8, 2004.
12. Wendell Berry, *What Are People For?* (New York: Farrar, Straus & Giroux, 1990), 117.

## One   The Measure of a River

1. N. Scott Momaday, *The Way to Rainy Mountain* (Albuquerque: University of New Mexico Press, 1969), 83.
2. *The Journal of Anthony Henday, 1754–55: York Factory to the Blackfeet Country,*" ed. Lawrence Burpee (Toronto: Canadiana House, 1978; first printed, 1907], 25. On the unreliability of Henday's geographic references see Eldon Yellowhorn, "The Never-Ending Journey of Anthony Henday," in *Alberta Formed Alberta Transformed*, vol. 1, eds. Michael Payne, Donald Wetherell and Catherine Cavanaugh (Edmonton: University of Alberta Press; Calgary: University of Calgary Press, 2006).
3. Wendell Berry, *The Long-Legged House* (New York: Ballantine Books/Audubon Society, 1971), 161.
4. Wallace Stegner, "The Sense of Place," in *Where the Bluebird Sings to the Lemonade Springs: Living and Writing in the West* (New York: Random House, 1992), 204.
5. My historical sources include J.G. MacGregor, *The Battle River Valley* (Saskatoon: Western Producer Books, 1976); Stan Hambly, ed., *The Battle River Country: An Historical Sketch of Duhamel and District* (New Norway, AB: Duhamel Historical Society, 1974); *The Golden Trail* (Camrose, AB: The Camrose Canadian, 1955).
6. Berry, *The Long-Legged House*, 144.
7. Albert Borgmann, *Crossing the Postmodern Divide* (Chicago: University of Chicago Press, 1992), especially ch. 5, quotation at 117.
8. Borgmann, 126.
9. Martin Heidegger, "Building Dwelling Thinking," in *Poetry, Language, Thought*, trans. Albert Hofstadter (New York: Harper and Row, 1971).

## Two   Oklahoma

1. Linda Hogan, "Heritage," reprinted in *Red Clay: Poems and Stories* (Greenfield Center, NY: Greenfield Review Press, 1991.
2. Antonio Gramsci's injunction is cited from Edward Said's *Orientalism* (New York: Random House, 1978), 25, which gives a fuller version of the passage than does the standard English translation of *The Prison Notebooks* by Quintin Hoare and Geoffrey Nowell Smith (New York: International Publishers, 1971), 325.
3. The verse is my own.
4. While I first heard Black Kettle's story orally, his words here are those recounted from archival sources in Stan Hoig, *The Peace Chiefs of the Cheyenne* (Norman, Okla.: University of Oklahoma Press, 1980), ch. 7, *passim*, long quotations at pages 112, 114. See also Dee Brown, *Bury My Heart at Wounded Knee: An Indian History of the American West* (New York: Henry Holt, 1970), ch. 4.
5. Jacob Klaassen's words are from *Memories and Notations about My Life*, trans. Walter Klaassen (n.p., 1964). See also John W. Arn, *The Herold Mennonite Church, 70th Anniversary, 1899–1969* (North Newton, KS: Mennonite Press, 1969); and Allan Teichroew, "World War I and the Mennonite Migration to Canada to Avoid the Draft," *Mennonite Quarterly Review* 45 (1971): 219–49.
6. Lawrence Hart's account of the centennial re-enactment is from a short essay, "I am a Cheyenne Peace Chief," part of a packet of materials distributed by Mennonite Central Committee in the early 1990s.
7. White Buffalo Woman's story is recounted, e.g., in Henrietta Whiteman, "White Buffalo Woman," in Calvin Martin, ed., *The American Indian and the Problem of History* (New York: Oxford University Press, 1987), 162–70. See also Richard Hardorff, *Washita Memories: Eyewitness Accounts of Custer's Attack on Black Kettle's Village* (Norman, OK: University of Oklahoma Press, 2006).

**Three    Hanley, Saskatchewan**

1.  *Hanley: The Story of the Town and District*, Prepared by the Pupils of Hanley High School, Jubilee Year, 1955, 68.
2.  William Thorsell, "In a land where mobility means opportunity, denying children both is immoral," *Globe and Mail*, February 19, 1994.
3.  Wallace Stegner, *Wolf Willow: A History, a Story and a Memory of the Last Plains Frontier* (New York: Viking Press, 1962), 306.
4.  For historical detail I have relied primarily on *Hanley: The Story of the Town and District*, especially ch. 1–5.
5.  *Hanley: The Story of the Town and District*, 65–66.
6.  Glen Sorestad, "Hawarden Hotel," in Dennis Cooley, ed., *Draft: An Anthology of Prairie Poetry* (Winnipeg: Turnstone Press, 1981), 145.
7.  Joseph A. Amato, *Rethinking Home: A Case for Writing Local History* (Berkeley: University of California Press, 2002), 3.
8.  Kathleen Norris, "Can You Tell the Truth in a Small Town?" in *Dakota: A Spiritual Geography* (Boston: Houghton Mifflin, 1993), 83.
9.  One exception is Guy Vanderhaeghe's *Homesick* (Toronto: McClelland and Stewart, 1989). Another is Bonnie Burnard's *A Good House* (Toronto: HarperCollins, 1999), which contains a wonderfully recognizable description of the cultural skill and characteristic way of a group of men who are renovating a main-floor bathroom for the dying wife of one of them, and who "toned down" the rough language of a younger newcomer "by declining to respond in kind, by taking the trouble to choose their own words. They were in the habit of controlling talk this way and they didn't think badly of him, they just assumed he'd been raised differently." (41–42)
10. Raymond Williams, *The Country and the City* (Oxford: Oxford University Press, 1973), 298.
11. Kieran Bonner, *A Great Place to Raise Kids: Interpretation, Science and the Rural-Urban Debate* (Montreal and Kingston: McGill-Queen's University Press, 1997), ch. 10.
12. Walter Klaassen, *"The Days of Our Years": A History of the Eigenheim Mennonite Church, 1892–1992* (Rosthern, SK: Eigenheim Mennonite Church, 1992), 1.
13. Alistair MacLeod, *No Great Mischief* (Toronto: McClelland and Stewart, 1999), 160.
14. Ed White, "Old towns fade away, but will never die," *Western Producer*, 16 December 1999.
15. Ian Doig, "The party's next door," *FFWD Weekly* (Calgary), 30 June 2005.
16. The Lawrence house was described in 1955 as "one of the best testimonies to Hanley's vanished grandeur" (*Hanley: The Story of the Town and District*, 68). Its interior was the subject of great childhood speculation. I was never inside it.


**Four    "Their Own Emancipators"**

1.  One of the two "boys" in question was Morris Jevne (1915–2005). Before he died, it was my great, coincidental pleasure to meet him, escort him across my campus—his *alma mater*—and ask him to confirm the details of the story I had heard. He did.
2.  *Camrose Canadian*, 15 February 1933.
3.  *Camrose Canadian*, 26 July 1933. A UFA Sunday picnic at Avonroy is described in the same paper on 14 June 1933.
4.  Sheldon Wolin, *The Presence of the Past* (Baltimore: The Johns Hopkins University Press, 1989), 34.

5. "Dr. Chester A. Ronning, O.C., C.C.," inducted 1983, Alberta Order of Excellence *http://www.lieutenantgovernor.ab.ca/bio/ronning.htm* (accessed 11 July, 2006).

6. David Laycock, *Populism and Democratic Thought in the Canadian Prairies, 1910 to 1945* (Toronto: University of Toronto Press, 1990), 3. Laycock's book remains the best introduction to prairie agrarian ideas. See also Lorne Brown's introduction to the reissue of Paul Sharp, *The Agrarian Revolt in Western Canada: A Survey Showing American Parallels* (Regina: Canadian Plains Research Center, 1997; originally published, Minneapolis: University of Minnesota Press, 1948).

7. Bradford Rennie, *The Rise of Agrarian Democracy: The United Farmers and Farm Women of Alberta, 1909–1921* (Toronto: University of Toronto Press, 2000), 4, 5.

8. Rennie, *Agrarian Democracy*, ch. 1–2.

9. Sharp, *The Agrarian Revolt in Western Canada*, 75.

10. Wood is difficult to position ideologically. During the Cold War, his biographer William Kirby Rolph was anxious to point out that while Wood was sometimes accused of being a "red" and a "dangerous agrarian radical," "he was in fact a conservative." See *Henry Wise Wood of Alberta* (Toronto: Univeristy of Toronto Press, 1950), 217. While Wood had distanced himself from certain radical and labourite elements in the UFA by the late 1920s, backing John Brownlee as premier, he was steeped in the work of Marx, the social evolutionism of Herbert Spencer, and the turn-of-the-century American social reformers. Moreover, Wood was no friend of the "soft Liberal" Manitoba Progressives under T.A. Crerar.

11. William Irvine, *The Farmers in Politics* (Toronto: McClelland and Stewart, 1920; repr. 1976), quotations at 24, 57, 117, 146–47, 171, 191, 206.

12. Mary Parker Follett, *The New State: Group Organization, the Solution of Popular Government* (New York: Longmans, Green & Co., 1918), quotations at 3, 5, 11. Follett cites the NPL in North Dakota as one "interesting instance" in the U.S. of political organization along occupational-group lines, "from which we may learn much" (329).

13. *How to Organize and Carry on a Local of the United Farmers of Alberta?* (Calgary: United Farmers of Alberta, 1919), quotations at 12, 14. This pamphlet is part of the University of Alberta Library's digital archive at *http://peel.library.ualberta.ca/ bibliography/4540.html*.

14. Nanci Langford, "'All that Glitters': The Political Apprenticeship of Alberta Women, 1916–1930," in Catherine Cavanaugh and Randi Warne, eds., *Standing on New Ground: Women in Alberta* (Edmonton: University of Alberta Press, 1993), 75–76; Rennie, *Agrarian Democracy*, ch. 5.

15. Rennie, *Agrarian Democracy*, ch. 4–6. The movement culture was also built by a common songbook, including its anthem, "Equal Rights for All," with songs and music written by H.W. Gothard (1920).

16. See, e.g., Carl Betke, "The United Farmers of Alberta, 1921–1935," in Carlo Caldarola, ed., *Society and Politics in Alberta* (Toronto: Methuen, 1979).

17. R.J.E. Cook, *The UFA Experiment: 1920–35* (Edmonton: Alberta Woodsworth House Association, 1985), 8.

18. Betke, "The United Farmers of Alberta," 25.

19. Quoted in Carl Betke, "The UFA: Visions of a Co-operative Commonwealth," *Alberta History* 27 (Summer 1979): 9.

20. W.L. Morton, *The Progressive Party in Canada* (Toronto: University of Toronto Press, 1950), says that the Alberta MPs were the 'doctrinaire group in the Progressive caucus" (168). See also Sharp, *The Agrarian Revolt in Western Canada*, ch. 9. Needless to say, Preston Manning might have identified himself in a long tradition of western-based populist reformers, but he would have been distinctly out of place in the Alberta-based Ginger Group.

21. From a 1926 editorial by Walter Smith in *The UFA*, quoted in Laycock, *Populism and Democratic Thought*, 89.

22. Cf. Donald Wetherell and Irene Kmet, *Town Life: Main Street and the Evolution of Small-town Alberta* (Edmonton: University of Alberta Press, 1995), ch. 2.

23. See, e.g., Laycock, *Populism and Democratic Thought*, ch. 5; C.B. Macpherson, *Democracy in Alberta: Social Credit and the Party System* (Toronto: University of Toronto Press, 1953); John Irving, *The Social Credit Movement in Alberta* (Toronto: University of Toronto Press, 1959); Alvin Finkel, *The Social Credit Phenomenon in Alberta* (Toronto: University of Toronto Press, 1989); Bob Hesketh, *Major Douglas and Alberta Social Credit Ideology, 1932–1948* (Toronto: University of Toronto Press, 1997). This section of the essay is extracted from Roger Epp, "The Political De-skilling of Rural Communities," 314–16.

24. Irving, *The Social Credit Movement in Alberta*, 317.

25. Laycock, *Populism and Democratic Thought*, 293.

26. Morton, "A Century of Plain and Parkland," in Richard Allen, ed., *A Region of the Mind* (Regina: Canadian Plains Research Center, 1973), 178.

27. Doug Owram, "1951—Oil's Magic Wand," in Michael Payne, Donald Wetherell and Catherine Cavanaugh, eds., *Alberta Formed, Alberta Transformed* (Edmonton: University of Alberta Press; Calgary: University of Calgary Press, 2006), vol. 2, 566–86; Ed Shaffer, "The Political Economy of Oil in Alberta," in David Leadbetter, ed., *Essays on the Political Economy of Alberta* (Toronto: New Hogtown Press, 1984); John Richards and Larry Pratt, *Prairie Capitalism: Power and Influence in the New West* (Toronto: McClelland and Stewart, 1979), ch. 3–4.

28. Finkel, *The Social Credit Phenomenon*, 122.

29. Norman Priestley and Edward Swindlehurst, *Furrows, Faith and Fellowship* (Edmonton: Alberta Agricultural Centennial Committee, 1967); Grace Skogstad, "Farmers and Farm Unions in the Society and Politics of Alberta," in Caldarola, ed., *Society and Politics in Alberta*, 226–27.

30. Macpherson, *Democracy in Alberta*, ch. 8.

31. Macpherson, *Democracy in Alberta*, 226. Reg Whitaker once scolded the academic left for the "injustice" of dismissing farmers, historic farm movements and their "petit-bourgeois mentality": "They went down before the implacable onslaught of the market, of industrialization and urbanization, but they went down fighting, with some dignity and not a little imagination in their stand against the forces oppressing them. Certainly they and their leaders mounted a more impressive counterattack than the organized working class or its leaders have ever mounted against some of these same forces." Introduction, *The Farmers in Politics*, xii.


## Five   Statues of Liberty

1. *Twenty-One Years of Progress, 1924–1945* (Saskatoon: Saskatchewan Co-operative Producers, 1946), n.p.

2. On the contested history of modern property in land, see James C. Scott's *Seeing Like a State* (New Haven: Yale University Press, 1998), ch. 1.

3. "The Twelve Articles of the Upper Swabian Peasants" [1525], reprinted in Michael Baylor, ed., *The Radical Reformation*, Cambridge Texts in the History of Political Thought (Cambridge: Cambridge University Press, 1991), Appendix B.

4. "To the Assembly of Peasants' [1525], in Baylor, ed. *Radical Reformation*, 107–8.

5. Hans Hergot, "On the New Transformation of the Christian Life," in Baylor, ed. *Radical Reformation*, 217–8. Emphasis is mine.

6. Christopher Hill, *The World Turned Upside Down* (London: Temple Smith, 1972).

7. Gerrard Winstanley, *The Law of Freedom and Other Writings*, ed. Christopher Hill (Cambridge: Cambridge University Press, 1983), 102, 287. *The Law of Freedom* was published in the same year as Thomas Hobbes's *Leviathan*. For those familiar with the latter, Winstanley's reasoning around authority and freedom is strikingly different.

8. Hill, *The Law of Freedom*, quotations at 295, 380–81, 383.

9. John Locke, *The Second Treatise of Government,* ed. C.B. Macpherson (Indianapolis: Hackett, 1980), ch. 5. While Locke is often associated with doctrines of limited government and unlimited accumulation, it is clear to me that he develops his position on the difficult ground prepared by the Levellers.

10. Barbara Arneil, "The Wild Indian's Venison: Locke's Theory of Property and English Colonialism in America," *Political Studies* 44 (1996): 60–74. Deploying the standard of productive use, Locke asked rhetorically "whether in the wild woods and uncultivated waste of America, left to nature, without any improvement, tillage, or husbandry, a thousand acres yield the needy and wretched inhabitants as many conveniences of life, as ten acres of equally fertile land do in Devonshire, where they are well cultivated."

11. Jean de Crevecoeur, *Letters from an American Farmer*: Letter II, "On the Situation, Feelings and Pleasure of an American Farmer" (New York: E.P. Dutton, 1957), 17–18. On these points Crevecoeur attracted the notice of the philosopher Jean-Jacques Rousseau's followers in pre-revolutionary France.

12. Catherine McNicol Stock, *Rural Radicals: Righteous Rage in the American Grain* (Ithaca, NY: Cornell University Press, 1996).

13. Hannah Arendt, *On Revolution* (New York: Viking, 1996). Note her relevant remarks on Jefferson and the "lost treasure" of the American Revolution (ch. 6), as well as Crevecoeur's dissent (132–37).

14. Thomas Jefferson, "Notes on the State of Virginia" [1781–82], in Merrill D. Peterson, ed., *The Portable Thomas Jefferson* (New York: Penguin, 1975), 227.

15. Paul B. Thompson, "Thomas Jefferson and Agrarian Philosophy," in Paul B. Thompson and Thomas C. Hilde, eds., *The Agrarian Roots of Pragmatism* (Nashville: Vanderbilt University Press, 2000), 118.

16. Thomas Jefferson, "Letter to James Madison," in *The Portable Thomas Jefferson*, 396–97.

17. Simon Hornblower, "Creation and Development of Democratic Institutions in Ancient Athens," in John Dunn, ed., *Democracy: The Unfinished Journey* (Oxford: Oxford University Press, 1992); Victor Davis Hanson, *The Other Greeks: The Family Farm and the Agrarian Roots of Western Civilization* (New York: Free Press, 1995).

18. See, e.g., Xenophon, *Oeconomicus*, trans. E.C. Marchant (London: William Heinemann, 1979); Aristotle, *The Politics,* trans. T.A. Sinclair (Harmondsworth: Penguin, 1962), 240–43. There is, in fact, an intriguing historical correlation between agrarian communities in their early stages and strong democracy, whether the *landgemeinde* colonies of the late-medieval north-European frontier or the homestead settlements on the North American prairies. On the former see William TeBrake, *Medieval Frontier: Culture and Ecology in Rijnland* (College Station, TX: Texas A & M University Press, 1985).

19. Hannah Arendt, *The Human Condition* (Chicago: University of Chicago Press, 1958), 65. See also Jill Frank, who attributes to Aristotle a very similar middle position on property of "holding things as one's own *for common use*." See *A Democracy of Distinction: Aristotle and the Work of Politics* (Chicago: University of Chicago Press, 2005), ch. 2.

20. Thomas Jefferson, "Notes on the State of Virginia, in *The Portable Thomas Jefferson*, 217. Similar alarm about the coming age of manufactures is sounded in Alexis de Tocqueville's *Democracy in America* [1831], ed. Thomas Bender (New York: Modern Library, 1945), vol. 2, 450–54. Note also Tocqueville's comments on the well-read farmers he met on the frontier, 189–90.

21. Thomas Jefferson, "Letter to Brother Handsome Lake," and "Second Inaugural Address," in Bender, ed., *The Portable Jefferson*, 307, 318.

22. Lawrence Goodwyn, *The Populist Movement: A Short History of the Agrarian Revolt in America*, (New York: Oxford University Press, 1978), 69.

23. This was true, for example, of the Missouri-born Alberta farm leader Henry Wise Wood, whose library included volumes of Marx's work.

24. Karl Marx, *Capital*, vol. 1 (New York: Modern Library, 1906), 555–56; "The Eighteenth Brumaire of Louis Bonaparte," in *Selected Writings*, ed. Lawrence Simon (Indianapolis: Hackett, 1994, 202–03). Like Locke, Marx himself was no agrarian. He shared the conventional Victorian prejudices about the achievements of industrial capitalism—not least its having rescued people, in that infamous phrase in the *Communist Manifesto*, from the "idiocy of rural life."

25. Quoted in James Bissett, *Agrarian Socialism in America: Marx, Jefferson, and Jesus in the Oklahoma Countryside* (Norman, OK: University of Oklahoma Press, 1999), 66.

26. See, e.g., C.B. Macpherson, *Democracy in Alberta: Social Credit and the Party System* (Toronto: University of Toronto Press, 1953); Gavin Burbank, "Agrarian Socialism in Saskatchewan and Oklahoma: Short-run Radicalism, Long-run Conservatism," *Agricultural History* 51 (1977): 173–80. As Scott shows in *Seeing Like a State*, ch. 6, the greatest interest in North America in Soviet-style collectivization came from agronomists impressed by the experiment in farming on an industrial scale. The Soviets, in turn, had learned much from the largest frontier farms in the American plains.

27. Goodwyn, *The Populist Movement*, vii.

28. See Georgina Taylor, "'What Can We, the Plain Common People, Do?': Violet McNaughton and the Hillview Local of the Saskatchewan Grain Growers' Association," in Murray Knuttila and Bob Stirling, eds., *The Prairie Agrarian Movement Revisited* (Regina: Canadian Plains Research Center, 2007), 31–59.

29. William Irvine, *The Farmers in Politics* (Toronto: McClelland and Stewart, 1920, repr. 1976), 202.

30. Edward A. Partridge, *Manifesto of the No-Party League of Western Canada* (Winnipeg: DeMonfort Press, 1913), 1, 5, 7.

31. Edward A. Partridge, *A War on Poverty* (Winnipeg: Wallingford Press, 1925). See also Murray Knuttila, *"That Man Partridge": E.A. Partridge, His Thoughts and Times* (Regina: Canadian Plains Research Center, University of Regina, 1994).

32. Irvine, *The Farmers in Politics*, quotations at 117, 146, 24.

33. Wood, like many others, had read or absorbed Herbert Spencer on social evolution and adaptation. I am quoting from Wood's short articles (including "RE the U.F.A.—How Organized and Purposes") and the transcript of the Medicine Hat speech found in the Walter Norman Smith and Amelia Turner Smith fonds (M-1157-102; M-1157-50) at the Glenbow Museum's digital archive, accessed at *http://asaback.archivesalberta.org:8080/access/asa/documents/display/GLEN-257.*

34. W.C. Clark, "The Country Elevator in the Canadian West," Bulletin of the Departments of History and Political and Economic Science, Queen's University, No. 20, July 1916, 1.

35. See, e.g., Brett Fairbairn, "A Century of Prairie and Saskatchewan Farm Co-operatives," in Knuttila and Stirling, eds., *The Prairie Agrarian Movement Revisited*. He makes clear that co-operation was not a natural expression of prairie character and that "harsh circumstances do not by themselves produce idealistic co-operators" (96). See also the essays on various Canadian co-operative leaders and thinkers in Part I, "Memory," of Brett Fairbairn, Ian Macpherson and Nora Russell, eds., *Canadian Co-operatives in the Year 2000* (Saskatoon: Centre for the Study of Co-operatives, University of Saskatchewan, 2000).

36. Quoted in David Laycock, *Populism and Democratic Thought in the Canadian Prairies, 1910–1945* (Toronto: University of Toronto Press, 1990), 122–23. See also Parlby's radio talk, "Farm Women and the Co-operative Movement," in *The Canadian Wheat Pools on the Air*, a series of short national broadcasts published by the three prairie pools in 1935.

37. See, e.g., *The Wheat Pools in Relation to Rural Community Life in Western Canada* (Winnipeg: Canadian Wheat Pool, 1935).

38. Richard Levins, *Willard Cochrane and the American Family Farm* (Lincoln: University of Nebraska Press, 2000), 5.

39. Vernon Fowke, *The National Policy and the Wheat Economy* (Toronto: University of Toronto Press, 1957), 292.

40. See Deborah Fitzgerald's fine essay, "Accounting for Change: Farmers and the Modernizing State," in Catherine Stock and Robert D. Johnston, *The Countryside in the Age of the Modern State: Political Histories of Rural America* (Ithaca, NY: Cornell University Press, 2001).

41. In 1934, for example, while the prairies were ravaged by drought, drifting soil and grasshoppers, the president of the Manitoba Wheat Pool, Paul Bredt, carefully raised some fundamental questions in a national radio broadcast: "Is this a warning by Nature herself that we should take stock? Have we failed to make the best use of our fertile acres?...Is it possible that we have produced too much? Are we injuring instead of helping ourselves by producing more of some products than the world will buy, even when it is freely offered below the cost of production?" Bredt's concern was not just economic. While he defended farmers against charges of "wheat mining," he stated that "the land we live on is not merely a field for careless exploitation." He called for better farming practices and questioned, in particular, the conversion of "excellent ranching lands" into "poor farming areas." See "The Land We Live On," in *The Canadian Wheat Pools on the Air*, 20–22.

42. Wendell Berry, *The Unsettling of America: Culture and Agriculture* (San Francisco: Sierra Club, 1977), 41.

43. Berry, *Unsettling of America*, 19.

44. Wendell Berry, *Another Turn of the Crank* (Washington, DC: Counterpoint Books, 1995), 33.

45. Berry, *The Unsettling of America*, 191.

46. Berry, *Another Turn of the Crank*, 33–34, 13. For a collection of recent essays including Berry's retrospective on *The Unsettling of America* see Norman Wirzba, ed., *The Essential Agrarian Reader: The Future of Culture, Community and the Land* (Lexington: University of Kentucky Press, 2003). The collection is introduced by the writer Barbara Kingsolver, who has emerged as a leading voice of the new agrarianism.

47. Cody McCarroll, unpublished review. See also James Montmarquet, "American Agrarianism: The Living Tradition," in Thompson and Hilde, eds., *The Agrarian Roots of Pragmatism*. While regarding Berry as the "leading agrarian writer of our times" (51), Montmarquet says that the "relief of drudgery" especially for farm women has been no small achievement. McCarroll is now engaged in an important PhD study on the figure of the smallholder.

48. Darrin Qualman, "Corporate Hog Farming," in Roger Epp and Dave Whitson, eds., *Writing Off the Rural West: Globalization, Governments and the Transformation of Rural Communities* (Edmonton: University of Alberta Press, 2001), 22. In recent years the NFU has produced a series of research studies challenging the association of scale with efficiency. See *http://www.nfu.ca/briefs.html*.

49. See, e.g., Vandana Shiva, *The Violence of the Green Revolution: Third World Agriculture, Ecology and Politics* (London: Zed Books, 1991); *Monocultures of the Mind: Perspectives on Biodiversity and Biotechnology* (London: Zed Books, 1993); *Biopiracy: The Plunder of Nature and Knowledge* (Boston: South End Press, 1997).

50. Wendell Berry, "The Prejudice Against Country People," *The Progressive*, April 2002.

51. The book is *A Survey of Chinese Peasants*, by Chen Guidi and Wu Chuntao. See Wenran Jiang, "Prosperity Based on Poverty and Disparity," *China Review*, Spring 2004.

52. José Bové, "A Farmers' International?" *New Left Review* 12 (November–December 2001): 89–101; and, with Francois Dufour, *The World is Not for Sale* (London: Verso, 2001).

53. See the interview with leader Joao Pedro Stedile, "Landless Battalions," *New Left Review* 15 (May–June 2002): 77–104.

54. "The Struggle for Agrarian Reform and Social Changes in the Rural Areas" [2000], accessed at *http://rds.org.hn/via/theme-agrarian.htm*. See also Annette Aurelie Desmarais, *La Via Campesina: Globalization and the Power of Peasants* (Halifax: Fernwood, 2007).

55. "Biodiversity, Biosafety and Genetic Resources" [2000], accessed at *http://rds.org. hn/via/theme- biodiversity.htm*.

56. Thomas Frank, *What's the Matter with Kansas? How Conservatives Won the Heart of America* (New York: Henry Holt, 2004).

57. Eric Freyfogle, "Introduction," in Freyfogle, ed., *The New Agrarianism: Land, Culture, and the Community of Life* (Washington, DC: Island Press, 2001).

58. In a fascinating book, Richard Sennett suggests that the traditions of craft and work might sustain an egalitarian, self-governing citizen-politics along Jeffersonian lines. See The Craftsman (New Haven: Yale University Press, 2008), ch. 10.

59. There is a wonderfully articulate example of the rural-urban culture divide—all about work–in a published essay by a 12-year-old Manitoba girl whose family was forced off its farm. Meighan Bambridge, "My father used to be a farmer," *Western Producer*, June 1, 2000. The genius of older communal rural practices of work, including barn-raising and butchering bees, was that they moderated conflict among people who had to live together by engaging them in shared work. See, e.g., Daniel Kemmis, *Community and the Politics of Place* (Norman, OK: University of Oklahoma Press, 1990), ch. 6. Any account of the rural culture of work, however, would also have to acknowledge how hard it can be on its own members. It can reinforce a harsh, debilitating honour-and-shame code that assigns respect in relation to apparent prosperity—"*he* worked for it"—or blame when farm failure comes to light. It can also privilege "men's" work, and the social standing and household authority derived from it, over against "women's" work.

60. I am indebted to Jacie Skelton of Brandon, Manitoba for the parallelism in Western Canada that is book-ended by the *Dominion Lands Act* and the *Indian Act* in the 1870s—creating two separate legal, political, and social identities–and by the Task Force on Agriculture and the federal White Paper that in 1969 promised to abolish "special status" for Indians. In other words, there were too many farmers and too many Indians. Both needed to be integrated into the urban mainstream. I have developed a larger argument on related points in "We Are All Treaty People," also in this volume. The historical record is complex. See, e.g., Sarah Carter, *Lost Harvests: Prairie Indian Reserve Farmers and Government Policy* (Montreal and Kingston: McGill-Queen's University Press, 1993); and, in the U.S., Benjamin Heber Johnson, "Red Populism? T.A. Bland, Agrarian Radicalism, and the Debate over the *Dawes Act*," in Stock and Johnston, eds., *The Countryside in the Age of the Modern State*.

## Six    Populists, Patriots and Pariahs

1. Michael Baylor, ed., *The Radical Reformation,* Cambridge Texts in the History of Political Thought (Cambridge: Cambridge University Press, 1991); Hans-Jürgen Goertz, *The Anabaptists*, trans. Trevor Johnson (London: Routledge, 1996); Peter Blickle, *From the Communal Reformation to the Revolution of the Common Man*, trans. Beat Kümin (Leiden: Brill, 1998), and *The Revolution of 1525: the German Peasants' War from a New Perspective*, trans. Thomas A. Brady Jr. and H.C. Erik Midelfort (Baltimore: The Johns Hopkins University Press, 1981).

2. Hans Hergot, "On the New Transformation of the Christian Life," in Baylor, ed., *The Radical Reformation*, 210–11.

3.  Hannah Arendt, *The Origins of Totalitarianism,* vol. 1, *Anti-Semitism* (San Diego: Harcourt Brace Jovanovich, 1951), 23. Cf. David G. Rempel, "The Mennonite Commonwealth in Russia: A Sketch of its Founding and Endurance, 1789-1919," *Mennonite Quarterly Review* 48 (1974): "The overwhelming majority of Mennonites were absolutely apolitical. Few of them read Russian newspapers; they knew little of the seething cauldron of agitation that was threatening the Czarist regime, except insofar as they...heard it from their seasonal laborers" (52).
4.  Johann Jantzen, *Accounts of Various Experience in Life: A Diary Begun in the Year 1839*, trans. 1976, 1-2.
5.  *The Diaries of David Epp*, 1837-1843, trans. and ed., John B. Toews (Vancouver: Regent College, 2000), 2 October 1841, 158.
6.  *The Diary of Jacob Klaassen*, trans. Henry Klaassen, ed. Marie Spencer (Saskatoon: n.p., 1997), 24 May 1939, 540.
7.  *A Mennonite in Russia: The Diaries of Jacob D. Epp*, trans. and ed. Harvey L. Dyck (Toronto: University of Toronto Press, 1991), 11 June 1867, 232.
8.  *The Diary of Jacob Klaassen*, 12 May 1937, 480.
9.  *Old and New Furrows: The Story of Rosthern* (Rosthern, SK: Rosthern Historical Society, n.d.), 609.
10. William Lyon Mackenzie King, Personal diaries, Public Archives of Canada, 16 February 1926.
11. *The Diary of Jacob Klaassen*, 9 August 1928, 248.
12. Gavin Burbank, *When Farmers Voted Red: The Gospel of Socialism in the Oklahoma Countryside, 1910-1924* (Westport, CN: Greenwood, 1976); James Bissett, *Agrarian Socialism: Marx, Jefferson, and Jesus in the Oklahoma Countryside, 1904-1920* (Norman, OK: University of Oklahoma Press, 1999).
13. *The Diary of Jacob Klaassen*, 18 May 1938, 509.
14. Catherine Stock, *Rural Radicals: Righteous Rage in the American Grain* (Ithaca, NY: Cornell University Press, 1996).
15. "Schleitheim Confession of Faith," in J.C. Wenger, ed., *Glimpses of Mennonite History and Doctrine* (Scottdale, PA: Herald Press, 1947), 206-13.
16. "The Augsburg Confession [1530]: Preface to the Emperor," trans. F. Bente and W.H.T. Dau, in *Triglot Concordia: The Symbolical Books of the Evangelical Lutheran Church* (St. Louis: Concordia Publishing House, 1921), 37-95. Accessed 14 July 2006 at "Project Wittenberg," <http://www.iclnet.org/pub/resources/test/wittenberg/concord/web/augs-000.html>
17. William Keeney, *The Development of Dutch Anabaptist Thought and Practice from 1539 to 1564* (Nieuwkoop: B. de Graaf, 1968), ch. 7, at 185.
18. Cornelius Krahn, *Dutch Anabaptism* (Scottdale, PA: Herald Press, 1981), 238. Amsterdam would have been a partial exception to the norm. After independence from Spain, Mennonites achieved a degree of commercial wealth and social prominence, as well as a qualified citizenship, though they would not be eligible to hold public positions for two centuries.
19. I have not seen the volume. It is the subject of Walter Klaassen, "A Belated Review: Martin Klaassen's *'Geschicte der Wehrlosen Taufgesinnten Gemeinden,'*" *Mennonite Quarterly Review* 49 (1975): 43-52. According to the summary, the volume reflects "an attitude of awe and reverence bordering on obsequiousness towards the monarchs of the time" (48)—Prussian, Russian and Austrian—and a hostility towards the recent constitutional reforms in Prussia that had interposed a "sheet of paper" between the king and his subjects, not least Mennonite ones.
20. Walter Klaassen, *"The Days of Our Years": A History of the Eigenheim Mennonite Church, 1892-1992* (Rosthern, SK: Eigenheim Mennonite Church, 1992), 55-56.
21. J.S. Woodsworth, *Strangers Within Our Gates* (Toronto: F.C. Stephenson, 1909), 287.
22. On the targeted recruitment of German-speaking immigrants see David Smith, *Prairie Liberalism: The Liberal Party in Saskatchewan, 1905-1971* ((Toronto: University of Toronto Press, 1975), ch. 2; J. William Brennan, "Wooing the 'Foreign

Vote': Saskatchewan Politics and the Immigrant, 1905–1919," *Prairie Forum* 3 (Spring 1978): 61–77.

23. I am relying on a poll-by-poll analysis of election results completed as research for an unpublished B.A. Honours thesis, "Mennonite Involvement in Federal and Provincial Politics in Saskatchewan, 1905–1945," Department of Political Science, University of Alberta, 1984.

24. Fred Richard Belk, *The Great Trek of the Russian Mennonites to Central Asia, 1880–1884*, Studies in Anabaptist and Mennonite History, No. 18 (Scottdale, PA: Herald Press, 1976). Great-grandfather Jacob Klaassen recounts this journey in his *Asienreise* [1941], translated into English as *Grandfather's Description of the Trip to Central Asia, 1880* (n.p., 1964). His rationale for the journey is entirely about the introduction of compulsory military service in the 1870s, the failure of Mennonite delegations to St. Petersburg—his father among them—to change policy, and the invitation from the Russian military governor in Tashkent to settle where they would be able to live according to their faith and exempt from taxation. A version of this story that follows closely on my family's history told in Rudy Wiebe's novel, *Sweeter than All the World* (Toronto: Alfred A. Knopf Canada, 2001), ch. 12: "The Holy Community of the Bride." In the novel, a wayward character in the novel, beside his Oklahoma-born father's hospital bed in 1941, observes that the "enormous stupid madness of a trek...has lain over my life like a blanket" (184). Some of us can glimpse what this means even unto the third and fourth generations.

25. On Roosevelt's popularity, see James C. Juhnke, *A People of Two Kingdoms: The Political Acculturation of the Kansas Mennonites* (Newton, KS: Faith and Life Press, 1975), ch. 6.

26. Quoted in Burbank, *When Farmers Voted Red*, 57–58.

27. Burbank, *When Farmers Voted Red*, 36–37.

28. Quoted in Burbank, *When Farmers Voted Red*, 19–20.

29. Quoted in Burbank, *When Farmers Voted Red*, 143.

30. Klaassen, "A Belated Review," 49–50.

31. Jacob Klaassen, *Memories and Notations About My Life, 1867–1948*, trans. Walter Klaassen (n.p., 1964), 29.

32. Charles Tilly, ed., *The Formation of National States in Europe* (Princeton: Princeton University Press, 1975).

33. On this particular controversy in early 17th-century Holland and its relation to modern political philosophy and international law, see Roger Epp, "'To Enlighten Artless Innocence ...': Grotius, the Law of Prize, and the Idioms of Political Exclusion," *Conrad Grebel Review* 12 (Winter 1994): 63–78.

34. Frank H. Epp, *Mennonites in Canada*, vol. 1 (Toronto: Macmillan, 1975), ch. 15.

35. John Herd Thompson, *The Harvests of War: The Prairie West, 1914–1918* (Toronto: McClelland and Stewart, 1978), 37–38.

36. The respected Canadian parliamentary scholar Norman Ward once described the legislation as "the most remarkable franchise act ever passed in Canada, and even possibly in the democratic world," since it was devised to exclude those least likely to support the national government. *The Canadian House of Commons: Representation* (Toronto: University of Toronto Press, 1963), 226.

37. Quoted in Epp, *Mennonites in Canada*, vol. 1, 381.

38. Jean Bethke Elshtain, *New Wine and Old Bottles: International Politics and Ethical Discourse* (Notre Dame: Notre Dame University Press, 1998), 8–9. See also James H. Fowler, "Creating an Atmosphere of Suppression, 1914–1917," *The Chronicles of Oklahoma* 59 (summer 1981): 202–23.

39. Burbank, *When Farmers Voted Red*, ch. 6–7; Bissett, *Agrarian Socialism*, ch. 7; James H. Fowler,"Tar and Feather Patriotism: The Suppression of Dissent in Oklahoma During World War I," *The Chronicles of Oklahoma* 56 (winter 1978–79): 409–30.

40. Fowler, "Tar and Feather Patriotism"; O.A. Hilton, "The Oklahoma Council of Defense and the First World War," *The Chronicles of Oklahoma* 20 (1942): 18–42.

41. Hilton, "The Oklahoma Council of Defense and the First World War," *The Chronicles of Oklahoma* 20 (1942), 36.

42. The diary of John Klaassen's father Michael is excerpted and translated in Rose M. Klaassen, "Mennonite Diary," *Liberty*, September/October 1985, 8–10. It was at Fort Leavenworth that two Hutterite men from South Dakota who had made similar principled refusals died as a result of prolonged physical abuse. A valuable resource is Bethel College's on-line oral history collection of interviews with Mennonite World War I draftees. Accessed 16 July 2006 at *http://www.bethelks.edu/ services/mla/holdings/ohww1*.

43. Epp, *Mennonites in Canada*, vol. 1, ch. 16. There are mixed reports about an incident in the town of Rosthern involving veterans who forced their way into the Mennonite church, flung the pulpit Bible and hung a black flag—the anarchist flag?—from the church steeple. Apparently, they also tried to coax a "converted" cow into the church in order to make a point about how easy and expedient it had been for some to avoid military service. See Frank H. Epp, *Mennonite Exodus: The Rescue and Resettlement of the Russian Mennonites since the Communist Revolution* (Altona, MB: Canadian Mennonite Immigration and Relief Council, 1962), 98–99. There is a much more circumspect account of the incident in the local history, *Old and New Furrows* (291), which suggests that the veterans had themselves been raised as Mennonites.

44. Statutes of British Columbia, *Provincial Elections Amendment Act*, 1919, 9 George V, ch. 25.

45. Frank H. Epp, *Mennonites in Canada*, vol. 2 (Toronto: Macmillan, 1982), 183.

46. Adolf Ens, "Mennonite Relations with Governments, Western Canada, 1870–1925," unpublished PhD dissertation, University of Ottawa, 1979), 373.

47. J. Winfield Fretz, "Recent Mennonite Community-building in Canada," *Mennonite Quarterly Review* 18 (1944): 5–31; Epp, *Mennonites in Canada*, vol. 2, ch. 5.

48. House of Commons, *Debates*, 14 April 1927, 2530.

49. T.D. Regehr, "Bankers and Farmers in Western Canada, 1900–1939," in John Foster, ed., *The Developing West* (Edmonton: University of Alberta Press, 1983), 324.

50. "Not Soulless," *Lethbridge Herald*, 21 September 1937, 4; also 20 September 1937, 1, 3. It might be pointed out that in 1919 one of the most unequivocal parliamentary supporters of a ban on Mennonite immigration was the Liberal W.A. Buchanan, whose family also published the *Herald*. See House of Commons, *Debates*, 30 April 1919, 1912–13.

51. Williams's articles appeared in the *Leader-Post* October 17, 19, 21, 22, 23, 24, 26, 27 and 28—always beginning on the front page. Toews's initial letter appeared November 7 under the headline, "Soviet Russia in a Different Light." See also Epp, *Mennonite Exodus*, 273–74; and Ivan Avakumovic, *Socialism in Canada* (Toronto: McClelland and Stewart, 1978), 52.

52. "Barrage of Queries as Williams Speaks Here," *Saskatoon Star-Phoenix*, 5 December 1931.

53. See Patrick Kyba, "Ballots and Burning Crosses–the 1929 Election," in Norman Ward and Duff Spafford, eds., *Politics in Saskatchewan* (Don Mills, ON: Longmans, 1968); Smith, *Prairie Liberalism*, ch. 4–5. Interestingly, the Klan had a brief and influential moment in Oklahoma politics, too, in the mid-1920s. Burbank, *When Farmers Voted Red*, ch. 8.

54. Howard Palmer, "Nativism and Ethnic Tolerance in Alberta: 1920–1972," unpublished PhD dissertation, York University, 1973, 96–97, 152, 155–56. There is a subtler tendency to blame the victims for the "dangers," "suspicions" and "discord" created by racial and religious settlements, as encouraged by the

214    Notes

railways, in the *Report* of the Saskatchewan Royal Commission on Immigration and Settlement (Regina: King's Printer, 1930), quotations at 188. The *Report* is available through the digital archive at <http://peel.library.ualberta.ca/bibliography/5500.html>.

55.  William Calderwood, "Pulpit, Press and Political Reactions to the Ku Klux Klan in Saskatchewan," in S.M. Tominenkoff, ed., *The Twenties in Western Canada* (Ottawa: National Museum of Man, 1972), 213.

56.  Seymour Martin Lipset, *Agrarian Socialism: The Cooperative Commonwealth Federation in Saskatchewan* (Berkelely, CA: University of California Press, 1950), 208.

57.  Andrew Milnor, "The New Politics and Ethnic Revolt, 1929–1938," in Ward and Spafford, eds., *Politics in Saskatchewan*, 160–61.

58.  This is true in my family as well though they had not lived in Russia for half a century. Jacob Klaassen records such news on two occasions in May 1930 (*Diary of Jacob Klaassen*, 295–96). He also mentions sending money to a cousin still in Russia (28 April 1933, 371) and to the one remaining minister in his former village there (26 March 1934, 395).

59.  Ulrich's ministerial papers, speeches and pamphlets in the Provincial Archives of Saskatchewan are filled with examples.

60.  *Saskatchewan Valley News*, 24 May 1944. For the flavour of Tucker's rhetoric see his speech in the Commons, *Debates*, 7 March 1944, 1287–88.

61.  C.A. Dawson, *Group Settlement: Ethnic Communities in Western Canada* (Toronto: Macmillan, 1936), 146–47.

62.  Nova Scotia MP Clarence Gillies, for example, urged respect for the exemption from military service given as a "solemn undertaking" by the Canadian government in 1873: "Unless we want to go further than we have gone in imitating Hitler we should not start off by tearing up these obligations." House of Commons, *Debates*, 12 November 1941, 4312.

63.  Epp, *Mennonites in Canada*, vol. 2, ch. 2.

64.  *Saskatchewan Commonwealth*, 10 April 1940.

65.  *Saskatoon Star-Phoenix*, 2 June 1952.

66.  Stock, *Rural Radicals*, 148–49. I have a distant familial interest in the U.S. militia movement. In 1985, a young man who was raised essentially as a son by relatives in southeast Nebraska was sexually abused, tortured—skinned alive—and fatally shot in the head when he attempted to leave the Posse Comitatus farm compound to which he had been drawn amid the rural anger of the times. See the *New York Times*' coverage: "Torture and Murder Tied to Survivalist Group Stun a Nebraska Farming Community," 24 August 1985; "Cult Leader and Son Convicted in Nebraska Torture and Murder," 11 April 1986.

67.  Charles Taylor, *Modern Social Imaginaries* (Durham, NC: Duke University Press, 2004), ch. 8: "The Sovereign People," quotation at 136–37.

68.  Michael Walzer makes a particularly interesting attempt to reconcile liberal, pluralist and egalitarian principles in *Politics and Passion: Toward a More Egalitarian Liberalism* (New Haven: Yale University Press, 2004). He highlights the importance of "involuntary associations"—particular families, class positions, nationalities, often religious and ethnic communities—in which we develop a sense of self and of agency, and whose "constraints" on our self-generative freedom we can disavow, at a cost, but which continue to shape our moral horizons and associational patterns in later life.

69.  Hannah Arendt, *The Human Condition* (Chicago: University of Chicago Press, 1958). See also her essays, "Truth and Politics" and "What is Freedom?" in *Between Past and Future: Eight Exercises in Political Thought*, rev. ed. (Harmondsworth, UK: Penguin, 1977).

Seven    We Are All Treaty People

1.  "Notes for an Address," Hon. Jane Stewart, minister of Indian Affairs and
    Northern Development, Ottawa, January 7, 1998. The government's full response
    is *Gathering Strength: Canada's Aboriginal Action Plan* (Ottawa: Minister of Supply
    and Services, 1998).
2.  "Notes for an Address".
3.  Royal Commission on Aboriginal Peoples, *Final Report*, vol. 1, *Looking Forward,
    Looking Back* (Ottawa: Minister of Supply and Services, 1996), quotations at 7–8,
    xxiv.
4.  *Final Report*, 602.
5.  Paul Bunner, "On the Brink," *Report Magazine*, October 25, 1999, 12–17.
6.  *Vancouver Sun*, February 2, 1998, A1.
7.  Ken Coates, *The Marshall Decision and Native Rights* (Montreal and Kingston:
    McGill-Queen's University Press, 2001), 169, 127.
8.  "Portraits of Canada 2000," Centre for Research and Information on Canada, 8.
9.  Bruce Wallace, "The politics of apology," *Maclean's*, January 19, 1998, 33.
10. Menno Boldt, *Surviving as Indians: The Challenge of Self-Government* (Toronto:
    University of Toronto Press, 1993), 18–21.
11. Tom Flanagan, *First Nations? Second Thoughts* (Montreal and Kingston:
    McGill-Queen's University Press, 2000). It is no surprise that Flanagan's book
    amplifies the ideas expressed in various iterations of the Reform Party's policy
    Blue Book in the 1990s. Indicatively, it makes one passing reference to residential
    schools.
12. In addition to anthologies of past judgments, see *Delgamuukw: The Supreme Court
    Decision on Aboriginal Title* (Vancouver: Douglas and McIntyre, 1998).
13. Taiaiake Alfred, *Peace, Power, Righteousness: An Indigenous Manifesto* (Don Mills,
    Ontario: Oxford University Press, 1999).
14. *Sovereign Injustice: Forcible Inclusion of the James Bay Crees and Cree Territory
    into a Sovereign Quebec* (Eeyou Astchee/Nemaska, Quebec: Grand Council of the
    Crees, 1995).
15. Alan Cairns, *Citizens Plus: Aboriginal Peoples and the Canadian State* (Vancouver:
    University of British Columbia Press, 2000).
16. Peter Nabokov, "Present Memories, Past History," in Calvin Martin, ed., *The
    American Indian and the Problem of History* (New York: Oxford University Press,
    1987), 151.
17. The shorter, published version is Roger Epp, "At the Wood's Edge: Toward a
    Theoretical Clearing for Indigenous Diplomacies in International Relations," in
    Robert Crawford and Darryl Jarvis, eds., *International Relations–Still an American
    Social Science?* (Albany: State University of New York Press, 2001).
18. This story is told in Murray Mandryk, "Uneasy Neighbours: White-Aboriginal
    Relations and Agricultural Decline," in Roger Epp and Dave Whitson, eds.,
    *Writing Off the Rural West? Globalization, Governments, and the Transformation of
    Rural Communities* (Edmonton: University of Alberta Press, 2001). See also Ken
    Coates's chapter on northern British Columbia in the same volume and, on New
    Brunswick, his *The Marshall Decision and Native Rights*.
19. John Locke, *The Second Treatise of Government* (Indianapolis: Hackett, 1980), ch. V,
    para. 49.
20. Catherine McNicol Stock, *Rural Radicals: Righteous Rage in the American Grain*
    (Ithaca, NY: Cornell University Press, 1996), ch. 1.
21. Locke, *The Second Treatise*, para. 37.
22. Emmerich Vattel, *The Law of Nations, or the Principles of Natural Law*, trans.
    Charles Fenwick (New York: Oceana Publications, repr. 1964), 7, 81, 207–9.

23. George Grant, *Technology and Empire: Perspectives on North America* (Toronto: House of Anansi, 1969), 17. Locke is a central figure in the essay cited.

24. Flanagan, *First Nations? Second Thoughts*, 39. See also Gordon Gibson, "A Principled Analysis of the Nisga'a Treaty," *Public Policy Sources*, a Fraser Institute Occasional Paper, Number 27 (1999), 12.

25. This point is compellingly made in James C. Scott, *Seeing Like a State* (New Haven: Yale University Press, 1998).

26. Epp, "At the Wood's Edge," 306–11, 313–14; C. Parry, ed., *Consolidated Treaty Series, 1648–1918*, 170 vol. (Dobbs Ferry, NY: Oceana Publications, 1969); Martin Wight, *International Theory: The Three Traditions*, ed. Brian Porter and Gabriele Wight (Leicester: Leicester University Press/Royal Institute of International Affairs, 1991), ch. 4.

27. Michael Ignatieff, *The Warrior's Honour: Ethnic War and the Modern Conscience* (Toronto: Penguin, 1998), quotations at 170, 167, 64.

28. Cairns, *Citizens Plus*, 8–9.

29. See, e.g., James (Sakej) Youngblood Henderson, "First Nations Legal Inheritances in Canada: The Mikmaq Model," *Manitoba Law Journal* 23 (1996), 1–31; Francis Jennings, ed., *The History and Culture of Iroquois Diplomacy* (Syracuse: Syracuse University Press, 1985); Harold Cardinal and Walter Hildebrandt, *Treaty Elders of Saskatchewan* (Calgary: University of Calgary Press, 2000).

30. James Tully, "A Just Relationship between Aboriginal and Non-Aboriginal Peoples of Canada," in Curtis Cook and Juan Lindau, eds., *Aboriginal Rights and Self-Government* (Montreal and Kingston: McGill-Queen's University Press, 2000), 59.

31. Sheldon Wolin, *The Presence of the Past: Essays on the State and the Constitution* (Baltimore: The Johns Hopkins University Press, 1989), ch. 2: "Injustice and Collective Memory"; ch. 8: "Contract and Birthright," quotations at 144–45, 37, 139.

32. Wolin, *The Presence of the Past*, 137, 139, 146. This work is for newcomers too. The ethos I have in mind is expressed well in a different context, by a Welsh writer, anxious to instruct the many English retirees moving into her countryside, buying pastoral scenery at affordable prices:

    > When you move to an old house in the Welsh countryside, you are taking on more than a nice place to live, in a beautiful landscape. The siting of houses, the materials used to build them, and the people who lived there in the past, are all part of the continuing story of a locality, and a new owner has the responsibility to acknowledge this. One way is to try to understand the way of life, past and present, in these old houses, and their relationship with the broader sweep of history....

    Noragh Jones, *Living in Rural Wales* (Llandysul, Wales: Corner Press, 1993), 281.

33. One such position is developed at length in Charles Taylor, *Sources of the Self: The Making of the Modern Identity* (Cambridge, MA: Harvard University Press, 1989), Part I.

34. Ignatieff, *The Warrior's Honour*, 188; Martha Merritt, "Forgiveness, Despite the Pressures of Sovereignty and Nationalism," in Jean Bethke Elshtain, *New Wine and Old Bottles: International Politics and Ethical Discourse* (Notre Dame: University of Notre Dame Press, 1998).

35. Cairns, *Citizens Plus*, 7.

36. Paul Tennant, "Delgamuukw and Diplomacy: First Nations and Municipalities in British Columbia," Paper presented to a conference of the Fraser Institute, Ottawa, 1999, quotation at 9. Tennant does not mean to shrink First Nations to the present status of municipalities ("undignified creatures kept on a rather short leash") but to enhance the political-legal status of each.

37. One optimistic initiative in this context is the Federation of Saskatchewan Indian Nations' report, *Saskatchewan and Aboriginal Peoples in the 21st Century: Social, Economic, and Political Changes and Challenges* (1997).

38. See Mandryk, "Uneasy Neighbours," and Cameron Harder, "Overcoming Cultural and Spiritual Obstacles to Rural Revitalization," both in *Writing Off the Rural West*.

39. Wolin, *The Presence of the Past*, 45. This is precisely Flanagan's advice in *First Nations?*.

40. Cardinal and Hildebrandt, *Treaty Elders*, 14, 39.

## Eight    What is the Farm Crisis?

1. See, e.g., Joe Friesen and Marcus Gee, "The World's Hottest Commodities are in Your Cereal Bowl," *The Globe and Mail*, February 16, 2008.

2. This column first appeared as "'Farm crisis' not just a matter of net income," *Edmonton Journal*, December 17, 1999. It was based on remarks made as an invited witness to the House of Commons' Standing Committee on Agriculture and Agri-Food, in Vegreville, AB, earlier that same month.

3. This column first appeared as "Farmers have no future in Ottawa's vision," *Edmonton Journal*, September 24, 2001. I first found the futuristic *National Geographic* image in a fine book written from rural sympathies, James C. Scott's *Seeing Like a State: How Certain Schemes to Improve the Human Condition Have Failed* (New Haven: Yale University Press, 1998).

4. See, e.g., Lawrence Solomon, "Buffalo, not farmers, belong on the prairies," *National Post*, September 11, 2001; "Brian Kappler, "Family farm wrongly treated as 'sacred cow,'" *Edmonton Journal*, August 7, 2001; "Singin' the Farm Blues," *National Post*, January 18, 2000; Terence Corcoran, "Boom and gloom down on the farm," *National Post*, January 15, 2000; Terence Corcoran, "Farm subsidy is robbery no matter how you say it," *Globe and Mail*, July 11, 1990.

5. See, e.g., "Agriculture: food and much more," *The Globe and Mail*, October 29, 2001; Scott McKeen, "Revolutionizing the farm," *Edmonton Journal*, June 6, 2001.

6. This column first appeared in the *Parkland Post*, Summer 1999.

7. This column first appeared as "Hard choices for rural Alberta," *Edmonton Journal*, October 21, 2000. It has been revised to take subsequent developments into account, including the unexpected outcome in the County of Flagstaff. One other unexpected outcome deserves mention: in the new meat-packing towns like Garden City and Brooks, a multi-ethnic workforce has brought a valued cultural and culinary diversity, not just challenges.

8. This column first appeared as "Spare a thought for your councillor," *Farmers' Independent Weekly* (Winnipeg), October 3, 2002. It was based on talks given to the Alberta Association of Municipal Districts and Counties' fall convention and earlier to the Association's zone 4 meetings in Grande Prairie.

9. This text is adapted from a presentation made to a panel entitled "The Changing Characteristics of Urban and Rural Canada" at the national conference of the Institute of Public Administration of Canada, Vancouver, August 2004.

10. This text is adapted from a keynote address given to a community supper and seminar on the future of the family farm that attracted close to 300 people to the hall in Viking, Alberta in November 2003. Since then, versions of this talk have been given in several places across the prairies, including the National Agriculture Awareness Conference in Edmonton, November 2005, and the Agriculture Renewal Alliance conference in Winnipeg in October 2005. Notions of rural culture and farm knowledge are explored in a preliminary way in the second hour of the CBC Radio *Ideas* programme I co-produced with Dave Whitson, "The Canadian Clearances," first broadcast September 2004. Some of the best work on the growing gap between gross and net farm income and on the extractive role of new technologies has been done by the National Farmers' Union (Canada). See,

e.g., "The Farm Crisis: Its Causes and Solutions" (2005) and "The Farm Crisis, Bigger Farms and the Myths of 'Competition' and 'Efficiency'" (2003).

11. This point is powerfully made in the NFU study, "The Farm Crisis, Bigger Farms, and the Myth of 'Competition' and 'Efficiency'".

# Nine    Two Albertas

1. Quoted in Roberta Rampton, "Urban West growing," *Western Producer*, December 7, 2000.
2. George Melnyk, *New Moon at Batoche: Reflections on the Urban Prairie* (Banff: Banff Centre Press, 1999), 101.
3. *Calgary Herald*, January 1, 2000.
4. See, most famously, C.B. Macpherson, *Democracy in Alberta* (Toronto: University of Toronto Press, 1953).
5. Dave Pommer, "Duerr: Share taxes fairly," *Calgary Herald*, January 28, 1998.
6. Canadian Broadcasting Corporation, Radio One, *This Morning*, November 3, 1998. As the program log notes: "More and more, cities seem to be rebelling against their provincial governments. They feel they are misunderstood and mistrusted by their provincial protectors who are often kept in power by rural voters. We visit Calgary to see if cities are, in fact, outgrowing their provinces, *http://www.radio. cbc.ca/insite/THIS_MORNING_TORONTO/1998/11/3.html,* accessed October 16, 2004.
7. Nick Lees, "How to party the cowboy way," *Edmonton Journal*, November 4, 1996.
8. Charlie Gillis, "Chariots of the cowboys: pickups part of the culture," *Edmonton Journal*, November 7, 1996; Monica Andreeff, "Urban cowboys joining pickup lines," *Financial Post*, July 17, 1998.
9. Statistics Canada, *Census of Agriculture, Alberta Highlights. www.statcan.ca/ english/censusag/ab.htm,* accessed July 27, 2004.
10. See the Ludwig family's record, with index and commentary by Wiebo Ludwig, which was widely distributed throughout Alberta under the title "Partial and Abridged Anecdotal Record of Oil and Gas Activities as These Invade our Privacy and Peace, Threaten Our Safety, Jeopardize Our Health, Kill the Unborn and the Grown." My copy came from a former oil-patch worker.
11. Alberta Agriculture, *Grain Handling and Transportation: Freedom to Choose*, 1990, 1. I am grateful to Michael Broadway for this material.
12. Agriculture and Agri-Food Canada, *Western Grain Transportation: Why Change?*, brochure mailed to grain producers, 1995, 1.
13. Nellie Oosterom, Canadian Press, "Farmers expect record bounty; retailers prepare for spending splurge," *Edmonton Journal*, September 22, 1996.
14. Agriculture and Agri-Food Canada, *Western Grain Transportation Reform and Agricultural Diversification*, draft discussion paper, September 9, 2002, 9.
15. Michael Broadway, "Bad to the Bone: The Social Costs of Beef Packing's Move to Rural Alberta," in Roger Epp and Dave Whitson, eds. *Writing Off the Rural West: Globalization, Governments, and the Transformation of Rural Communities* (Edmonton: University of Alberta Press/Parkland Institute, 2001).
16. Statistics Canada, *Census of Agriculture, Alberta Highlights*.
17. Statistics Canada, *Census of Agriculture* (1996): *Characteristics of Farm Operations*; *Alberta Highlights*; and "Operators, Classified by Number of Operators on the Farm, Selected Variables, 1991 and 1996."
18. Statistics Canada, "Farmers leaving the Field," *The Daily*, February 22, 2002.
19. *Rural Alberta: Land of Opportunity*, Report of the MLA Steering Committee on Rural Development, March 2004.

20. Alberta Economic Development, *Regional Disparities in Alberta: Resource Package*, March 4, 2002; also, Mary MacArthur, "Report tells tale of two Albertas," *Western Producer*, May 30, 2002.
21. This did not go unnoticed. On March 6, 1996, for example, a front-page article appeared in the *Camrose Canadian* under the headline "VLTs take $3.9 million from Camrose."
22. In the mid-1990s, for example, Talisman Energy paid $800,000 in taxes to the Municipal District of Wainwright alone. In the Municipal District of Provost, 80 percent of taxes came from the oilpatch. See the *Provost News' Oil Patch Guide*, 1997–98.
23. Arn Keeling, "The Rancher and the Regulators: Public Challenges to Sour-Gas Industry Regulation in Alberta, 1970–1994," in Epp and Whitson, eds., *Writing Off the Rural West*, 295–6. See also Thomas Marr-Laing and Chris Severson-Baker, *Beyond Eco-terrorism: The Deeper Issues Affecting Alberta's Oilpatch* (Drayton Valley: Pembina Institute for Appropriate Development, 1999); and Andrew Nikiforuk, "Flare Up," *National Post Business*, October 2002; "The Killing of Patrick Kent," *Canadian Business*, December 2000.; and *Saboteurs: Wiebo Ludwig's War Against Big Oil* (Toronto: Macfarlane Walter & Ross, 2001).
24. Alberta Energy, *Annual Report, 1996–97 http://www.energy.gov.ab.ca.com/ Department/Annual+Reports/*, accessed August 14, 2004.
25. Canadian Association of Petroleum Producers, "Industry Facts and Information," 1996–2003 *http://www.capp.ca/default.asp?V_DOC_ID=675*, accessed September 4, 2004.
26. Andrew Nikiforuk, "Oh Wilderness, The Promise of Special Places Betrayed," *Alberta Views*, Fall 1998.
27. Eva Ferguson, "Pollution killed cattle, judge rules; oilpatch loses round in environmental battle," *Edmonton Journal*, July 9, 1999; Andrea Maynard, "Second study links poor cattle health to sour gas leak," *Western Producer*, January 14, 1999; David Staples, "Faceoff over Flaring," *Edmonton Journal*, July 23, 2000.
28. M. Strosher, Alberta Research Council, "Investigations of Flare-Gas Emissions in Alberta," Final Report to Environment Canada Conservation and Protection, the Alberta Energy and Utilities Board, and the Canadian Association of Petroleum Producers, November 1996.
29. See, for example, Ashley Geddes, "Speculation about election follows Klein on mainstreeting forays into rural Alberta," *Calgary Herald*, January 14, 1996; Marta Gold, "Klein gets back to the roots: Folks in rural districts see election in the political wind," *Edmonton Journal*, January 12, 1996; Mark Lisac, "Feedback from Klein road trip likely to mirror the Tory line," *Edmonton Journal*, January 9, 1996; Don Martin, "Klein stays home for this?" *Calgary Herald*, January 9, 1996.
30. Don Martin gives a frank summary of the Multi-Corp controversy in his generally friendly biography *King Ralph* (Toronto: Key Porter, 2002), ch. 14.
31. Geddes, "Speculation about election follows Klein."
32. Bradford Rennie, *The Rise of Agrarian Democracy: The United Farmers and Farm Women of Alberta, 1909–1921* (Toronto: University of Toronto Press, 2000).
33. This interpretation is developed at greater length in Roger Epp, "The Political De-skilling of Rural Communities," in Epp and Whitson, eds., *Writing Off the Rural West*, 301–24. See also Mark Lisac's *Alberta Politics Uncovered: Taking Back Our Province* (Edmonton: NeWest Press, 2004), 73–87.
34. Alvin Finkel, *The Social Credit Phenomenon in Alberta* (Toronto: University of Toronto Press, 1989), 122.
35. Helga Martyniuk, "The rape of rural Alberta: government ignores impact of facility closures on small communities," *Edmonton Journal*, May 21, 1996.
36. A copy of this correspondence is in the possession of the author. Like many others of its kind, it circulated within the surface-rights movement during the late 1990s.

37. David Bercuson and Barry Cooper, "Electoral Boundaries: An Obstacle to Democracy in Alberta," in John Courtney, Peter MacKinnon, and David Smith, eds., *Drawing Boundaries* (Saskatoon: Fifth House, 1992), quotation at 118.
38. Alberta Court of Appeal, Reference *Re Electoral Divisions Statutes Amendment Act,* 1993, *Dominion Law Reports* 119 (4th Series), judgment issued October 24, 1994.
39. Davis Sheremata, "Say It for the Farmers," *Alberta Report*, September 16, 1996, 10.
40. Adrienne Tanner, "Riding boundaries dispute a burr in rural saddles," *Edmonton Journal*, September 22, 1996.
41. Raymond Williams, *The Country and the City* (Oxford: Oxford University Press, 1973).
42. Melnyk, *New Moon at Batoche*, 88.
43. Melnyk, *New Moon at Batoche*, 103.
44. Melnyk, *New Moon at Batoche*, 87.
45. Renato Rosaldo, *Culture and Truth: The Remaking of Social Analysis*, 2d ed. (Boston: Beacon,1993), ch. 3, quotation at 69. I am grateful to Cody McCarroll for this reference.
46. Wallace Stegner, *Wolf Willow* (New York: Viking, 1962), especially Part I.
47. Bryant Avery, "Dream lifts Paradise Valley," *Edmonton Journal*, June 22, 1996.
48. William Kittredge, *Who Owns the West?* (San Francisco: Mercury House, 1996), 158.

## Ten    A University at Home in the Rural

1. Patrick Kavanagh, *The Parish and the Universe: Collected Prose* (London: MacGibbon and Kee, 1967), 282. I am grateful to John Johansen for this reference.
2. The CBS network in the United States dropped plans for a new Beverly Hills reality show featuring an Appalachian farm family, in response to public opposition, including a threatened rural boycott of advertisers, some of it generated through the Kentucky-based Center for Rural Strategies. Its advertisement appeared in the January 7, 2003 editions of the *New York Times, Washington Post* and other papers.
3. Richard Florida, *The Rise of the Creative Class* (New York: Basic Books, 2002); and also *The Flight of the Creative Class* (New York: HarperCollins, 2005).
4. Jane Jacobs, *The Economy of Cities* (New York: Random House, 1970); *Cities and the Wealth of Nations* (New York: Random House, 1984); *Dark Age Ahead* (New York: Random House, 2004), especially ch. 8. In this otherwise grim prophecy, Jacobs coolly declares the times to be "post-agrarian."
5. Lawrence Solomon, "Coast-to-Coast Subsidies Trap Canada," *Financial Post*, 19 June 2001; Michael Rushton, "Economics, Equity and Urban-Rural Transfers," in Raymond Blake and Andrew Nurse, eds., *Trajectories of Rural Life: New Perspectives on Rural Canada* (Regina: Saskatchewan Institute of Public Policy/Canadian Plains Research Center, 2003).
6. "When you picture a global university, you picture urban," says Princeton University's President, Amy Gutmann. See Alan Finder, "Rural colleges seek new edge and urbanize," *New York Times*, February 7, 2007.
7. Alexander John Watson makes a related, intriguing point about the common rural provenance of previous generations of Canadian scholars in *Marginal Man: The Dark Vision of Harold Innis* (Toronto: University of Toronto Press, 2006).

8. Eric Zencey, "The Rootless Professors," in William Vitek and Wes Jackson, eds., *Rooted in the Land: Essays on Community and Place*, (New Haven: Yale University Press, 1996), 19; Wes Jackson, *Becoming Native to this Place* (Lexington: University Press of Kentucky, 1994). Pamela Banting makes a spirited point about the inclusion of all possible identities, except rurality, in post-structuralist criticism in "How Rural Settings Can Unsettle Prairie Critics: Deconstructing the Politics of of Location," *International Journal of Canadian Studies* 32 (2005): 237–68.

9. Clifford Geertz, *Local Knowledge: Further Essays in Interpretive Anthropology* (New York: Basic Books, 1983), 153.

10. *The Works of Aristotle*, ed. David Ross, vol. 12: *Selected Fragments* (Oxford: Clarendon Press, 1952), 33–34.

11. Edward Said, *Representations of the Intellectual* (London: Vintage, 1994), 46.

12. One critic, however, later characterized the field as "a field of strangers," each a lone horseman or itinerant late-Renaissance *condottiere*, "a stranger to every place and faith, knowing that he can never be at home among the people who dwell there," yet searching for places where his "strategic art" could be performed. Richard Ashley, "The Achievements of Post-Structuralism," in Steve Smith, Ken Booth and Marysia Zalewski, eds., *International Theory: Positivism and Beyond* (Cambridge: Cambridge University Press, 1996), 240–53 *passim*.

13. Brooks Blevins, "Back to the Land: Academe, the Agrarian Ideal, and a Sense of Place," in , Zachary Michael Jack, ed., *Black Earth and Ivory Tower: New American Essays from Farm and Classroom* (Columbia, SC: University of South Carolina Press, 2005), 305.

14. Geertz, *Local Knowledge*, 158–59.

15. Wendell Berry, *What are People For?* (New York: Farrar, Straus & Giroux), 117.

16. David W. Orr, "Re-ruralizing Education," in Vitek and Jackson, eds., *Rooted in the Land*, 228.

17. See, e.g., Sarah Kennedy, "University not an option for many rural students," *Globe and Mail*, 24 June 2002; Marc Frenette, "Too Far to Go On: Distance to School and University Participation," *Research Paper* No. 191, Statistics Canada, Business and Labour Market Analysis, 19 June 2002; Statistics Canada, "Rural and Urban Educational Attainment: An Investigation of Patterns and Trends, 1981–1996," *Rural and Small Town Canada, Analysis Bulletin*, June 2003; Canadian Council on Learning, "The Rural-Urban Gap in Education," *Lessons in Learning*, 1 March 2006.

18. Zencey, "Rootless Professors," 15.

19. Linda Elizabeth Peterson, "Holding Ground," in Jack, ed., *Black Earth and Ivory Tower*, 89–90. Somewhere the cultural theorist Raymond Williams writes about the Cambridge professor who, in the 1930s, felt obliged in a course on Shakespeare to explain the meaning of the anachronistic word "community," the reality of which, he pronounced, had long passed from lived experience. As a young student and knowing otherwise, just arrived from his native Welsh village, Williams was compelled to offer a spirited reply. See also Pamela Banting's introduction as editor to the book, *Fresh Tracks: Writing the Western Landscape* (Victoria: Polestar Books, 1998), 10–14.

20. This point is borrowed from my essay, "The Call of the University," *Journal of Curriculum Theorizing* 15 (Spring 1999): 47–61.

21. Orr, "Re-ruralizing education," 231.

22. Laura Rance, "Local food goes to school in Toronto," *Farmers' Independent Weekly*, 28 September 2006, 6.

23. Bill Readings, *The University in Ruins* (Cambridge, MA: Harvard University Press, 1996).

# Index

Aberhart, William, 67–69, 98, 156
aboriginal peoples
    agrarianism and, 81, 185
    alterity of, 128
    assimilation of, 124
    in British Columbia, 123, 125, 133, 138
    British diplomatic relations with, 132
    cultivation of land, 128, 130
    cultural continuity, 138
    cultural renewal, 185
    eclipse of, 185
    farmers and, 139
    global economy and, 140
    government transfers and, 139–40
    homestead settlement and, 81
    as immigrants, 124
    land claims, 123, 133, 138
    as nations, 132, 133
    and place names, 14, 183
    reconciliation with, 121–24, 125–27,
        132, 134–35, 137–38
    rights, 123–24, 125, 127, 133, 139
    as rural, 157
    rural communities and, 5, 138, 139–41
    in Saskatchewan, 138–39
    self-government, 124, 125, 128, 129,
        130, 139
    treaties with, 14, 123, 130, 132–33, 135
    in U.S., 130
    White Paper on Indian policy and,
        211n.60
age
    in Alberta, 168
    of farmers, 172
agrarian activism, 92, 160
    international, 89–90
agrarian populism, 5
    in Alberta, 59–71, 116–17, 184

    as culture, 139
    plasticity of, 117
    Roger Epp's ancestors and, 98–99
    and Russian Mennonite refugees, 110
agrarian socialism, 82–83, 98
*Agrarian Socialism* (Lipset), 112
agrarianism, 4–5
    and aboriginal peoples, 81
    in ancient Greece, 80
    history of, 75–83
    in U.S., 78–81
agribusiness, 5, 74, 88, 104, 149, 172
agriculture
    corporations and, 87
    employment in, 172
    link with rural, 6
    specialization of, 87
Alberta
    age of population in, 168
    agrarian populism in, 59–71, 116–17,
        184
    agricultural employment in, 172
    agricultural industry in, 159
    cities, 167, 168–69
    co-operatives in, 69
    crop diversity in, 171
    education levels in, 168
    electoral boundaries in, 167, 180–81
    electrical utility·in, 167
    government of, 167, 174
    hospitals in, 174, 177–78
    identities in, 182–83
    incomes in, 157, 168, 172, 173
    industrial meat production, 152
    land-use conflicts in, 169–70
    livestock industry, 171–72
    livestock numbers, 169
    Mennonite immigrants in, 110–11, 112

non-delivery strike in, 70
numbers of farms/farmers in, 172
oil and gas industries, 69–70, 170,
175–76, 179
population, 69, 168, 173
populism in, 166–67
Progressive Conservatives in, 167
regional disparities in, 173
rural mythology in, 168–69, 184
rural-urban tensions in, 167
Russian Mennonite refugees in, 110
taxation in, 179
triumphalism in, 167, 182
two divisions of, 167–68
unity against threats to, 184
urbanization of, 60
workforce composition in, 69
*See also* rural Alberta
Alberta Advantage, 172, 174
Alberta Energy and Utilities Board, 175–76
Alberta Farmers' Union (AFU), 70
Alberta Wheat Pool, 60, 65, 67
Alexander II, Tsar, 97
Almighty Voice (Cree), 135
America, colonization of, 127–29
Amsterdam, Mennonites in, 212n.18
Anabaptists, 99–100
anti-mnemonic society, 134
Arapaho, 30
Arendt, Hannah, 3, 118
*The Origins of Totalitarianism*, 96
Aristotle, 80, 193, 208n.19
Augsberg Confession, 100
Augustana University College, Camrose. *See*
University of Alberta
Avonroy Hall, 59–60

Bambridge, Meighan, 211n.59
Batoche rebellion, 1885, 18
Battle River, 2, 3, 11–13
rail trestle bridge, 16, 17
valley, 16, 17–18, 195
Battle River Research Group, 73
Beatty, Sir Edward, 110–11
Berry, Wendell
on choice of place, 18, 19
on details of place, 16
on local vs. global economy, 156
on universities' need for beloved
country, 8–9, 195
*The Unsettling of America*, 87–88
and V. Shiva, 89
Betkowski, Nancy, 177
Big Jake Crossing, 30, 33
Big Sky Pork, 153

biofuels, 145
biotechnology, 147, 150–51, 160
bio-serfdom, 75, 146, 150, 161
Black Kettle, 25–27, 30, 31
Bogle, Bob, 180
Bonner, Kieran, 50–51
Borgmann, Albert, 19–20
Bové, José, 89
bovine spongiform encephalopathy (BSE), 6,
159, 162–63, 172
Brazil, Sem Terra squatter movement, 89
Bredt, Paul, 210n.41
Britain
biotechnology in, 151
relations with aboriginal peoples,
132–33
*See also* England
British Columbia
aboriginal peoples in, 123, 125, 133, 138
conscientious objectors in, 109
Brooks, Garth, 169
Brownlee, John, 65, 67
Buchanan, W.A., 214n.50
buffalo economy, 14, 17
Burnard, Bonnie. *A Good House*, 205n.9

Cairns, Alan, 138
*Citizens Plus*, 132
Calgary, 165–66, 179, 180, 181–82
*Calgary Herald*, 165–67, 182
Camrose, 2, 189, 190, 191
Canadian National Railway, 17, 74
Canadian Northern Railway, 38
Canadian Pacific Railway (CPR), 110, 170
Canadian Wheat Board, 65, 89
canola, 151
Cargill, 151–52, 172
Charles V, Emperor, 100
Cheyenne people, 30, 135
China, peasant struggles in, 89
churches
burning in Vauxhall, 117
Hanley Mennonite, 45–47
Herold Mennonite, 28, 29, 32–33
cities
of Alberta, 167, 168–69
allocation of resources to, 191
of future, 165–66
new deal for, 156, 157, 158
population growth, 157
rural communities vs., as centres,
190–91
universities in, 191
wealth and labour of rural people and,
156

See also Calgary; rural vs. urban

*Citizens Plus* (Cairns), 132

citizenship
  accommodation of differences in, 118
  rural, 4, 85, 89, 159
  rural-based universities and, 195, 202
  rural political tradition and, 5
  self-government and, 84
  wheat pools and, 86

co-operation, 5
  capitalist competition vs., 84–85
  farmers and, 86–87
  and liberty, 63, 85

Co-operative Commonwealth Federation
    (CCF), 110
  and electrification under public
      ownership, 70
  D. Epp and, 119
  founding of, 61
  as government, 115
  and land ownership, 113
  membership in, 114–15
  and Mennonites, 112, 114
  newspaper, 113–14
  organizational character, 114–15
  receptivity to, and religion and
      ethnicity, 112–13
  Regina Manifesto, 59
  Ronning as leader, 60
  in Rosthern, 115
  in Saskatchewan, 61, 69, 115, 117
  social gospel and, 114
  and socialism, 113–14
  UFA and, 61, 68

co-operative commonwealths, 62–63,
    83–84, 85

co-operatives
  in Alberta, 69
  in Oklahoma, 103
  in Saskatchewan, 69

cod fishery, 159

Columbus, Christopher, 132

commons, enclosure/loss of, 75, 90, 95

communism, 87, 95, 113

community
  definitions of, 48
  farm people and, 161–62
  survival, 185
  UFA and betterment of, 63–64
  See also rural communities

computerization, 160

conscientious objectors, 109, 117

conscription, 105, 106
  in U.S., 106–7, 107

*Consolidated Treaty Series, 1648–1918*, 130

consumption
  agricultural revolution and, 149
  separation of production from, 199

Cordell, OK, 34

Cree, 135
  around Hobbema, 14
  sun dance, 17

Crevecoeur, Jean de. *Letters from an
    American Farmer*, 78–79

Cromwell, Oliver, 77

Crow Rate, 60–61, 139, 144, 147, 149, 169,
    170, 172

cultivation
  aboriginal, 128, 130
  hunting/herding/ranching vs., 78, 128
  Jefferson and, 79–80
  and property ownership, 128

cultural renewal, 185

*Culture and Truth* (Rosaldo), 183

curricula
  attentiveness to place in, 198
  liberal arts, 199
  physicality in, 198–99

Custer, General, 25–27, 31, 135

Daws, S.O., 103

Daysland, AB, 50

de Crevecoeur, Jean. *See* Crevecoeur,
    Jean de

de Tocqueville, Alexis. *See* Tocqueville,
    Alexis de

Debs, Eugene, 104

Decore, Laurence, 177

*Delgamuukw* decision, 126

democracy
  farming and, 80
  land acquisition and, 80
  plebiscitarian, 68, 70, 167
  rule by farmers and, 63
  rural municipal councillors and,
      155–56
  UFA and, 63

*Democracy in Alberta* (Macpherson), 70–71

Depression. *See* Great Depression

Diggers, 77

diversity
  and equality, 117–18
  and immigration to Canada, 118

*Dominions Land Act*, 211n.60

Douglas, C.H., 68

Douglas, T.C., 115

Doukhobors, 106, 109, 115

Dried Meat Hill *(Kahkewak)*, 14–15, 20–21

Driedmeat Hill, 137

drought, 6, 172

Dunbar-Ortiz, Roxanne. *Red Dirt: Growing Up Okie*, 34n.
dust storms, 46

eco-feminism, 89
Edmonton, 180
*Edmonton Journal*, 166–67
Eigenheim, SK, 1, 30, 31–32, 97, 101, 102, 119, 135
El Reno, 30
electoral boundaries, 158, 167, 180–81
electrification, 70, 167
Elizabeth II, Queen, 38
*Empire Wilderness* (Kaplan), 6
employment
    part-time off-farm, 49, 144–45
    relocation for (*see* relocation)
Energy Resources Conservation Board, 175
Engels, Friedrich, 95
England
    civil war, 77, 131
    rural resistance in, 77–78
    *See also* Britain
Ens, Gerhard, 101–02
environment
    food growing and, 163
    genetic manipulation and, 150
    hog-barn complexes and, 145
    intensive livestock operations and, 152, 153
    meat packing industry and, 151
Epp, Clarence, 15, 40–42
Epp, David, 96–97
Epp, Diedrich (grandfather), 119
Epp, Diedrich (grandfather's uncle), 119
Epp, Jacob, 97
Epp, Peter, 45
Epp, Roger
    and aboriginal peoples, 136–37
    and beloved country, 195
    choice of return to prairies, 18–20
    and Eigenheim, 31–32
    father as schoolteacher, 40–42
    and Hanley, 31–32, 37–47, 53–56
    and Oklahoma, 23, 32–34
    teaching at University of alberta, Augustana Campus, 189–90, 195
Epp family, 4, 135
    and Liberal Party, 97
    settlement in North-West Territories, 101
Esau (biblical person), 134–35
European Union, 148

Fairbairn, Brett, 209n.35
family farms
    agricultural crisis and, 146
    destruction of way of life on, 7
    energy development and, 176
    industrial meat production and, 152
    and ownership of economy, 89
    as social units, 87
Famous Five, 62
farm incomes, 86, 160, 172
farm knowledge, 162
farmers
    age of, 172
    as bio-serfs (*see* bio-serfdom)
    and biotechnological revolution, 150
    as business stakeholders, 87
    and co-operation, 86–87
    as contract workers, 150
    demands on, 88
    freedom of, 87–88
    income, 145
    Jefferson on, 79–80
    and land ownership, 82–83
    movement, 5, 83–85
    numbers of, 6, 85, 86, 172, 211n.60
    off-farm employment, 144–45, 146, 172
    population, 144
    as producers, 86
    self-government, 5, 63, 67, 84
    and socialism, 82–83
    *Via Campesina* on rights of, 75
    *See also* smallholders
*The Farmers in Politics* (Irvine), 62–63, 83, 84
farming
    and democracy, 80
    in European Union, 148
    federal government and, 147–48
    freedom and, 78
    future of, 74, 86
    good work of, 146, 161
    money from, 159, 173
    as subsidy industry, 158
farms
    crisis, 143–63
    failures of, 42
    family (*see* family farms)
    number of, 144, 172
    1960s policy, 86
    size of, 171
federal government
    and aboriginal self-government, 125
    and farming, 147–49
    and grain, 147
    and new deal for rural communities, 158

and Canadian pluralism, 118
in Eigenheim, 31
farm, 33, 34
and First World War, 108
and Hanley Mennonite church, 45
and Herold Mennonite Church, 29–30,
   32
and King, 98
leaves Oklahoma, 27–31
life of, 28
marriages, 33
and Mennonite trek to Central Asia,
   213n.24
in Oklahoma, 24, 32
and politics, 98, 103, 104
and relatives in Soviet Union, 215n.58
Klaassen, John, 28, 108
Klaassen, Lizette Jantzen (grandmother),
   23, 30, 34
Klaassen, Martin (grandfather), 29, 30,
   108, 135
Klaassen, Martin (great-great-grandfather),
   97
Klaassen, Michael, 214n.42
Klaassen, Rose M. "Mennonite Diary,"
   214n.42
Klaassen, Walter, 52
Klaassen family, 4, 102–03, 108, 135
Klein, Ralph, 174, 177–78, 178, 180, 184
Ku Klux Klan, 112

Lacombe, Father, 14
land claims, 123, 133, 138
land ownership, 78–79
   absentee, 162
   ccf and, 113
   cultivation and, 128 (see also
      cultivation)
   and democracy, 80
   dispersed vs. concentrated, 162
   farmers and, 82–83
   freedom and, 79, 80–81
   and future of farming, 148
   of individual farms, 91
   lease-use arrangements, 66, 83
   and liberty, 128
   Via Campesina on, 90
land use
   conflicts, 6, 154, 169–70
   multiple, 176
Law of Nations (Vattel), 128–29
Laycock, David, 60, 68–69
leadership, and farm crisis, 146, 148
Lennoxville, QC, 191
Lethbridge Herald, 110–11

Letters from an American Farmer
   (Crevecoeur), 78–79
Levellers, 77–78, 79, 89
liberal education, 199
Liberal Party
   as brokerage party, 114
   D. Epp and, 119
   Epp family and, 97, 101–02
   Mennonites and, 109
   organizational character of, 114
liberty
   co-operation and, 63, 85
   farming and, 78, 87–88
   free enterprise and, 87
   independence and, 87
   land ownership and, 79, 80–81
   political, 118
   property and, 128
   See also independence
Lipset, Seymour Martin. Agrarian Socialism,
   112
livestock industry
   in Alberta, 169, 171–72
   and environment, 152, 153
   intensive, 152–53
      hog-barn complexes and, 145
   in Saskatchewan, 153
local government, 153–56
   See also rural municipal councils
Locke, John, 78, 126, 129, 130, 131, 139
   Second Treatise of Government,
      127–28
Lougheed, Peter, 174
Ludwig, Wiebo, 170, 184
Luscar coal mine, 169
Luther, Martin, 96, 100

MacLeod, Alistair. No Great Mischief, 52
Macpherson, C.B. Democracy in Alberta,
   70–71
Makaroff, Peter, 115
Manifesto of the No-Party League (Partridge),
   83
Manning, Ernest, 70–71
Manning, Preston, 206n.20
Marx, Karl, 82–83, 95
McIntyre, Alasdair, 7
McKinney, Louise, 62
McNaughton, Violet, 83
meat industry, 151–53
   See also bovine spongiform
      encephalopathy (bse)
mechanization, 85
Melnyk, George, 165, 185
   New Moon at Batoche, 182–83

Parlby, Irene, 61, 62, 65–66, 85
particularism, 193
Partridge, E.A.
    *Manifesto of the No-Party League*, 83
    *A War on Poverty*, 83–84
Paul I, Tsar, 97
Peace River region, 171, 172
peasants
    in China, 89
    in Germany, 76–77, 83, 95–96, 99
    march to London, 75–76
    *See also* serfdom
Persons Case, 62, 65–66
Peters, Henry, 46–47, 51
place
    attachment of rural people to, 185
    dwelling in, 20
    influence of, 19
    knowledge of, 19
    nostalgia of, 31
    principled indifference to, 193–94, 195
place-names, 14, 53
plebiscitarian democracy, 70, 167
plebiscitarian populism, 68
*polis*, 51, 80
*Politics and Passion* (Walzer), 215n.62
population
    of Alberta, 69, 168, 173
    of cities, 157
    farm, 144
    of Hanley, 39, 54
    in rural communities, 49, 139, 152,
        157, 173
    of Saskatchewan, 157
populism
    1896 campaign
    in Alberta, 166–67
    American, 62
    Mennonites and, 95
    plebiscitarian, 68
    of rural people, 8
    Social Credit and, 68–70
    "sour side" of, 116
Posse Comitatus, 215n.66
post-mnemonic society, 60, 134
post-secondary education
    rural students and, 157, 196
    structural inequality bween rural and
        urban, 196
    *See also* universities
Prairie Farm Rehabilitation Administration,
    46
prairie towns, 37–38
*The Presence of the Past* (Wolin), 121

prices
    commodity, 91
    oil, 176
    parity in, 70
    and rural communities, 49, 159
    wheat, 145
Priestley, Norman, 110
*Prison Notebooks* (Gramsci), 24
producer-citizens, 5, 75, 80, 82, 90, 91
producers
    agrarian populism and, 184
    as citizens, 91–92
    farmers as, 86
    financial return to, 160, 173
    in food system, 159
    freedom of, 87
    policy shift from, 5, 149
    self-identity of, 75, 91–92
    serfdom and, 74, 75
production
    industrialization of, 86
    policy shift from producer to, 5, 149
    separation from consumption, 199
    volume of, 86
professoriate
    and "beloved country," 8–9, 195
    dual citizenship in academy and
        community, 201
    job markets for, 194
    local involvement, 201
    in rural setting, 190, 192
    sense of place, 194–95
Progressive Conservative Party, 167, 174,
    178
Progressive Party, 66, 112
property. *See* land ownership
protectionism, 151, 158
provincial government(s)
    centralization of power in, 69
    cost cutting by, 154
    industrial livestock operations and,
        153
    and local government, 156
    and municipal politics, 154
    and new deal for rural communities,
        158
    rural Albertans and, 178–79
    UFA as, 65–67
public ownership, 70

racial segregation, 47, 117
railroads, 12, 18, 74, 75, 147, 170, 171
rain, 46
"Re-ruralizing Education" (Orr), 196

reconciliation
  with aboriginal peoples, 121–24,
    125–27, 132, 134–35, 137–38
  history and, 131–32
*Red Clay* (Hogan), 23
*Red Dirt: Growing Up Okie* (Dunbar-Ortiz),
    34n.
Red River diaspora, 17
Reform Party, 216n.11
*Regina Leader-Post*, 111
Regina Manifesto, 59–60
relocation
  aboriginal peoples and, 140
  of farm people for employment, 161
  nostalgia and, 7
  rural communities and, 50, 140
  of rural people to cities, 191
Rennie, Brad, 64, 65
*Report Magazine*, 123, 127
research, agricultural, 147
residential developments, 154
residential schools, 122, 136
resource-based economies, 158
Richard II, King, 75–76
*The Rise of the Creative Class* (Florida), 190
Rolph, William Kirby, 206n.10
Ronning, Chester, 59–60
Roosevelt, Theodore, 103
rootedness
  farms and, 161
  rural communities and, 52–53
Rosaldo, Renato. *Culture and Truth*, 183
Rosthern, SK, 1, 97, 98
  CCF in, 115
  Mennonite refugees arriving in, 110
  Mennonites of, 112
  and provincial elections, 113, 115
Rousseau, Jean-Jacques. *The Social
    Contract*, 117
Royal Commission on Aboriginal Peoples
    (RCAP), 121–22, 126, 130, 132
Royal Proclamation of 1763, 133
rural, the
  displacement by urban, 7
  images of, 190
  link with agriculture, 6
  reclamation as site of politics, 4
  urban vs., 190–91
rural Alberta
  community survival in, 185
  electoral boundaries and, 180–81
  and government, 178–79
  Klein Revolution and, 174–75, 178
  legacy of unity and, 184
  mass media and, 182

mythology in, 168–69, 184
oil and gas industry and, 175
population of, 173
Progressive Conservatives and, 178
and provincial government, 178–79
self-defence initiatives, 185
self-image of, 182–83
University of Alberta and, 190, 191–92
voting patterns in, 178
rural-based universities, 8–9
  curricula, 198–99
  as good neighbour, 201
  graduates of, 199–200
  regional business of, 200
  relationship with community, 201
rural communities, 47–53
  *ad hoc* organizations and, 154–55
  characteristics of, 47–48
  commodity markets and, 49
  complexity of, 48
  cultural capital of, 50–53
  cultural projects, 185
  culture of, 160–62
  distance from decision-making
    regarding, 91
  food production and, 51–52
  formative stories of, 48–49
  future of farming and, 149
  global economy and, 140
  government transfers and, 139–40
  historic connections to, 52–53
  and identity, 48, 52
  inter-generational contact within, 51
  involvement in, 50–51
  landmarks of, 52
  new deal for, 158–59
  outside decision making and, 158
  parallels with aboriginal peoples,
    139–41
  part-time work in, and farm survival, 49
  population demographics, 49, 139,
    152, 157
  prices and, 49, 159
  reinstatement of place names for, 53
  relationship of rural-based universities
    with, 201
  relocation from, 50, 191
  resentment of government-dependent
    groups, 92
  resource-based economies of, 158
  romanticization of, 162
  and rootedness, 52–53
  sentimentality regarding, 50
  survival of, 185
  university graduates in, 200

*Via Campesina* on rights of, 75
  web of silence in, 48–49
  work on farms, 51–52
rural municipal councils
  and democracy, 155–56
  election to, 153
  importance of, 155–56
  limitation on powers of, 153
  residential developments and, 154
rural municipalities
  aboriginal people and, 138
  global economy and, 154
  industrial livestock operations and, 152
  infrastructure, 154
  land-use conflicts in, 154
  politics, 49
  provincial governments and, 154,
    155–56
  Social Credit and, 69
rural students
  at University of Alberta, Augustana
    Campus, 190, 196
  costs for, 196
  estrangement from background,
    197–98
  in post-secondary education, 157,
    196–97
rural vs. urban
  and displacement of rural, 7
  identities, 182
  in location of universities, 191
  in location of university graduates,
    199–200
  and social theory, 2
  structural inequality, 196
  tensions, 167
Russia
  Mennonites in, 96–97
  revolution and civil war, 109
  *See also* Soviet Union
*Russlaender*, 45, 46

Said, Edward, 193
  *Orientalism*, 204n.2
Saskatchewan
  aboriginal people in, 138–39
  CCF in, 61, 69, 115, 117
  co-operatives in, 69
  Conservative Party in, 112
  economic conditions, 138–39, 157
  industrial livestock operations in, 153
  Mennonite immigrants in, 111, 112
  number of farmers in, 172
  place-names in, 53
  population of, 138, 157

Progressive Party in, 112
public vehicle insurance in, 70
Royal Commission on Immigration
  and Settlement, 214–15n.54
*Saskatchewan Commonwealth* (CCF), 114
Saskatchewan Valley Land Company, 42
Saskatchewan Wheat Pool, 38, 73, 119
Schleitheim Confession, 100
Schmidt, Eddie, 33
Schmidt, Helen, 34
Schmidt, Robert, 32, 33–34
Scott, James. *Seeing Like a State*, 209n.26
Scott, Walter, 119
*Second Treatise of Government* (Locke),
    127–28
Second World War, pacifism and, 115
seeds
  diversity of, 147
  saving of, 150
*Seeing Like a State* (Scott), 209n.26
self-government
  aboriginal, 124, 125, 128, 129, 130, 139
  of farmers, 5, 63, 67, 84
Sem Terra squatter movement, 89
Sennett, Richard, 211n.58
serfdom, 74, 75
  *See also* bio-serfdom
settlement
  Crow Rate and, 170
  of prairies, 129, 147, 170
  Western, 81
settler, as designation, 3–4
Sharp, Paul, 62
Shiva, Vandana, 89
Sifton, Clifford, 101
Simons, Menno, 101
smallholders, 79, 80, 81, 82, 103
  *See also* farmers
Smith, David G., 2
social contract, 128, 131, 134
*The Social Contract* (Rousseau), 117
Social Credit, 67–70
  and electrification under public
    ownership, 70
  failure of promised reforms, 117
  implications of joining, 114–15
  J. Klaassen and, 98
  Macpherson on, 70–71
  and municipal government, 69
  and populism, 68–70
  and radical populism, 184
  and UFA, 61, 68
social gospel, 114
socialism, 82
  agrarian, 82–83